Angels&DEMONS

Angels&DEMONS

One Actor's Hollywood Journey

An Autobiography by Ray Stricklyn

BELLE PUBLISHING

Printed in the United States of America

Library of Congress Cataloging-in-Publication Data:
Stricklyn, Ray.
   Angels & demons : one actor's Hollywood journey : an autobiography /
by Ray Stricklyn — 1st ed.
   p. cm.
   Includes index.
   ISBN 0-964-9635-4-X
   Preassigned LCCN: 98-74501

   1. Stricklyn, Ray.   2. Actors–United States–Biography   3. Gay actors and actresses–
United States–Biography.   4. Williams, Tennessee, 1911-1983–Friends and associates.
I. Title.

   PN2287.S775A3 1999   791.43'028'092
                        QBI99-900313

Belle Publishing
Los Angeles, California

Book and cover design by Sparrow Advertising & Design

DEDICATION

For all the fine actors who didn't get the
opportunities their talents deserved.

TABLE OF CONTENTS

ACKNOWLEDGEMENTS

First, my grateful thanks to David Galligan, who suggested he submit my manuscript to a literary agent.

To my wondrous surprise, that agent, the most generous Dorris Halsey, offered to represent the book. In record time (would you believe six weeks?), she had a publisher.

Third, a special thanks to Lee Melville, the first to read my scribblings. I appreciate his expert advice, assisting me with making the necessary additions, deletions, and corrections.

My thanks also to Kim Garfield for jogging my memory, and to Jamie Anderson, John Beaird, Jeffrey Bloom, Harry Prongue, and Deborah Nishimura for their frustrating attempts in trying to teach me how to use a Macintosh computer.

And the praise or blame falls on Joe Seiler, who suggested I put these words to paper.

Also, I'd like to acknowledge artist Heather Buchman, with Sparrow Advertising & Design, for the many striking cover jackets she created. My ego wants to frame each one.

And last, but not least, a resounding thank you to Tray Burk, with Belle Publishing, for making *Angels & Demons* a revealing reality.

PROLOG

Let me begin, as Hollywood often does, at the end.

As I put this pen to paper, it is a chilly Sunday afternoon. The date is December 7, 1997. I am seated at an elegant French desk in a luxurious suite at the Sterling Hotel in Sacramento, California. Only two blocks away, on the same street, Avenue H, is the old Governor's mansion. You know, the one Nancy Reagan refused to live in. One block away on the opposite side of the street, is the Sacramento Theatre Company, where I am closing in a play tonight. It has been an exhausting engagement; one that I am not sorry to see end. I never thought I would feel that way, as closing nights are usually a bittersweet experience for me. But tonight is different. As I am about to make my entrance, for the 1,501st time, I turn to an assistant stage manager and say, "I have a feeling this may be my final performance."

Why do I have this sudden compulsion to put words to paper? Already the waste basket is overflowing with discarded sheets of crumpled, yellow-lined paper, abortive attempts at starting this formidable task. Why bother to write about the ups and downs of Ray Stricklyn? Who could possibly be interested? I'm not a world-famous actor—although I might qualify as one who has had his fifteen minutes in the limelight; perhaps even twenty. But I have no illusions of a publisher beating down my door for the literary rights. Regardless, I still feel the *need* to write. To purge myself? To make an attempt at sorting out a life that is ebbing away? Or was Tallulah Bankhead right when she said, "If I had my life to live over again, I would make the same mistakes, only sooner."

Perhaps, through this journey, I will find an answer.

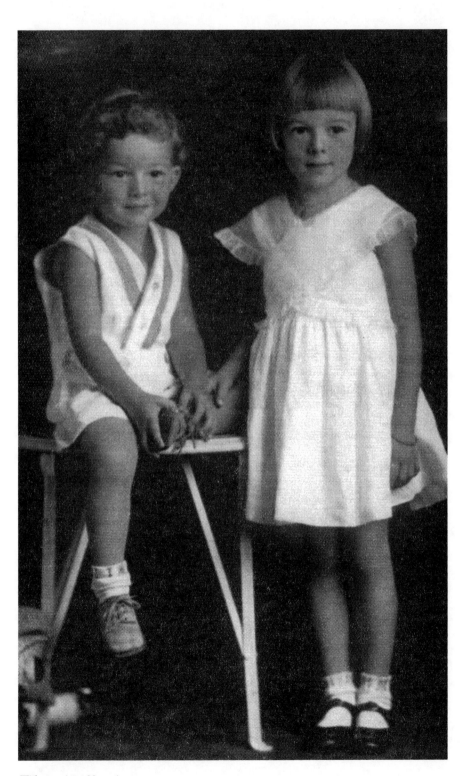

With my sister Mary Ann

TAKE ONE

"Without a past, we are children.
To be grown up is to have a memory."
Kundera

I entered the world, reluctantly, on October 8th. The year was 1928. A Depression baby. The birth was in a bedroom of a modest white-framed house located at 6709 Avenue O in Houston, Texas, with my grandmother as mid-wife. It was a difficult delivery, the baby fighting not to leave the warm, safe womb. He did not arrive kicking and screaming, however. He emerged upside down, feet first, with his delicate head refusing to make an entry. Was he rebelling even then? When the head finally oozed out, there was a dead silence. Even when the grand-mother's firm hand swatted his bottom, there was no sound. Finally, with one last whack, Raymond Stricklin gave his first outcry. The first of many to come.

I wonder if being born upside down contributed to my early decision to be an actor? It was a dramatic entrance. I *had* made an impact.

Mother—Ina was her given name—was past forty when I was born. In those days, having a baby at that age was considered quite dangerous, although she had had my sister, Mary Ann, three years earlier. Despite the love and attention my mother showered on me, I have sometimes wondered if my birth was a "mistake." As I lay in her warm womb, I'm sure I heard constant bickering between my parents, arguing that they couldn't afford to have another child. Perhaps that is why the birth was such a struggle. I didn't want to enter a world where I wasn't wanted.

The house on Avenue O was a very simple white framed abode, located in an unfashionable section of the city. "I only have to go a block to P," was my childish answer when asked where I lived. I thought that was quite naughty. The house consisted of the standard six rooms—a living room, dining room, two bedrooms,

1

kitchen and bath, plus a small back porch area. A large front porch, however, covered the width of the house, with an inviting swing hanging from the ceiling. Many a childhood fantasy was played out on that porch.

I'm told I was a delicate, sickly child, with mother doting over me every step of the way. My first three years are a blank now, although I do recall a traumatic experience at the age of four. As a child I was often called "beautiful." I had a regular halo of blond curls tumbling about my head. They attracted attention and compliments. I liked that. My sister, Mary Ann, had straight brown hair, which often caused her to wail, "I'm the girl, I should have the curls!" Therefore, it was devastating when I was taken to the local barbershop for my first haircut. Mother had to physically hold me in the barber's chair, for I was yelling and kicking as each golden curl cascaded to the floor. "'Now, now," the barber said, "*men* don't have curls." Without my curls, I no longer felt I was special.

As I was growing up, I don't remember any real affection between my parents. I did, however, overhear, as I thought I had in the womb, a lot of crying and arguing; usually over the mounting bills, lack of money and my father's drinking. I would often hear him coming in late at night, stumbling as he banged into a chair and then the inevitable exchange of heated words. I may have been christened Lewis Raymond Stricklin Jr., but that was the only similarity I wanted with my father. To avoid confusion, I was called Raymond, a name I always hated. When I had a son, I said, I would name him Gregory or David or Michael. Those were beautiful names.

My father, Lewis, was a sometime sign painter. An expert one too. He would hand letter each placard. I remember new trucks sitting in our driveway, with dad skillfully lettering and painting the company's name and logo on their sides. But despite his talent, the work wasn't steady. Sort of like an actor, waiting for the telephone to ring. He had a studio over the garage where he would spend a good deal of his time. It was a rundown building with a shaky staircase leading to the upper story. Once inside, the floorboards were very weak and you had to be careful where you stepped or you might go crashing to the concrete below. This studio was his haven. There, with his paints and his easel, he could create the things he really wanted to paint—a landscape, a snow scene, pictures of animals, and a dramatic forest fire. To be an artist had been his dream, but one he had sadly brushed away. It was a frustration that was eating away at his very soul. In the realities of the Depression, dreams are not easily fulfilled. And so he settled, out of necessity, for the pittance he earned as a sign painter. He didn't particularly like it when Mary Ann or I would intrude in his private domain, although I think part of his concern was that we might fall through the rotten floor. Also, since mother didn't allow liquor in the house, I'm sure he had his bottle of bourbon stashed away in some hidden alcove. He was a quiet man, sullen, moody, rarely speaking, except late at night when the arguments with mother would filter through the walls. I hated hearing her cry and blamed him for making her life, and ours, frequently miserable. He had let life defeat him, he didn't fight back. Of course, at that time, I didn't understand the pain and anguish he must have been suffering.

Out of necessity, mother became the primary bread earner in the family. Once Mary Ann and I were old enough, she returned to her old profession—the millinery world—making hats. She had a certain flair for fashion, at least where hats were concerned, and she also made some very pretty dresses for Mary Ann to wear, sewing away on some new frock every weekend. Mother worked so hard, rising early to fix our breakfasts, pack our lunches, and get us ready for school. Then she would be off to the bus stop where she would often have to wait in the bitter cold and rain for her tardy transportation. On top of that, it was a two-hour ride to work. She would return home around 7 P.M., understandably tired, but always continuing her day-in-day-out routine of preparing dinner, cleaning the house, washing the dishes, and ironing. Once Mary Ann was old enough she tried to assist as much as she could. It had to have been an exhausting existence, but one mother did with stamina and guts. She couldn't have been very happy as a woman either, devoting her life completely to her children.

Fortunately, her parents, Mary and Oliver Hatfield, were able to help out a great deal and not only with money. They owned a grocery store and meat market, so we always had sufficient food. The store was located in the Fifth Ward, on Dowling Street, which is an almost entirely Negro district. But they were loved in the area, not accepting pay if they knew it was a particularly needy family. Their living quarters were behind the market and some of my happier childhood memories were spent there. Also, it was a great luxury to have all the store's goodies at my fingertips. Imagine, all the ice cream and candy you could eat! It was a childhood fairyland.

I had two friends that I particularly liked to play with—two black sisters with the odd names of Beebee and Baybay. Minutes after I would arrive at the store, I would dash down the back alley to the old shack where they lived and invite them over. Then we would improvise movie plots and act them out; or cut the stars' pictures out of the movie magazines and paste them into scrapbooks. Though segregation was still very evident in Houston, I never felt a part of it— thanks to my friendship with Beebee and Baybay. The fact that I could also bribe them with free candy didn't hurt either. Every evening they would go home with their pockets filled with bubble gum and tootsie rolls and a shiny new apple.

* * * * *

Since television was still in the distant future, my fantasies were fanned by the radio serials and the movies. What a marvelous escape! The people in the movies and on the radio seemed to live such adventurous, exciting lives. Each Saturday morning I would dash off to the local movie house, either the Navaway or the Boulevard, to catch the latest episode of the newest serial. Then we would see a couple of main features—usually a 'B' picture or a Gene Autry Western—all for a nickel. I particularly liked two serials—*Jungle Girl*, with Frances Gifford as Nyoka, Queen of the Jungle, and my absolute favorite, *Flash Gordon*, with Buster Crabbe and Jean Rogers. Weekly, I would share every harrowing moment Flash and Dale were subjected to.

The first major motion picture I remember seeing was the 1935 tearjerker *Magnificent Obsession,* based on a Lloyd C. Douglas best seller. It probably stands out because I only saw half of it. An electrical storm, frequent in Texas, blew out all the power and the screen went blank. I remember being very distraught. Would Irene Dunne regain her eyesight after Robert Taylor had accidentally run her down with his car? I wouldn't find out the answer to that cliffhanger until 1954 when the film was remade with Jane Wyman and Rock Hudson.

How could I possibly have known, way back then when I was only seven years old, that I would one day play a leading role in another Lloyd C. Douglas movie; that I would appear in a Western with Buster Crabbe; that I would co-host a benefit with Jane Wyman; that I would visit with Irene Dunne in her home; or that Rock Hudson would figure prominently in my early Hollywood years? Only Robert Taylor escaped my future.

By 1939, I was an avid movie fan. I bought every fan magazine I could afford, even stooping to stealing an occasional quarter out of mother's purse to buy the latest issue of *Photoplay*. It was also the year I fell madly in love with a movie star. I had gone to the downtown Metropolitan theatre to see a new 20th Century Fox release, *Hotel for Women*. I had particularly wanted to see it because Jean Rogers, my beloved Dale Arden from *Flash Gordon*, was featured in the film. But it was the movie's young leading lady that I became completely enamored with. Her name was Linda Darnell. She was from Dallas and this was her debut film. She was only sixteen, although she appeared slightly older, and I thought she was the most beautiful girl I had ever seen. From that moment on, I eagerly awaited every new film she made—*Daytime Wife, The Mark of Zorro, Brigham Young, Blood and Sand*—all opposite Tyrone Power; or *Chad Hanna* with Henry Fonda; or *Stardust* with John Payne. Over the years I collected thousands of photos of her, meticulously pasting every article and picture in dozens of scrapbooks.

Maybe Linda wasn't the greatest actress in the world, but you couldn't have argued that with me then. One time my sister made the mistake of saying Olivia de Havilland was a better actress. I was furious, not speaking to her for two days. A few years later I finally admitted that Mary Ann was right, but I think I waited until Miss de Havilland had two Oscars on her mantle. But Linda Darnell could be a very good actress, particularly when she was directed by Joseph Mankiewicz in *A Letter to Three Wives* and *No Way Out*. Back in the 1940s, I saw every movie she made; usually several times. I'm almost ashamed to admit that I viewed *Forever Amber* sixteen times! It really wasn't that good a movie, but she was so breathtakingly beautiful in it (and as a blonde yet). My other big favorite was Lana Turner. She came close to dislodging Linda a couple of times, but I managed to remain loyal. As you can see, my taste in actresses veered toward their physical beauty. All was not lost, however. Slowly, I was beginning to appreciate the more mature talents of such really great film actresses as Bette Davis, Vivien Leigh, Ingrid Bergman, Katharine Hepburn, Olivia de Havilland, Jean Arthur and Irene Dunne.

Years later, in 1961, I finally met Linda Darnell. Even then, I must admit, I was rather excited about meeting my childhood idol. I had been asked to co-host, with Jane Wyman, a charity benefit for the Boys' Town of Italy, being held in San Diego, and Linda was one of the stars scheduled to entertain. By the 1960s, her movie career was basically over and she had been appearing in summer stock in plays like *Tea and Sympathy* and *A Roomful of Roses*. Now she was embarking on a hoped-for new venue—nightclubs. She had prepared a new act, that paired her with a handsome younger singer. The benefit was to be their initial appearance. Prior to our meeting, she had been forewarned that I was her "biggest fan." When we finally met, at an afternoon rehearsal, she just looked at me and said, "You should have known me then." Her face was still lovely, if a bit bloated, and she had put on a little weight. However, I noticed that her arms and legs were painfully thin. I was later told that she had contracted some bone disease while filming in Italy. Of course, on stage her long-sleeved, floor length gown covered any figure flaws and she looked lushly beautiful.

At the lavish dinner before the entertainment started, the celebrities were seated at one large table. I was assigned a seat next to Connie Stevens, who was enjoying considerable popularity with her television series, *Hawaiian Eye*. I, however, wanted to sit across from Linda, who was at the opposite end of the table. I arranged with the event's organizer to switch my seat with Linda's singing partner.

All the fan magazines and newspaper photographers were clamoring around Connie, but even as publicity conscious as I was, I was still willing to forego having my photo taken with Miss Stevens in order to be near my Linda. Unfortunately, the actress had had one drink too many and, suddenly, her already low voice descended another octave, and she loudly said to her young singing co-star, "Get your ass down here, immediately! I don't want you photographed with that young girl! Then they'll see you with me and it'll make me look that much older!" There was a silence at the table. Comedienne Carole Cook, who was also scheduled to entertain, looked at me, raising her eyebrow to an arch. Miss Darnell was now the center of attention (was that her intention?). She half-smiled, then mumbled, "Old movie stars never die. Like MacArthur, we just fade away." It was sad. Sometimes, perhaps, it is best not to meet your idols. Still, nervous as she was, and despite one too many drinks, she performed admirably. Her singing voice was pleasant, low and husky, and she even did a monologue from *Forever Amber.* (I could practically recite the dialogue along with her.) But somehow you sensed that the nightclub act wasn't going to go any further. When she died in 1965, following an awful apartment fire in Chicago, she was only forty-two. I was appearing in *The Knack* at Houston's Alley Theatre when I heard the news. I received a wire of condolence from a Hollywood acquaintance, John Carlyle, who knew of my youthful passion for Linda Darnell.

* * * * *

My desire to become an actor was, undoubtedly, forming at an early age. Exactly where that desire came from, I'm not sure. Escape? Certainly no one in my family was remotely interested in theatre or films. Perhaps it stems from my father's brush with art? Wherever the need came from, I was hooked.

I don't remember my elementary school years at all, and there isn't too much from my junior high days at Thomas A. Edison that stands out. I do recall having a crush on a girl named Billie Joyce Tinsley. She was very pretty and already developing quite a good figure. Occasionally we would attend a Saturday movie, where I would dare to put my arm around her and, when brave enough, I'd give her a kiss when I took her home. This was my first experience with a girl, and while it was innocent, it was the beginning of sexual stirrings. Not that I had any idea what that meant. I was terribly naive about anything regarding sex, as it was never discussed in our household; at least not with me. But the feeling I had for Billie Joyce was a new one; a growing affection that I'd never experienced before. Perhaps our relationship would have progressed, but mother put an end to it by insisting I was seeing too much of her. That, combined with our going to different high schools after graduation, ended our ripening friendship. But I have always remembered that first blush of adolescent affection.

There was *one* traumatic experience at Edison Junior High, however. I had overheard a group of older boys gossiping about a certain girl in school— Gloria—saying that she was going to have a baby. I was so naive I didn't see anything sinister in that—a baby was a nice thing—so I passed the rumor on to someone else. It got back to our homeroom teacher, and I was blamed for spreading this "vicious" rumor. I was given bloody hell for saying such a "disgusting" thing.

The teacher phoned my mother. After thoroughly chastising me, my mother then warned, "Girls can cause trouble." I doubt if I had even heard the word pregnant before.

Sometime later, now at Milby Senior High, I got myself into another mess. Perhaps because of my father's influence, I fancied myself a rather capable artist. I was constantly doodling, usually sketching the female figure. There was a nude picture in an issue of *Life* magazine that caught my attention. I decided to draw my own version (perhaps enlarging the breasts a bit). Anyway, one of the school's star football players saw it and asked if I'd draw one for him for his wallet. Since it was the first time an athlete had paid any attention to me, I was delighted. However, I made the mistake of passing the completed sketch to him across the room. The teacher, thinking it was a note, demanded that it be brought to her desk. Imagine her surprise when she opened it and saw a voluptuous nude! With high indignation she demanded to know *who* had drawn such a *disgusting thing*! Scared to death, I finally raised my hand. She immediately ordered me out of the classroom. There I was, all of fourteen years old, always the perfect little gentleman, as innocent as one could be, being accused of something *very dirty*. I was hauled off to the principal's office, where I was told I would be expelled until they had talked with my parents. Since it was a Friday afternoon that meant I would have all weekend to suffer. I cried all the way home. I explained to Mary Ann what had happened and she was very sympathetic, but that didn't ease my pain. When mother got home from work, Mary Ann told what had transpired. Of course she was very upset with me, but then she became angry that the teacher had over-reacted. Come Monday morning the situation was straightened out and I was able to resume my classes. But I paid a price. As a result of spreading "such filth" I was given a failing grade in deportment, ruining my nearly all-A report card.

It was a bitter lesson for an innocent kid. *Girls can cause trouble,* mother had said. Mrs. Simpson, the teacher, had indicated that there was something *disgusting* and *dirty* about the female figure. I was a very confused young man. Subconsciously, I think, this is when I began to be wary of the opposite sex. They could only cause me trouble. Yet, even with those warning signals, no sexual enlightenment ever came from my parents. True, sex wasn't openly discussed in those days, but it sure would have helped, believe me. When I first asked where babies came from, I was told, "From a seed." For days I was out digging in the backyard, searching for a newborn under a rose bush or an asparagus plant. Talk about someone needing help . . . .

Although I usually made very good grades in school, I did have a terrible time with algebra. The complicated problems seemed beyond my comprehension. Besides, I couldn't see how solving those formulas would possibly benefit my future life as an actor. Fortunately, or unfortunately, depending on how you look at it, the girl who sat in front of me in algebra class was a mathematical whiz. Rosemary Wilcox would whip through the tests, then was considerate enough to sneak me the problems she had solved and I would copy her answers. Not too ethical, I'll admit. Of course, those tactics soon backfired on me, as cheating always does. My test papers were always so neat and legible, plus the addition of Rosemary's correct answers that I'd always get an A+. Poor Rosemary, however, wasn't quite as neat, so she would only get an A. Understandably, this didn't set too well with her and she stopped saving my ass. Consequently, I failed the important algebra final and had to go to summer school to make up the credit. I didn't do too well there either. But the very attractive teacher, seeing my agony, ended up sitting in my chair with me solving the problems. She also passed me. My lack of interest in figures, except the human kind, is probably why my finances are frequently in shambles.

Of course the one class I did excel in was drama, taught by my favorite teacher, Roscoe Bayliss. Since I was his only student aspiring to be an actor, he was very helpful in my early stages of training, teaching me the value of the classics, introducing me to the works of Shakespeare, Anton Chekhov, George Bernard Shaw and Eugene O'Neill.

My biggest drawback in the drama class was my extremely youthful appearance, a bugaboo that would help and hinder me in the years ahead. Also, I hadn't reached my full height (5'9"), so my short stature only accentuated my "baby" look. This was most frustrating, because when the school plays were cast, I would always lose out. I was just too young looking and/or too short when matched up against my competitors. Unlike today, when high schools present their versions of hit Broadway plays and musicals, we would do innocuous little plays with titles like *Grandma Bunty Pulls the Strings*. Mr. Bayliss tried to help me, letting me perform in special playlets during assembly programs. Of course I would always pick some highly dramatic scene, where I could scream and go crazy. This was *acting*, I thought. I'd begun to see Bette Davis movies, you see. But despite my earnestness, Mr. Bayliss didn't encourage me to become an actor. Not because he didn't think I showed some talent, but because it was such a difficult and unreliable profession. Also, he probably thought I would outgrow this childhood obsession. I didn't heed his advice, however, for I knew there was only one road for me to follow.

* * * * *

Following graduation at the age of sixteen, I read in the local paper that the Houston Civic Theatre was holding auditions for Eugene O'Neill's one foray into warm comedy, *Ah, Wilderness!* I had read the play in school, so I knew that the leading juvenile role, Richard, was a choice part. Winnie Mae Crawford was the new artistic director at the theatre, having replaced a woman named Margo Jones, who had moved to Dallas to start her own professional theatre company. She would shortly make a name for herself, both in Dallas and New York, when she introduced a young playwright with the unlikely name of Tennessee Williams to the world.

My stage debut as Richard in Eugene O'Neill's Ah, Wilderness!

I was cast as Richard. I was thrilled, of course, a leading role my first time out. Surely stardom was just around the corner. Never mind that it was an amateur production in a little theatre located near Houston's bayou. The reviews were respectable with one paper, *The Houston Press,* singling me out as "a young player of promise."

Meanwhile, on the other side of town, a young woman named Nina Vance was entering the local theatre scene. She had been a teacher at Lamar High School and had acted in several plays around town, usually at the Houston Little Theatre, which was considered the best of the local groups. But Mrs. Vance had ambitions to be a director. She started by doing plays at the Jewish Community Center and they were encouragingly received. I read where their next production was to be a John Van Druten comedy, *The Damask Cheek,* and there was a good juvenile role in the script. I auditioned and got the part. The rehearsals seemed much more professional than they had been at the Civic Theatre, plus better actors seemed to be involved. One of the actresses, even younger than I, but appearing older, was a girl named Pat Horn. She had been a student of Mrs. Vance at Lamar High School and was an obvious pet. She also happened to be very gifted. We became friends immediately. The play opened to favorable reviews and attracted good audiences. Next, I appeared in Nina's production of *Junior Miss*, only this time we played in an arena space in the downtown Texas State Hotel.

Before long, Nina Vance had her own theatre. She was very ambitious and with a group of Houston friends—primarily Vivien and Bob Altfeld—she began organizing a new theatre group. Vivien was a very seductive and glamorous blonde dancer/actress (she had appeared in *The Damask Cheek*) and she offered her dance studio on Main Street for the site of the new arena playhouse. The studio was at the end of a long alley, hence the eventual name of the theatre. The arena had one particularly distinguishing feature—a large tree that grew right inside the building, its branches shooting through the roof. One evening, along with Pat Horn and about forty other interested parties, I attended the first meeting to form the Alley Theatre. We sent out hundreds of penny postcards soliciting funds and subscriptions. The response was quite encouraging.

The first production was an all-male war melodrama entitled *A Sound of Hunting* (which had featured a young Burt Lancaster in its Broadway presentation). The Alley's version topcast a young actor by the name of Larry Blyden. He was terrific, and you just knew he had a future. He did too, becoming a successful Broadway actor (co-starring, for one, with Barbara Harris and Alan Alda in *The Apple Tree*), and several motion pictures. His career was cut short when he was killed in an auto crash in Morocco. As there wasn't a role for me in *A Sound of Hunting*, I ended up doing odd jobs around the theatre, taking tickets, etc. But mainly, I watched the play nightly, looking and learning. The reviews were wonderful and the Alley began its upward climb. Immediately, there was a rivalry between the new upstart and the older, more established Houston Little Theatre. Quickly, the Alley outgrew its small dance studio space and began raising money to build a new theatre. They found an old fan factory building and, eventually, converted it into an absolutely charming arena theatre. Within a few years they'd outgrow this space too, but by then they had become a professional Equity house. In time, after a massive fund-raising drive, they would build a large castle of a building in downtown Houston, with both a large proscenium stage as well as a smaller arena space. Today, all these years later, the Alley is considered one of the finest regional theatres in the country. I, however, wouldn't appear at the theatre for quite a while, but the Alley and Nina Vance would figure importantly in my life.

Since there were no roles for me at Nina's theatre, I became an actor with the Houston Little Theatre, under the artistic guidance of Ralph Mead. It was an elegant old playhouse, seating around three hundred, with a sold-out subscription audience. Although classified as a non-professional theatre, the productions were tastefully done with expert set designs. But, catering to their audience, they didn't usually offer anything too offbeat or exciting, as the Alley frequently did. Still, it was a very popular playhouse during the 1940s and 1950s. I appeared in several of their productions: I played Lysander in *A Midsummer Night's Dream*, and I was Ferdinand in *The Tempest*, regretfully my only attempts at Shakespeare. I also had roles in the popular comedy, *George Washington Slept Here*, in *Cradle Song*, and I also had several small roles in the world premiere of Angna Enters' *Love Possessed Juana*. My best exposure was probably as the spoiled son in Shaw's *You Never Can Tell*, and I was cast as professor John Brook, you know, the teacher who marries Meg in *Little Women*. It was a ludicrous piece of casting, though I didn't think so at the time. I looked ridiculously young, despite the addition of a moustache, and at the top of Act II when I made an entrance carrying baby twins that Meg had given birth to, the audience roared with laughter. *The Houston Post* reviewer, a widely admired critic named Hubert Roussel, wrote: "Raymond Stricklin's performance is quite a feat for so young an actor." At the time I thought that was a good review, not realizing he was making a crack about my very youthful appearance.

It was during this Houston Little Theatre period that I became close friends with several other young, would-be actors. They were Billy Herman, John B. Shanks, Bill Gideon and Jerry Scales. We all had one goal—to become professional actors and take Broadway by storm! Another good friend I made was John Stevens. John, at the time, was employed by a Houston oil company and later would be quite successful in real estate. He was older and had no ambitions to follow the theatre as a career, though he appeared in a play from time to time. He would become a life-long friend, until his death in 1995.

John Shanks, called J.B., was the "mature" one of our group, at least in appearance. He was very thin, with black hair, and excelled in playing eccentric comedy. Even at his young age he was already a character actor—sort of a road company version of movie actor Edward Everett Horton. He was also the most experienced having appeared in several musical stock productions back east. Bill Gideon was the "pretty one" with blond hair and long eyelashes, which looked as if he curled them. Jerry Scales attracted a bit of attention when a Warner Bros. talent scout saw him in a Houston Civic Theatre production of *Our Town* and he went to Hollywood for a screen test. Although nothing came of the test, I was most envious of his opportunity. Billy Herman, with whom I became closest, was also a young character actor. He was quite short in stature with a thin, wiry build. He was also, even at his age, beginning to lose his hair. Billy was the bright one in the group. As a matter of fact, he'd been in my sister's graduation class at Milby High and he also lived on Avenue O.

Into this male group came a redheaded bombshell named Michelle Condre. Her flaming tresses bounced as she walked, attempting not to trip in her too high heels. She fancied herself as Rita Hayworth in *Gilda*. Her real name was Wendell Lee Nowlin, but her mother read some French novel and changed their surname to Condre. Wendell Lee became Michelle, while the mother, who had long, jet-black dyed hair, took the exotic name of LaVe. Michelle wore provocative, tight-fitting dresses often cut rather low at the bosom. She wasn't really pretty—she had a slightly crooked nose—but she had a certain flair and I thought she was glamorous. Others, behind her back, ungallantly called her "cheap." While she appeared to be worldly, she was really quite an innocent, and not at all promiscuous as was assumed. Especially by my mother.

Following our late night rehearsals, Michelle and I would take the bus downtown to the Rice Hotel, then sit for a couple of hours in the all-night coffee shop, dreaming of the day we could go to New York. At one A.M. we'd catch our respective busses, the last ones to leave the terminal.

My late nights caused mother some alarm, however. Some busybody crone phoned her and said she had seen me coming out of the Rice Hotel in the wee hours of the morning with a "redheaded tootsie"—a more polite way of saying prostitute. I explained to mother that it was only Michelle and that we had just been talking and drinking coffee. Still, mother never liked her and didn't approve of our friendship. *Girls can cause trouble* she reminded me. When I would sass back, asking why the old crone was out so late I was told it was none of my business; that she was an adult. Once again, women had gotten me in hot water. If truth be known, mother should have been concerned about my growing attraction to my own sex. But that experimentation was yet to come.

It was during my rehearsals at the Houston Little Theatre that I had my first cigarette. I had a crush on a beautiful blonde girl who played Amy in *Little Women*, Carol Jean Rosaire. She was from a wealthy River Oaks family and, though still in high school, was already smoking. I thought that was very sophisticated and, to impress her, I started to light up. I wasn't inhaling, I told myself. Besides, smoking was very "in" in those days—the product constantly being promoted on the radio and in magazines. Of course I never smoked at home, but I'd make up for it the minute I'd get to the theatre. It was the start of my lifelong slavery to nicotine.

Around this time, a woman named Minerva Black came into my life. Minerva was a monologist, performing at various functions around town, and she taught drama classes. She'd seen me in a few plays and one evening approached me. She said she'd been impressed by my potential and, particularly, my dedication. Each year, she said, she gave two six-week summer scholarships to a drama school in New York—the Theodora Irvine Studio for the Theatre. Would I like to come? She also asked Pat Horn. We were thrilled. Of course, Minerva explained, while she'd pay for our tuition, we'd have to have extra money for our food and lodgings.

I couldn't wait to get home to tell my mother my exciting news. While she thought it was a nice gesture, she said there was no way we could afford such an expense. "You *can't* say no," I childishly screamed, "this is the break of my life!" "Raymond, we can't afford it, now that's final!" "We *must!*" I selfishly yelled back. I cried myself to sleep, knowing that I was forever doomed to stay in Houston. How could my mother be so cruel, I silently screamed, pounding my pillow. When we're young, we can be pretty selfish, thinking our wants are the only important ones in the world. The fact that the family was struggling to make ends meet never entered my one-track mind. This stubborn, headstrong, spoiled child *had* to go.

And I did. With mother's small savings and, no doubt, an assist from grandma and grandpa, this seventeen-year-old took off for the wilds of New York and Broadway.

It was a summer I still remember. My first trip, *anywhere*, and it was to New York and Broadway! My dream was becoming a reality. On the train trip east, Minerva mentioned that she had arranged tickets for a play called *The Glass Menagerie*, written by the writer with the funny name, Tennessee Williams. Minerva's old friend, Margo Jones, had co-directed it with Eddie Dowling, who was also co-starring in the play. I stood outside the theatre reading review quotes. They were staggering. And who was this Laurette Taylor? "The performance of a lifetime!" one notice said. "Perhaps the greatest performance of all time!" raved another.

I sat in the balcony, eager for the play to begin. It started quietly. A man walked downstage in a spotlight. He was dressed as a merchant sailor. He slowly strolled across the front of the stage to a fire escape. He stopped, lit a cigarette and began to address the audience:

> Yes, I have tricks in my pocket. I have things up my sleeve. But
> I am the opposite of a stage magician. He gives you illusion

that has the appearance of truth. I give you truth in the pleasant disguise of illusion.

The magic had begun. I sat there, enthralled. Laurette Taylor's performance, of
course, is now legendary. But I was too young, too inexperienced to really know
what I was witnessing. I knew I was seeing acting that was different from anything I'd ever seen before. At first I thought she didn't know her lines—every
utterance seemed to be on the spur of the moment, as though she were making
up the words as she went along. It was all so spontaneous, so natural, and so real.

Then, Tom, the son, spoke the final lines of the play:

Blow out your candles, Laura—and so goodbye.

She blows out the candles. Dissolve. End of play.

The audience sat there in stunned silence. There was no applause, just quiet.
I'd never experienced that kind of reaction before. Don't New Yorkers know
you're supposed to applaud at the end, I wondered? Then, slowly, the stage lights
came up and the players—Julie Haydon, Anthony Ross, and Eddie Dowling—took
their bows. Then Miss Taylor stepped forward. Suddenly, the audience, who had
been so quiet only moments before, started screaming and stomping their feet.
Next they were standing. I'd never seen a reaction like that, not in Houston. It was
electric. I remember shivering. I've never forgotten it.

Of course, I'd seen theatrical magic. Whatever it was, I wanted more. And I
wanted some for me too.

"If you work hard, study, then work even harder," Minerva said, "who knows?
The theatre is a mysterious place. Occasionally miracles happen. It's the toughest
business in the world to crack—thousands try—a few sometimes succeed. And
you've got to want it more than anything in the world, because there are many
heartbreaks ahead. There can also be many joys."

It was difficult to sleep that night. Imagine, your first night in New York, your
first Broadway play, and you're exposed to both Tennessee Williams *and* Laurette
Taylor. It's mind boggling!

* * * * *

Theodora Irvine was an elegant lady, a tall, handsome dowager, who must have been in her early seventies. Her school had been in existence for many years and, at one time, was considered one of the foremost drama studios. Even Clark Gable had been a former student. More recent graduates had been Anne Baxter and Cornel Wilde, who, by the mid-forties, were enjoying considerable success as popular movie stars. Ms. Baxter had recently won an Academy Award for her performance in *The Razor's Edge* and Mr. Wilde had a best actor nomination for playing the role of Chopin in *A Song to Remember*. To show their gratitude to Miss Irvine, each year they gave $500 scholarships for a year's study to a promising young actor and actress.

By today's standards, the school would probably be considered old-fashioned. But we had valuable lessons in speech, projection, dance, fencing, history of theatre, etc. Skills that I think the young actor of today could still use. Projection alone, for one thing. Today, even in the smallest theatres, it is sometimes impossible to hear or understand the actors. I find that particularly annoying.

At the end of the six-week course, Pat Horn and I did a scene from a Tennessee Williams one-act, *Moony's Kid Don't Cry*. We were both ecstatic when we were announced as the winners of the Wilde-Baxter scholarships. Looking back, I'm sure Pat was a deserving recipient, but they must've given it to me for sheer guts. There I was, baby face and all, attempting to play one of Mr. Williams' pre-Stanley Kowalski characters. Sensitive I was—butch I wasn't.

There is one amusing footnote to my being awarded the Cornel Wilde scholarship. Upon graduation from the Irvine Studio, I saw where the noted Broadway producer Guthrie McClintic was planning a revival of Shaw's *Candida*, to star his wife, Katharine Cornell, one of the reigning theatre stars of the day. Since I'd played Marchbanks in scenes from the play in class, I thought it only natural that I should do the challenging role in Mr. McClintic's production (ah, the bravado of the young!). I went to his office and requested to see him. His secretary said he wasn't interviewing, but casually asked me what experience I had had. Since that was minimal, I mumbled something about the Cornel Wilde scholarship. The secretary, who had been preoccupied, suddenly raised an eyebrow and said, "Hold on a minute." In a few seconds she returned and said Mr. McClintic *would* see me. I was thrilled. As I entered his office, he looked up, tersely saying, "Now what's this about a Cornell scholarship? Miss Cornell does not give scholarships!" I gulped. "Oh, no sir, your secretary must have misunderstood me. I said the Cornel Wilde scholarship." He hastily rose from his desk and rudely escorted me to the exit. Before slamming the door, he added, "Mr. Wilde should still be in acting school himself!" Shortly thereafter, *Candida* was revived, with some young upstart named Marlon Brando playing Marchbanks.

* * * * *

Pat Horn and I returned to Houston, basking in our scholarship victories. I made sure it was played up in the Houston press. I was learning at an early age the value of publicity. Our enthusiasm was infectious, and Billy, Michelle and J.B. were all planning to enroll at the Irvine Studio. It would be a Texas invasion. Our other buddy, Bill Gideon, opted instead to join the University of Texas's drama department in Austin. He was a little more practical than the rest of us.

Being ambitious, Pat Horn and I decided to form our own Houston theatre company. And we did too, using a small auditorium at a local Women's Club for our Little Stages productions. The venture was short-lived, but we got off to a healthy start with a double-bill of William Saroyan's *Hello Out There*, in which I played the lead and Tennessee Williams' *Hello from Bertha* which featured Pat.

Billy Herman and I became increasingly close during this period. It was with him that I had my first sexual experience. It was really quite innocent; two guys playing around, which led to mutual masturbation. The earth didn't shake, but it was a pleasant sensation. Certainly I had never heard the word *gay* or *homosexual* before. It was just two youths horsin' around, a stage that I think most boys go through. I was just more naive than most. However, a few months later I did have my first real homosexual experience—with my older friend, John Stevens, though I was pretty passive throughout. I do remember the strains of Nat "King" Cole's *Nature Boy* playing in the background. It seemed a most appropriate number.

Though sex had briefly entered the equation, my main objective was getting the money to return to New York. Even with my family's assistance, they couldn't afford to support me for a whole year. Fortunately, I had two enterprising friends, Rosemary Clark and Jimmie Wallace. We'd known each other since childhood, attending weekly prayer services at the Methodist Church. We were all quite active in church activities, but Rosemary and Jimmie were the real leaders. Why not, they asked—just like Mickey and Judy—put on a show in the church basement? A brilliant idea, I thought; particularly when they said the proceeds would go to me. After obtaining permission from the church board, we decided to stage a variety show, ending with me doing a dramatic reading from the *Knock On Any Door* novel, in which I enacted a young delinquent about to be electrocuted (perhaps you saw the movie version with Humphrey Bogart and John Derek? The one with the famous catch phrase—"Live fast! Die young! Have a good looking corpse!") It was a rather heavy, shocking piece for a church basement, and I'm sure I was quite ridiculous, but my sincerity seemed to carry me through. Happily, we raised several hundred dollars. Being greedy, we decided to do another evening, only this time I'd do something a bit more religious. Our "box-office" take was considerably better with my reading from *The Song of Bernadette.* As you can see, I was quite shameless. Jennifer Jones won her Oscar playing Bernadette; I won my bus fare to New York.

* * * * *

Before I took off for New York, however, there was a family incident that stands out. My mother's older sister, Aunt Ada, whom I adored, was married to Uncle Elliott. It was her second marriage. Divorce was frowned upon in those days and the family never quite accepted Uncle Elliott. He also was Jewish. He was quite short and Aunt Ada towered over him. They both had good jobs—she in the tire business, he in the furniture trade. While they were far from rich, I still referred to them as my "wealthy" relatives. I know they slipped money to mother on more than one occasion. Uncle Elliott and my father couldn't stand one another, though they'd tolerate each other at necessary family functions. He couldn't understand why my father wouldn't find a decent job, nor could he understand my crazy desire to be an actor. Moving to New York was totally beyond him. "Raymond is going to be just like his father," I heard him say, "a lazy good-for-nothing bum." I was furious. If there was *one* person I wouldn't be like, it was my father! His beer drinking had progressed to an almost daily ritual, and then he'd come home and start fighting with mother. I swore then that I'd never drink. I particularly couldn't stand the smell of beer. As a young boy I frequently had to run to the corner pool hall and drag him home for supper. Whenever I'd enter the bar the fumes of stale beer would immediately overwhelm me. Dad, however, was a good pool player. One time he was in the middle of a game, so I had to wait. Being bored, I picked up another cue stick and started to randomly hit the balls on an adjoining table. With one stroke, I pushed too hard, ripping a hole in the pool table's green felt. At seven years old, I'm sure I was the youngest person to be eighty-sixed from a bar. But to this day, I've never had a beer.

* * * * *

With my church money in my pocket, Michelle Condre and I boarded the Greyhound bus for our long anticipated journey to New York City. In tears, mother saw us off, along with my friends Rosemary and Jimmie. Of course, mother wasn't happy about my being with the "redheaded tootsie," but there was little she could do about it then.

Once in New York, J.B. Shanks and I rented a very small one room flat. There was no kitchen and the toilet was down the hall. There was just room enough for two twin beds, a chair and a small desk. That was it. Eventually, a friend of J.B.'s moved in—John George—a redheaded dancer. Talk about being crowded! But splitting the rent three ways was a big help, even if we had to double up in the twin beds. But what-the-hell, we were young and it was an exciting adventure. Despite the closeness our relationships were strictly platonic. Fortunately, when Billy Herman and Pat Horn arrived, they found their own accommodations.

The year at Irvine was wonderful. Robert Hartung and Leonard Altobell were our primary instructors, with a handsome young assistant, Richard Dunlap, often joining them. Years later, Dunlap would direct several of the Academy Award television broadcasts. Miss Irvine, of course, still held forth with the speech classes. For an hour each day, we'd all try to speak properly—not easy to do with a cork in your mouth.

Every few months, we would mount a full production of a play, inviting an audience. I remember appearing as the son in Kaufman & Hart's *The Man Who Came To Dinner*, with Michelle cast as the glamorous actress, Lorraine Sheldon. We also did a good production of Irwin Shaw's powerful anti-war play, *Bury the*

Dead. But my biggest opportunities came when I attempted the role of Mio in Maxwell Anderson's difficult verse play, *Winterset*, and in Patrick Hamilton's thriller, *Rope*, loosely based on the infamous Leopold-Loeb murder case.

I particularly enjoyed the dance class held across the hall in Anita Peters Wright's studio. While I was only a passable dancer, I did try hard, and I became a pet of Mrs. Wright's. Like Miss Irvine, she was also along in years, but she moved so gracefully, almost gliding when she walked. She had a massive head of grey hair piled upon her head. She also had a rather large mole protruding from her lower lip, with one long hair jutting from it. I always had the urge to pull that hair. Knowing I was with limited funds, she'd frequently invite me for dinner in her quarters, which were attached to the studio. It was while dining there one evening that I met Kent Barnes. He was fresh from Los Angeles and he'd come east to study with Mrs. Wright. Besides being a most promising dancer, he also happened to be quite attractive—with blond hair and the remnants of a Santa Monica tan. And, of course, he had one of those hard firm bodies that only a dancer can produce. I'd watch him workout and, eventually the attraction between us began to grow. Before long I was having my first "affair." Alas, it only lasted a month as he returned to Los Angeles. We corresponded for a while, but that was the end of our brief union.

The year at Irvine was coming to an end. During the summer months, Leonard Altobell, one of our teachers, ran a summer stock theatre in Litchfield, Connecticut. It was a professional Equity house with guest stars from Hollywood usually playing the leads in the weekly productions. Altobell, always looking to save a buck, would recruit some of the better students from Irvine to be apprentices at his theatre. The best thing about being an apprentice for him, however, was that he'd usually cast his in good roles throughout the summer. Then, after they'd appeared in three productions, they could qualify to join Actors Equity, the professional union. A major step for any young actor starting out. The lucky ones from our group included Pat, Billy and Michelle. No room for Raymond Stricklin, however. I was very disappointed and more than a bit jealous. Altobell explained to me that I just looked "too damn young" to be castable every week.

Not to be outdone, I'd read an ad in Theatre Arts magazine about the Ivoryton Playhouse, also in Connecticut. The ad was promoting their apprentice program: "Come act with the stars! Helen Hayes! Tallulah Bankhead!" the come-ons blatantly stated. Well, gullible as I was, I thought this was far superior to going to Litchfield. I applied, not knowing, of course, that you had to pay them $100 if you were accepted. I don't think many apprentices were turned down. Somehow I scraped together the money and went off to Ivoryton, fully expecting to act with Helen Hayes and Tallulah Bankhead. Wrong. As an apprentice, you were expected to do all the menial back stage jobs such as building the scenery, painting the flats, collecting the props—everything I hated. I also wasn't very good at it.

The first production of the summer didn't offer much chance for an apprentice to appear, being John Van Druten's three character play, *The Voice of the Turtle*, with movie stars John Payne and Joan Caulfield starring. The next show had a much larger cast; a restoration comedy called *The Beaux Stratagem*, with Brian Aherne as guest star. But still no role for Raymond Stricklin. In a huff, I told the management I was going to leave. They tried to talk me out of it, hinting there might be a juvenile role in the next play, *Laura*, with the Swedish actress Signe Hasso. There *was* a juvenile role, but I didn't play it as Ms. Hasso brought her own actor. This was the final straw, so I quit. Oh, yes, I had a very high opinion of myself. I must've been terribly cocky for a young actor with limited experience. Looking back, I wish I *had* learned to build sets, etc. It could've saved me a small fortune in carpentry bills!

On a chance, I took off for Litchfield. Once I was there, and it wasn't costing him anything, Altobell did use me—fleetingly—in three plays. The first was my biggest role—one scene—in the macabre comedy, *Arsenic and Old Lace*. Old time movie horror star, Bela Lugosi, was guest starred, though Pat Horn played one of the crazy sisters, Abigail, and stole the show. Though she was much too young for the role, she was wonderful at character work and was an absolute delight. I, however, was badly miscast as one of the little old men she poisons with her elderberry wine. Even with an added moustache and gray powdered hair you couldn't disguise my youthful appearance. The second show was the farce *Room Service*. Conceivably I could have played the young playwright, but that was being enacted by guest star Jackie Coogan—who was past forty, I kept screaming to anyone who would listen. Coogan, of course, had been a very famous child movie star (though I knew him better because he had been Betty Grable's first husband). My bit in this opus consisted of one line—"Telegram!"—and that was delivered off stage. But I was remembered on opening night. I rang the doorbell on cue, Coogan slightly opened the door and I'm supposed to hand him the telegram. But I was so nervous, afraid that I'd miss my cue, that I shoved my arm in too fast, hitting the actor in the head and knocking off his toupee! It was the biggest laugh of the evening, but not one that had been anticipated. I was sure I'd be fired. Fortunately, I wasn't, but I gingerly handed Mr. Coogan the telegram for the remaining performances. My final shot at Litchfield was another offstage role, again with one line. This time I was Piles, a gangster in *The Petrified Forest.* Michelle got her chance in this one, playing the female lead, Gaby. Though comedy showed her off best, she was quite moving in her dramatic role. Anyway, as a gangster, I'm supposed to pound on the locked café door, shouting, "It's Piles!" I thought I gave an inspired reading on opening night when I said the line with a strained grunt. This too got an unwanted laugh. Altobell said I sounded like I was taking a shit. Even though I'd made all three of my small roles stand out—all for the wrong reasons—it confirmed my high opinion of myself: I wasn't meant to play bit parts. And that was the end of our Litchfield summer. Billy, Pat and Michelle got their prized Equity cards. I had to plead with Altobell to get mine, but he finally consented. Now all the Texans were card-carrying professionals. Tomorrow the world . . .

* * * * *

So what does a "professional" actor do? I went home to Houston. First of all, I couldn't afford to stay in New York, and second, Vivien and Bob Altfeld who had helped Nina Vance form the Alley Theatre, had now raised the money to open an opulent outdoor summer musical theatre. It would offer me my first opportunity as a new member of Actors' Equity, my first paying job. The musical was the collegiate comedy, *Good News*, with Ann Crowley and Biff McGuire, two engaging young talents from New York, brought in for the leading roles. I had a featured role with one scheduled song. My dancing was adequate, but my singing voice definitely didn't cut it. Finally, Vivien had to give my song to someone else. That relieved me, but I sang along with the chorus and delivered my lines with youthful aplomb. Next, I played a small role in the Sigmund Romberg operetta, *New Moon,* with opera star Marguerite Piazza. Movie comedian Sterling Holloway also had a top featured spot.

During this period a bus-and-truck company of *The Man Who Came To Dinner* played a one-nighter, featuring a cast of graduate drama students from Baylor University. The two female leads were played by Martha Hyer, who'd just signed a movie contract, and a hilarious redhead named Mildred Cook, who stole the show as the glamorous Lorraine Sheldon. Michelle had gone to Baylor, so I joined her to see her old classmates. I particularly enjoyed meeting Mildred Cook, who was even funnier offstage. We would become lifelong friends. She would also change her name to Carole Cook.

Once the summer was over, I didn't know what to do next. Of course I really wanted to return to New York, but that wasn't feasible, financially. Mother kept pleading for me to go to college, wanting me to have something to "fall back on" if I wasn't able to make a living as an actor. And the odds of doing that, of course, were quite slim. Though it was a financial strain, mother insisted, so I enrolled at the University of Houston. Of course, I was only interested in the drama department. I attended for about six months, but it was really a waste of mother's hard-earned money. I'd also started skipping my other classes.

Michelle's mother, the exotic LaVe, came up with the idea to open a hot dog stand in downtown Houston, across the street from where a giant department store was being constructed. They called it the *Hollywood Hot Dog.* To give it a movieland glitter, the dogs were extra large and wrapped in *gold* paper. The stand itself was nothing more than a little shack with four stools for customers. For a while though, they did a whopping lunch business, thanks to the construction workers. I'd skip school and help them hawk hot dogs. It was hilarious. There they were—the flaming redhead Michelle and the jet-black dyed LaVe—dressed in their finest cocktail wear—slapping the mustard and onions on the oversized dogs. They both looked as if they were dressed for a night on the town. Maybe they were. I know LaVe had several dates with a construction worker. One day, however, the health department showed up, demanding that they wear something over their long flowing hair. The next day, LaVe, dressed all in black, showed up with a fancy lace mantilla draped over her head. No unglamorous cook's cap for her. The Hollywood Hot Dog stand went out of business shortly thereafter, but it was fun while it lasted.

I felt very guilty about spending mother's money, particularly since I wasn't taking advantage of the education, and finally told her I couldn't continue the college scene. Of course she was very disappointed. As for me, I *had* to get back to New York somehow. The obvious solution was for me to get a job and save my money. I hated the thought, but that's what I did. I applied for a position with the National Tube Company, a subsidiary of the giant U.S. Steel Company. My future boss almost didn't hire me when he found out I was an actor. "You'll only quit the moment you get an acting job," he rightly said. But I lied and promised I wouldn't leave, so he hired me. Mostly, I was doing typing and filing work. Typing was the one thing I'd learned to do really well in high school. Mr. Earle, my boss, took a liking to me and asked me to join him for dinner one evening at his rather swank apartment. He was a bachelor, in his forties, and apparently had more than dinner on his mind. I managed to wriggle out of the touchy situation. Today it would be called sexual harassment in the workplace. I, however, found the attention flattering. I just didn't want to go to bed with him. Fortunately, the situation didn't occur again.

During my year's stay with the National Tube Company, I did get an acting job, but the rehearsals were in the evening, so I didn't have to quit my daytime work. The Alley Theatre, now located in the old fan factory, was going to stage the world premiere of a new comedy titled *Season with Ginger*, written by Ronald Alexander. At last, I was going to work with Nina Vance at the Alley. I would play one of the teenage suitors of the play's young heroine. Playwright Alexander flew in from New York for the rehearsals, which made it even more exciting, particularly when I'd overhear conversations about taking the play to New York if it were a success. A stunning brunette named Sherry Britton joined the playwright after a few weeks. She had the greatest figure I'd ever seen—"built like a brick shithouse," is that the expression? I didn't find out until later that Miss Britton was quite well known in New York, being a star stripper. The play turned out to be a real audience pleaser, a very commercial property. New York producers started flying in to check it out, and finally it was optioned by the producing team of

Joseph Hyman and Bernard Hart (brother of the famous playwright, Moss Hart). I didn't meet any of them, of course, but it was exciting to be a part of a new play.

* * * * *

The 1940s were coming to a close. With 1950 looming ahead, I knew it was time to make my permanent move to the Big Apple.

As mother was packing my clothes, I happened to look out the back bedroom window. My father was standing at the fence, all alone, staring off into space. He looked so desolate. "You must speak to your father," mother said, "you must say goodbye." It wasn't something I was looking forward to doing, but I knew it was necessary. We had never been close. Several times over the years I had tried to talk mother into leaving him, especially after he'd been abusive one more time. Once she almost did, but she never carried out her threat. She took her marriage vows very seriously. And so, they continued their suffering in silence.

I finally got up the courage to join him in the backyard. As I was walking toward him, I had a sinking feeling in the pit of my stomach. I was now almost twenty-one years old, yet in all that time, we'd never had a real conversation. How sad. I approached him. "Dad, it's almost time for me to leave. I wanted to say goodbye." He turned toward me; tears welled up in his eyes. Suddenly, he grabbed me, pulling me close to him. It was the only intimate moment we ever shared. "Be sure and write your mother," he said. Then, as though he too was anxious for the moment to end, he pushed a hundred-dollar bill into my hand. "Take care of yourself."

TAKE TWO

It was 1950. I was determined that I would find success as an actor. I had drive and I had ambition; a combination that is an absolute necessity in the cut-throat world of show business. I didn't waste any time in starting my pursuit of that illusive dream. Early each day, after shaving and showering, I'd hit the streets of New York City, walking from one casting office to the other, zigzagging across the city. I would walk at least six or seven miles a day, perhaps more. In those days you didn't need an appointment to enter most of the offices. You just walked in, asking if there was anything you might be right for that day.

There was one office, located on Broadway that was a beehive of activity. The Max Richards office. They were constantly hiring actors for industrial films, army training films, commercials, extra work. The tiny outer office was always so crowded you could barely get inside the door. I'd usually stop by there twice a day—early morning, then again in the late afternoon on my way home. Just like today, actors who could play teenagers were always in great demand. I became a familiar face to many a secretary, though at the Richards office there was no secretary—just a tiny hole in the wall. After fighting your way to "the hole," you'd poke your head in and ask, "Anything today?" Eventually, my persistence paid off. I don't know how many training films and industrials I did, but quite a few. I also did a couple of commercials—one for television, the other a print job. My typing came in handy when I did a "back to school" commercial for Remington Rand typewriters, which got a lot of airplay (as the sponsor of the *What's My Line?* television game show). The print ad was a bit less glamorous—it was for pimples—with a before and after photo. The pay was usually minimum, but I worked enough to be able to join the Screen Actors Guild.

One day the Richards office asked if I wanted to do any movie extra work? I hated the idea, but every little bit of money was always welcome, so I accepted a day's shoot on a new George Cukor film for Columbia, *The Marrying Kind*, starring Judy Holliday and Aldo Ray. The location was Central Park. I was paired with a young girl and was told to walk across one of the park's bridges. We were way in the background, at least a block away from where the action was taking place with Holliday and Ray. During the first take, instead of just walking across the bridge as we'd been directed to do, I decided it would be more interesting if we stopped, wandered over to the side of the bridge, then toss a couple of pebbles into the lake below. We were so far away from the camera, what possible difference could it make? Wrong. Suddenly, over a loudspeaker, you heard an angry voice scream, "Cut! You've ruined the take! Keep moving!" I vowed right then and there that I'd never do extra work again. But I *had* been noticed. I *did* stand out in the crowd.

My vow to never do movie extra work again didn't last very long, however. The Richards office asked me to be in a crowd scene on *The Thief*, a Ray Milland movie shooting at the Empire State Building. Again, I was noticed and, again, for the wrong reason. It was supposed to be a winter scene, but I had worn a light gray suit, which photographed white, so I was removed from the shot—I looked "too summery." I got my day's pay, however. This time I really meant it—no more extra work. The next time I saw Ray Milland the circumstances would be entirely different.

My daily round making continued. After pounding the pavements, day-in-day-out, you began to recognize certain faces that you'd see every day. One was a blond actor named James Terry. We met in a casting office and had coffee afterwards. You could tell he'd just arrived from Los Angeles—West Coast actors always looked so much healthier with their tans. After we'd known each other for a few weeks, he said he wanted to move from his hotel, as it was too expensive. We decided to share an apartment. We found one very large room with a small kitchen and bath. It was strictly a roommate situation and we became almost as close as brothers. Jim was sometimes mistaken for Burt Lancaster, a comparison he didn't seem to mind at all. But I didn't think he was too serious about an acting career.

Meantime, I continued my daily pursuit of new jobs. I appeared a couple of times on the very popular Ed Sullivan *Toast of the Town* television variety series. On the first one, I played a young sailor about to be shipped overseas. It was a television visual, no dialogue, but I got a good bit of camera time since Kate Smith was singing *The Last Time I Saw Paris* to me as I forlornly walked up the gangplank. My second appearance on the Sullivan show was somewhat more memorable. Film star Douglas Fairbanks Jr. was doing a dramatic reading of *The Battle Hymn of the Republic* downstage, while in the background behind him, in silhouette, was the famous pose of the marines raising the American flag over Iwo Jima. I was one of the marines. We're all bunched together, as shown in the famous photograph, when the actor behind me got a giant erection. The flagpole shook that day! The actor was named Val , who went on to become a well-known soap opera player. He was also known for having one of the bigger cocks, which he proudly displayed. His theory seemed to be—*if you've got it, flaunt it.*

I continued doing small parts on all sorts of "live" television programs. I appeared several times on *The Faye Emerson Show*, a sort of talk show/variety show combination. Miss Emerson was a bawdy dame, reeking with intelligence and a great sense of humor. She'd been a Warner Bros. contract actress for several years before finding fame on the small tube. Later she would marry Elliott Roosevelt, son of the late president. Another small effort was in a comedy sketch on Chico Marx's variety series (yes, *that* Chico Marx), as well as similar duties on the Mary Healy-Peter Lind Hayes show. Sometime during this period, I also did summer stock again—this time at the Woodstock Playhouse in upstate New York. I repeated my role as the son in Shaw's *You Never Can Tell*, which I'd done earlier at the Houston Little Theatre, and played the spoiled son in J.B. Priestley's *An Inspector Calls*.

During my Faye Emerson appearances, I met a man named Gus Schirmer. He was a talent manager and son of the man who owned the famous Schirmer Music Publishing Company. Gus was a roly-poly guy, looking like a plump cherub. He seemed quite sophisticated to me, as well as a bit of a snob. He asked me to dinner one evening at his plush eastside townhouse and I was very impressed because Carol Channing was one of his guests. Over the weeks he developed a crush on me, and while I enjoyed being with him socially, I didn't want the relationship to become more intimate.

Gus also had ambitions toward directing. And if his first effort was any indication, he was headed in the right direction. He put together a summer package of *Pal Joey*, one of the great musicals, and played a number of top theatres, including the Westport Playhouse in Connecticut, which was generally regarded at *the* summer theatre. Owned by the Theatre Guild, the playhouse attracted the biggest stage and screen stars, often trying out new scripts before they went on to Broadway (or not). I recall seeing Maureen Stapleton and Macdonald Carey in a tryout called *Wedding Breakfast* (which didn't transfer to Broadway), as well as a production of Kurt Weill's dramatic musical, *Down In The Valley. A*ppearing in it was a beautiful young blonde actress, who you just knew would become a film star. I first spied her sitting in a glorious field of yellow daisies—a spectacular sight—one that I'm sure David Lean would have used in *Doctor Zhivago*. Not only was she lovely to look at, onstage she was also a lovely actress. Her name was Eva Marie Saint. Within three short years she'd have an Oscar for her stunning debut performance opposite Marlon Brando in *On The Waterfront*. Gus's production of *Pal Joey* was a rousing success too. He'd cast the leads perfectly—Carol Bruce and Bob Fosse. Fosse was absolutely sensational in the title role.

Back in the city, Schirmer asked me to attend a very chi-chi cocktail party. It was being hosted by a woman named Jo Carstairs. She was reputedly one of the richest women in America, owning an island in the Bahamas. *Life* magazine had even done an elaborate photo spread on her. She also happened to be a very well known lesbian, with rumored romances with Greta Garbo and Marlene Dietrich. She was also quite "butch." Her mannish appearance was heightened by the expensive tailored suits she wore to match her boy's haircut. Despite her offbeat appearance, there was something very stylishly attractive about her. She also had a reputation for being quite generous with friends in need.

As the youngest one at the cocktail party, I felt quite out of place. It appeared to be a very elegant, wealthy crowd. Back in Houston I'd vowed never to touch liquor. I now changed my mind. Everyone was having a martini, seemingly to be having a glorious time, so I thought it was time I grew up and had a drink. The first one relaxed me; the second made me feel even better. I heard laughter and applause coming from another room, so I decided to checkout what the commotion was about. I noticed a group of very well dressed people standing around a piano, and I could hear a man and woman singing—sometimes together, sometimes solo. The music seemed quite sophisticated, and their voices were very unique. I didn't know who they were, but the group obviously adored them. T*hey* turned out to be Mabel Mercer and Bobby Short, two of café society's darlings who regularly entertained at chic eastside supper clubs.

While I was listening to this unusual duo, I noticed a young woman standing by herself at one side of the room. She was stunning and looked as much out of place in this crowd as I did. She was tall, athletic-looking, with short-cropped hair bleached from the sun, with a tan to match (Was she from Hollywood? I wondered.) She was simply, but tastefully dressed, wearing little makeup. In fact, she reminded me a little of Ingrid Bergman as she appeared in *For Whom The Bell Tolls*. So fresh and natural. She noticed me staring at her, then smiled. I walked over to her. "Hi," she said, extending her hand, "I'm Phyllis Gates." As we chatted, she revealed that she'd just arrived from Florida, which accounted for the tan, but said she was really from Minnesota, a farm girl, and she'd recently quit her job as an airline stewardess. We had another vodka martini. By the time the evening was ending we'd exchanged phone numbers and promised to meet the following morning for coffee. She was staying in a hotel on West 58th Street. "What a coincidence," I answered, "my roommate and I have just moved to an apartment-hotel right across the street."

The next morning I entered the corner drug store, which was attached to Phyllis' hotel. I noticed her immediately, seated at the counter with a handsome stud type, dressed in blue jeans and a black leather jacket. She greeted me warmly, then turned to the stud to introduce me, but she couldn't remember his name. "Marlon Brando," he offered. He seemed quite amused that she didn't know his name. Of course, I had recognized him immediately, twice having paid to stand to see his galvanizing performance as Stanley Kowalski in Tennessee Williams' masterpiece, *A Streetcar Named Desire*. It was the most exciting stage performance by an actor that I had ever seen. He told Phyllis he'd call her and left the drug store. "Phyllis," I asked incredulously, "don't you know who that is?" She didn't. I hastily explained that he was the hottest actor in America, even though the film version of *Streetcar* hadn't been released yet. She didn't seem overly impressed, however, as she was totally unaware about anything related to the theatre or movies. Shortly after this early morning meeting, she dated Brando a couple of times but said she found him rather crude, much preferring his roommate, comedian-actor Wally Cox.

We were now almost inseparable. We'd meet everyday for breakfast, for lunch, for dinner. With Jim Terry, we became like two brothers and a sister. She even started making the rounds with me, going from one office to the next. And she created quite a stir at practically every stop. But she had no interest in being an actress. After several weeks, and to save money, Jim and I asked her to move in with us. We had sufficient room, so the arrangement was quite satisfactory.

During one of my many round-making stops, an agent named Stephen Draper suggested that I shorten my name from Raymond to Ray. That appealed to me, as I'd always hated the name. He also said Stricklin spelled with a 'y' would look better on a marquee. I didn't know about that, but I liked his positive thinking. Thus, Raymond Stricklin's professional name became Ray Stricklyn. Draper was one of the better independent agents, shortly to gain in prestige when he had the foresight to sign a young unknown actress named Geraldine Page.

Besides the slight name alteration, my life was about to make a dramatic change in another way too. Through mutual friends, I met a young actor named Robert Casper, who was appearing on Broadway in a revival of Shaw's *Saint Joan* with Uta Hagen. He was about five years older than me, with a strong dominating personality. Before I knew what hit me, I had been seduced; both mentally and physically. As contented as I was living with Phyllis and Jim, I let him talk me into taking a small apartment with him on West 60th Street, which was a rather unsavory neighborhood. Located just off Tenth Avenue, the apartment was a fourth-floor walkup in a dingy brownstone building. But the monthly rent was right—$16.00! It consisted of two rooms—a kitchen, with the bathtub prominently located near the sink, and a combination living room/bedroom as well as a small walk-in closet. One window opened to a dirty fire escape. Our bathroom, however, was down the hall. It was our private bathroom, but we had to keep it padlocked to make sure it remained that way. Believe me, going to the bathroom during the freezing winter months was *not* a pleasant necessity.

Casper decided to paint the living-room/bedroom a deep burgundy color. It was attractive at first, but became increasingly dark and depressing after a while. He also didn't like my closeness with Phyllis and Jim and tried to alienate them. Although he didn't succeed, I did see less of them. In show biz terms, Bob Casper would be described as a "character juvenile." He was short, about 5'7", with dark brown hair. In appearance he reminded me a bit of actor Roddy McDowall. In fact, he'd replace Roddy in an upcoming tour of Shaw's *Misalliance*.

In the beginning, of course, our relationship was quite cozy. There were happy moments. But, increasingly I had the underlying feeling that he was always putting me down. Certainly he was better read than I , with his nose constantly stuck in some complicated book. He was considered by his friends to be a very good actor, studying diligently at the Uta Hagen-Herbert Berghof Studio. He was a *serious* actor, he'd remind me when I would come home thrilled that I'd gotten a television job, small though it may be. He wasn't interested in doing "such crap." I noticed, however, that my "crappy" television jobs came in handy when it was time to pay the monthly bills. Secretly, I think he was envious. I was a much more commercial type than he was, so I was a little more castable. It was during this period that I started drinking more too; mostly cheap wine, but there never seemed to be a lack of vodka either. But I was young and recuperated quickly from any hangover.

One night we started arguing about some actress; I don't recall who now (no it wasn't Linda Darnell), and he had disagreed with my opinion, which was usually the case. "If you want to see a really *good* actress," he said, "wait until you catch Geraldine Page." "I've never heard of her," I answered. He explained that they'd done stock together, had both attended the Goodman Theatre in Chicago and were currently studying together in Uta Hagen's class. "Gerry's about to open in a play in Greenwich Village," he said, "we'll go see it."

The play was a revival of Tennessee Williams' *Summer and Smoke*, which had been a critical failure when it had originally played on Broadway (directed by Margo Jones, incidentally). Now it was being revived at a fairly new theatre called Circle-In-The-Square. The Off Broadway movement was just getting started and, at that point, was rarely covered by the press. *Summer and Smoke* would change all that. The production opened quietly, with no fanfare. One night, however, the powerful *New York Times* critic, Brooks Atkinson, went to see it. A few days later his review appeared. It was a love letter. The direction by Jose Quintero was magnificent and a young actress named Geraldine Page, playing Alma, was absolutely breathtaking. He urged New Yorkers to see it. Before long, the rest of the theatrical press began covering it and the production became *the* thing to see in New York. Overnight, it seemed, this Geraldine Page was being heralded as giving perhaps the greatest performance seen in New York since the legendary Laurette Taylor in *The Glass Menagerie*. Lofty praise indeed. Geraldine Page and Jose Quintero. Two major careers had been launched.

I went to see it, skeptical that it could really be *that* good. But it was. For three hours I sat spellbound, returning to see it at least a half dozen times during its run. To this day, I consider Page's performance to be one of the finest I've ever seen. She quickly became my favorite actress and remained so throughout the years. We also became friends, thanks to Bob Casper. It was a most exciting time, watching her career flourish.

The Circle-In-The-Square would change my life too, but in a different way. While *Summer and Smoke* was still running, I read in the paper that playwright Tennessee Williams would be reading his poetry at a special Sunday afternoon event. I subwayed down to the Village theatre, only to be told that the performance was sold-out. Dejectedly, I stood outside the theatre, hoping there might be a cancellation. Suddenly, from out of nowhere, a birdlike gentleman approached, asking if he could help me. I explained that I couldn't get a ticket. Taking me by the arm, he said, "Come with me." With no questions asked, we sailed past the ticket taker, into the arena playhouse, where he seated me on a front row. "By the way," he said, "my name is Paul Bigelow." I told him mine, then he proceeded to introduce me to the people already seated on the row. "Mr. Stricklyn, this is Elia Kazan ... this is William Inge ... this is Cheryl Crawford ... and Audrey Wood." I was flabbergasted. It was a veritable "who's who" of important theatre names, all closely associated with Mr. Williams.

When the afternoon was over, Bigelow asked if I happened to be an actor? Silly question, I thought, as half of the audience was made up of actors, all adoring fans of Tennessee Williams. After I nodded in the affirmative, Bigelow explained that he was with the Theatre Guild and they were in the midst of casting a play for a summer production at Westport Playhouse, an old Viennese romance entitled *Fata Morgana,* which told the tale of a beautiful older woman's infatuation with a handsome youth. He thought I might be right for the role, suggesting I drop by the Guild's office and pick up a script. I sped home on a cloud, not mentioning the incident to Casper, however.

The following day I hurried to the Theatre Guild's imposing offices. Bigelow said to study the script and then he'd set up a reading. A couple of days later, he phoned, asking if I was available to stop by his apartment around 6 P.M.? He would "read" me then.

It was pouring down rain as the appointed hour neared, and I only had enough money on me to either take the subway *to* his eastside flat, or to use the funds for the ride home. Since it was raining so hard, I opted for the former. Even so, I was sopping wet when I arrived at his door. He greeted me, and as we started up a flight of stairs to a second floor, I heard the sound of laughter. He apologized, saying, "Oh, some friends of mine are just leaving. I'll read you as soon as they've gone." We had to pass through the dining room area, where several people were seated around the table. "Mr. Stricklyn, I'd like you to meet Carson McCullers, Bennett Cerf, Tennessee Williams." He poured me a glass of red wine and settled me in the living room. My God, I thought, he *knows* everybody! Of course I was awed by the celebrities in the adjoining room. Mrs. McCullers' *The Member of the Wedding* was one of the most beautiful plays I'd ever seen highlighted by the star-making performance of Julie Harris. Mr. Cerf, of course, was the head of Random House publishing, as well as being a celebrity panelist on the popular *What's My Line?* game show . . . and then there was Mr. Williams.

I tried looking at my script, but I was too nervous to concentrate. I happened to glance down the hall, and just as I did, I noticed a handsome young sailor strolling out of a back room, presumably going to the bathroom. Who's *that*, I wondered? Soon I heard the sound of his guests leaving. Then at the doorway, I heard Bigelow say, "Oh, Tenn, would you like to stay and hear this young man read?" *Please say no*, I said to myself. I was nervous enough without having to read in front of Tennessee Williams! But the southern drawl answered in the affirmative.

They settled in chairs opposite me, toasting me with their raised glasses. Bigelow explained that the Guild was negotiating with Greer Garson to star in *Fata Morgana*. I gulped. Miss Garson was a tremendously popular movie actress. Mary Hunter, he said, would be directing. I recognized her name as I'd seen her production of *The Respectful Prostitute*, which had caused quite a stir.

Bigelow picked a romantic scene between the youth and the woman for me to read. "Tenn, would you mind reading with Ray?" "I'd be absolutely charmed," Mr. Williams replied. Did I detect an attempt at a British accent in his answer? He's trying to be Greer Garson I decided. We read through the scene a couple of times, with Bigelow making suggestions. Eventually, we finished and he said, "Quite good." Again the wineglasses were raised. Then, bless him, Mr. Williams turned to Paul and said in that long, drawn-out southern drawl, "P-a-u-l, if I were you, I'd give this young man the part." From that moment on, I've always said Tennessee Williams was my first leading lady.

I was singin' in the rain all the way home.

A few days later, I was called to the Guild to meet the director, Mary Hunter. She greeted me with a warm smile, then said, "Well, you've certainly come highly recommended. Tennessee, himself, called to tell me about you." The reading went well. Bigelow told me that it looked favorable for me to get the role. Then days went by. There was a major snag; it seems the Guild couldn't get a firm answer from Greer Garson, who kept changing her mind. Finally, they gave up on her and made an offer to another beautiful film actress, Madeleine Carroll. She considered it for a while, but decided she didn't really want to act any more. The role called for an actress with class and style, one with real star magnetism. Although other actresses were discussed, like June Havoc and a musical comedy performer, Luba Malina, they weren't really ideal. When no suitable star was available, the Guild abandoned the project. I was, understandably, heartbroken.

But the experience had made Paul Bigelow a valuable friend and ally. I didn't realize it at the time, but he was almost a legendary figure behind the scenes in the New York theatre community. His talent for dissecting scripts and general knowledge was considered impeccable. He knew my disappointment when *Fata Morgana* was cancelled, and he also knew I needed a job. He arranged for me to start working at the Guild. I'd answer phones; type letters, read scripts, and write critiques. Eventually, because of my typing skills, I started working for the Guild's head honchos, Lawrence Langner and Theresa Helburn. They were getting ready to produce a comedy called *Heavenly Twins*, to star Faye Emerson and the French film actor Jean-Pierre Aumont. It would be his American stage debut. He was quite concerned about his French accent; afraid that he wouldn't be understood in

English. He asked the Guild to recommend someone to cue him and help him with his English pronunciation. I got the job. We'd meet at his hotel suite, going over his lines again and again, with me telling him when he wasn't intelligible. Thanks to my coaching, Jean-Pierre said he spoke English with a southern accent! A surprise visitor one day was British actor Laurence Harvey, who was also in New York to make his Broadway bow in *Island of Goats* opposite Uta Hagen. Neither play was successful. Jean-Pierre, in the years ahead, would become a longtime friend.

My various jobs at the Guild began to slacken, so Paul next had me working at the William Liebling-Audrey Wood agency. Audrey represented Tennessee and was a powerful force behind his career. Again, I answered phones and read scripts. One day Audrey asked me if I'd mind doing some extra work for Tennessee? *Mind!* I jumped at the chance. He needed someone to type script revisions on his new play, *Cat on a Hot Tin Roof.* Off and on for about a month, I'd go to his apartment and try to decipher his scribbling. I loved it though. Just being in his presence was an honor. This was at the height of his critical and popular success, so he was a joy to be around. I never saw any of his negative side. His demons hadn't yet begun their haunt.

Sometime later, through my connections with the Guild, I got my Houston friend, Billy Herman, a job there. Like Bigelow, Billy had a bright mind and was quite good at analyzing scripts. He'd decided his acting career wasn't going to happen, yet he wanted to remain in the business. It was the start of a productive relationship, and Billy eventually became an executive in the Guild's television department when they started producing plays for the *U.S. Steel Hour.* By the late 1950s, I had moved to the West Coast and I remember Billy calling me about a young actor named Warren Beatty, the first time I'd ever heard his name. They became good friends. Tragically, Billy contracted cancer and lingered for a while in the hospital. But when I'd speak with him, he'd always say how considerate Beatty was, frequently visiting him in the hospital. I always liked Warren Beatty a little bit more because of that story.

Billy wasn't my only Houston friend that died way too young. Both John B. Shanks and Bill Gideon also had the dreaded cancer and died at very early ages. We'd all had such ambitious dreams back at the Houston Little Theatre. Now they were gone. And my friend Pat Horn, who was so talented, decided that she couldn't take the constant rejection and returned to Houston to marry an attorney, Gerald Brown. However, years later, as Pat Brown, she would re-emerge on the theatre scene. That left crazy Michelle Condre and me battling the Broadway wars. She got there first, in a little farce called *Springtime Follies*, directed by Leonard Altobell, but it folded immediately and she too returned to Texas.

Meantime, Paul Bigelow continued in his efforts to help me. Tennessee's *The Rose Tattoo*, which had had a very successful Broadway engagement, was going to be done in Canada with the original stars, Maureen Stapleton and Eli Wallach. Paul thought the role of the young sailor was perfect for me (and it was). Tennessee agreed. Paul took me down to meet Eli in his Village apartment and he thought I'd be fine too. But once again, I had a bitter disappointment. The Canadian actors union refused to give working permits to anyone but the two stars, so that ended that opportunity. I had one more brief encounter with *The Rose Tattoo*. I was submitted for the movie version, but after meeting with director Daniel Mann, the part went to Ben Cooper.

I decided to ask Paul for one more favor. Could he possibly arrange for me to get an interview with Edith Van Cleve, a powerhouse legit agent at MCA? For months I'd tried to get past the receptionist, but was always rebuffed. Prior to this, I'd more or less been freelancing where agents were concerned, with different ones submitting me for various projects. MCA, along with the William Morris office, was the most powerful theatrical and motion picture agency in the business. MCA also had the most elegant offices, with expensive wood paneling lining the walls and plush carpeting beneath your feet. Among Van Cleve's prominent client roster—Marlon Brando and Tallulah Bankhead.

Paul immediately arranged an interview. One phone call from the *right* person made it so simple. It pays to have influential friends. On the appointed afternoon, I arrived at the MCA offices, only to be kept waiting for nearly an hour. Finally, Ms. Van Cleve buzzed the receptionist and I was allowed inside the hallowed inner sanctum. She was in her fifties, with white hair, horn-rimmed glasses and a very pleasant smile. She apologized for having kept me waiting, explaining that her secretary was out ill and she was swamped trying to juggle things by herself. I noticed several photographs on her wall, but not of her famous clients. They were pictures of thoroughbred horses. Tallulah was in one of the shots, but the horse was more prominently featured. Van Cleve was an avid horsewoman; owning several.

I liked her immediately, and she seemed to respond to me. She said Paul had spoken quite favorably about me. Unfortunately, she said she couldn't represent me at that time, but she'd keep her eyes open for any scripts that came in that I might be right for. I believed her, her straightforwardness not sounding like the usual bullshit. All during our interview, the phone kept ringing. "I'm going crazy without my secretary," she said. Half-jokingly, I replied, "Well, I'm an excellent typist." Among her friends and business associates, Miss Van Cleve was affectionately called Edie. Soon, I would be calling her Edie too.

A few days later, my home phone rang. Casper answered it. "It's MCA?" he questioned. I had learned not to tell him too much about my career activities, as he had a way of turning it into a negative. It was Miss Van Cleve. "Were you serious," she asked, "about being a good typist?" "The best," I replied. "Would you be interested in working with me until my secretary comes back?"

* * * * *

And so I began my sojourn in the theatrical agency business. I loved Edie Van Cleve. She could be tough, if the occasion called for it, but she was also great fun to be around. Our relationship just seemed to click. Also, I happened to be quite capable at the job.

Right next to Edie's office was the chamber of Maynard Morris, the other top agent at MCA. Though Morris handled some legit transactions for specific clients, he was primarily the liaison with the motion picture world. Among his top clients were Tyrone Power and Gregory Peck. His secretary's desk was directly opposite mine. Her name was Ina Bernstein. One morning, Maynard, who was a very nervous, fuss-budgety type, was in a state of panic. Ina, his secretary for many years, had been promoted to a new position within the agency (she would later become a top casting executive at one of the major television networks). Without her, Maynard was completely lost.

Suddenly, I had a brilliant idea. Since my friend Phyllis was looking for a job, why couldn't she temporarily fill in until Maynard found someone more experienced? He agreed to meet her. Of course, she charmed him. Her typing was only of the hunt-and-peck school, but she could answer the phones, a very important instrument in an agent's office. I *say* she could answer the phones. That may be an overstatement. "Ray," she would say, "It's Darryl Zanuck calling from Hollywood. Should I put him through?" "Yes!" I'd scream back, "he's only the head of 20th Century Fox!"

I'd probably been working for Edie about seven weeks when her secretary was finally able to return to work. Though I knew it was imminent, I hated to see the job end.

Then a near tragedy struck. Phyllis had stepped off a curb, ready to cross the street, when she was hit by a speeding car. She was seriously hurt, with internal injuries and a badly damaged leg. A steel plate was eventually placed in the leg. She was in the hospital for several weeks with mounting medical expenses soaring into the thousands of dollars. After recuperating for several weeks, Phyllis decided she needed a change of scenery and, after speaking with our former roommate, Jim Terry, who had returned to Los Angeles, made the decision to move to the West Coast. I hated to see her go, but we promised to keep in touch.

Back on the MCA front, while all the above chaos was going on, Edie's secretary returned. With Phyllis gone, Maynard was frantic again. Edie suggested that he use me. "You're the first male secretary MCA has ever hired," he said. I think he rather fancied the idea. While most thought Maynard extremely difficult to work with—mainly because he was so hyper—I managed to get along with him quite well. And, with me answering the phones, there was no delay in putting a call through from a Darryl F. Zanuck, or a Samuel Goldwyn, or a Dore Schary. I knew all their names. My early devotion to *Photoplay* magazine came in very handy.

Once Maynard began to relax with me, he opened up a bit, and we played a little game. While Maynard never admitted to being homosexual, there seemed to be a mutual understanding between us. When a young actor would request to see him, the receptionist would call me. Since I'd had so much trouble getting my initial interview, I was much more sympathetic to the actor's plight. Maynard would send me out to "scout" them. If I thought they were particularly attractive, I'd come back and tell him, and then he'd agree to see them. In those days, a Dustin Hoffman or an Al Pacino would never have gotten past the receptionist. It was the day of the conventionally handsome leading man, particularly in Hollywood, and offbeat types weren't considered potential star material. Now it's just the reverse, though good looks still have their distinct advantages.

One weekend Maynard took off for Yale University to see some stage production. He returned raving about a young actor named Paul Newman. He'd told Newman that he'd like to represent him once he'd finished college, presuming he was interested in pursuing a career. He was serious. Almost immediately Maynard had him working in the "live" television dramas, then got him cast in a supporting role in William Inge's hit play, *Picnic*. If you're going to have a major career in show business, there's usually someone with power behind you. Maynard Morris became that power at the start of Paul Newman's career.

* * * * *

My acting career was about to resume too. Edie said it must've come from my handling all her contracts.

I'd heard about a new Broadway play being cast. It was titled *The Climate of Eden* and was considered an important project because it was written by the great Moss Hart. He also was going to direct the production. Hart, with his partner, George S. Kaufman, had written some of the theatre's most popular and successful comedies, like *You Can't Take It With You* and *The Man Who Came To Dinner*. His book for the Kurt Weill musical, *Lady In The Dark,* had been a very successful star vehicle for Gertrude Lawrence, as well as making a star of Danny Kaye. Of course, Hart's direction of *My Fair Lady* would come much later. His new play, however, wasn't a comedy. It was a drama, adapted from a novel by Edgar Mittelholzer, *Shadows Move Among Them*.

By coincidence, *The Climate of Eden* was being produced by the team of Joseph Hyman and Bernard Hart (Moss's brother), the same producers who'd come to the Alley Theatre and optioned Ronald Alexander's comedy, *Season With Ginger*. The play had been retitled *Time Out for Ginger* and it was also scheduled for the 1952–1953 season.

I secured an interview with the producers and, eventually, they had me read for Moss Hart. The play's action took place in the house and church of Rev. Harmston in the jungle of British Guiana. Besides the Reverend and his wife, the

As I appeared in my Broadway stage debut for Moss Hart's The Climate of Eden.

play offered two very strong dramatic roles for their daughters, as well as two supporting roles for their younger brothers. I was auditioning for Garvey, the older of the two. The play had a large cast; twenty-one, and required British accents.

My first reading went well and I was called back a second and third time. Finally, I was told that it had been narrowed down to one other actor, James Lipton, and myself. After several anxious days, producer Hyman called and said how much they'd liked me, but they'd decided to go with Lipton. Of course I was devastated. I'd come *so* close.

I read in *The New York Times* that rehearsals had begun. Signed for the leading roles were John Cromwell, as the Reverend, with Isobel Elsom as his wife. Cromwell had been one of Hollywood's most esteemed directors, filming such movie classics as *Of Human Bondage,* the movie that established Bette Davis as an important actress; David O. Selznick's *Since You Went Away* with an all-star cast, including Claudette Colbert, Jennifer Jones, Joseph Cotten, Shirley Temple, Robert Walker, Monty Woolley and Lionel Barrymore. He'd also directed Irene Dunne, Rex Harrison and Linda Darnell in *Anna and the King of Siam* (long before it became *The King and I* musical). Sadly, he'd been caught-up in the frightening Communist witch-hunts of the day and his directing career was seriously damaged. Several years later he returned to films to do *The Goddess*, with the great Kim Stanley. Isobel Elsom was a handsome British character actress, who had been featured in many movies. For the all-important roles of the daughters, Hart had cast Penelope Munday and Rosemary Harris, two young actresses from London. Lee Montague, also British, was cast in the romantic lead. James Lipton and Ken Walken (his infant brother was Christopher Walken, a name for the future) would enact the young sons. There were also roles for several black actors—with Jane White, Earle Hyman, Leon Moore and Charles Gordone set for those. (Gordone would go on to win a Pulitzer Prize, no less, for his play, *No Place To Be Somebody.*)

Rehearsals had been under way for less than a week when I received a call from the Hyman & Hart office, requesting that I come to see them. I assumed it might be about repeating my role in *Time Out For Ginger.* But when I met with them they said they were thinking of replacing James Lipton and Moss wanted to hear me read again. I was to go to the Martin Beck Theatre, where they were rehearsing, sneak into the balcony and watch. They didn't want to take any chance of Lipton seeing me. It was all very mysterious. But I also had empathy for Lipton. As much as I wanted the role, my heart went out to him. He seemed a capable actor, but they'd decided his dark coloring might be too similar to Lee Montague, and Moss had decided to cast the role younger (as I write this, Lipton is the host of the very respected *Inside the Actors Studio* program on the Bravo cable network).

At noon the stage manager dismissed the cast for lunch. I was called to the stage. I couldn't see who was in the darkened auditorium, but I assumed it was Moss, as well as Hyman and Hart. I read a couple of scenes with the stage manager. When I'd finished, Moss came to the edge of the stage and said, "Very good. Thank you for coming in again. We'll be in touch." I didn't know what that meant, but, getting used to rejection, I assumed it was a polite way of dismissing me. Suddenly, from the darkened theatre, I heard a woman's voice: "Oh, Moss, why don't you tell the kid he's got the part! Why keep him dangling?" It was Kitty Carlisle, the playwright's wife. "You're right," he smiled. "The role is yours."

When the cast was re-assembled, Lipton was let go. Rosemary Harris later told me that his dismissal made them all very nervous, realizing that they, too, could still be given the heave-ho. Of course that didn't happen. But the situation only made me more anxious. Stepping into a cast that had already been in rehearsal becomes catch-up time.

Our first out-of-town stop was Philadelphia, where the reviews were decidedly mixed. This threw Moss for a loop. Next we played Wilmington, Delaware. The notices were much better, with a rave from one critic, who compared the play favorably with *The Member of the Wedding*. Every day we'd have rehearsals, with new scenes added, then discarded, and then added again. Or their order in the play would be reversed. It was very confusing. Moss loved the play so much, thinking it his finest work, that he couldn't get a proper perspective on what needed to be done. A good argument for a writer not staging his own script.

Our final pre-Broadway playground was the National Theatre in Washington, D.C. It's hard to fathom now, but *The Climate of Eden* was the first time in the nation's capital that a mixed cast had been allowed to appear on the National's stage. I know I caused a stir when my character patted Jane

White, a beautiful black actress on the ass. You could audibly hear the murmuring in the audience. Also, in the curtain call, I was holding her hand when we took our bows. Whites weren't supposed to be that familiar with people of color. It was eerie and appalling at the same time. Sometimes I'd have lunch with Leon Moore, an extremely handsome black actor, and we had to pick our dining spots very carefully.

While we were appearing in Washington, Bob Casper called, saying he wanted to come see the play. I really didn't want him to, but he was determined. I was still feeling insecure and I knew he would only make me more so. But he came, offering his unasked for critique of the play and my performance. I was very relieved when he returned to New York.

We officially opened at the Martin Beck Theatre on the evening of November 6, 1952. It was an exciting night for me; my long hoped-for Broadway debut. Our joy was short-lived, however, since the notices, while respectable, weren't the type to cause long lines at the box office. Brooks Atkinson in *The New York Times* gave it a good notice, but not a rave. It was obvious that we wouldn't have a long run. Moss Hart was bitterly disappointed and the play's failure disturbed him for a very long time. In fact, I don't think he ever wrote another play, eventually concentrating on direction and an occasional screenplay (Judy Garland's *A Star Is Born,* for one). The critics praised the actors, particularly Rosemary Harris and Penelope Munday. I received a couple of nice mentions. Rosemary decided to stay in America, signed with Edie Van Cleve at MCA, and was immediately besieged with movie offers. But she wasn't interested in becoming a film actress and turned all contract offers down. She did do one early film, *Beau Brummell,* with Stewart Granger and Elizabeth Taylor, but that was it. Instead, she concentrated on her stage work, becoming one of our very finest actresses. At the end of the season, when all the awards started being handed out, Brooks Atkinson re-reviewed the play. Now he called it "one of the best of the year." Too bad he hadn't done that when we first opened. We closed after only twenty performances.

I wouldn't have to wait too long before I had my next opportunity. The Circle-In-The-Square, after a year's run with *Summer and Smoke,* was preparing to do a revival of Truman Capote's *The Grass Harp*. The Off Broadway movement was really beginning to thrive now, and the Circle was leading the way. The press was also curious to see what director Jose Quintero would do next, and the critics had already catapulted Geraldine Page to stage stardom when she made her Broadway bow in *Midsummer*. Apparently in the original Broadway production of *The Grass Harp* the set, which included a giant tree house, had overwhelmed Capote's fragile story. Of course, Quintero's production would be much simpler. He cast two superb actresses, Clarice Blackburn and Ruth Attaway, in two of the script's leading roles, and I would play the other top role, Collin, a young lad who spent a good deal of time in the tree house.

The rehearsals were an absolute revelation to me. Jose Quintero was originally from Panama, and he would frequently get his tongue twisted between Spanish and English, so you had to listen carefully to what he was saying. He was probably around thirty years old at the time, but his wisdom seemed way beyond his years. His understanding of the characters and their relationships and motivations was remarkable. It was the first time I'd been directed so carefully, so lovingly. Not just me; the whole cast. He delved deeply into the human soul. Listening to him, and watching him, let alone being directed by him, was almost like a religious experience. It's not hard to understand why he became one of the most respected and distinguished directors in the American theatre. Besides *Summer and Smoke*, he became the foremost interpreter of Eugene O'Neill's works, starting with the Circle's production of *The Iceman Cometh*, which brought stage stardom to Jason Robards, then the original production of O'Neill's masterpiece, *Long Day's Journey Into Night*, and his award-winning presentation of *Moon for the Misbegotten*. He had an uncanny talent for bringing out the best in his actors. Of course, *The Grass Harp* was a slight work compared to the best of O'Neill and Tennessee Williams, but it was a lovely little tone poem and our production brought out all its charming qualities. The reviews were excellent and we ran for six months. It was a marvelous experience.

I wasn't prepared, however, for what happened next. It was time for the annual theatre awards for the 1952-1953 season. *The Climate of Eden* had opened at the end of '52, while *The Grass Harp* opened on April 27, 1953. Since 1944, editor Daniel Blum had started bestowing annual Theatre World Awards on the "Most Promising Personalities" of the season, given to actors making their

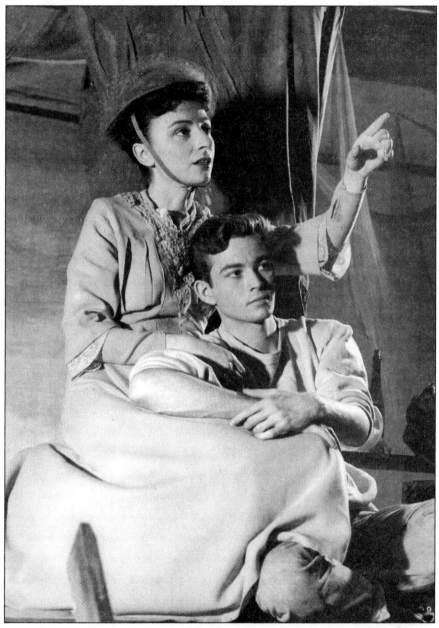

Co-starring with Clarice Blackburn in Truman Capote's The Grass Harp, *directed by Jose Quintero.*

Broadway bows. Judy Holliday had been a first recipient in '44, and the second year had brought attention to Marlon Brando and Burt Lancaster. The ensuing years awarded the likes of Julie Harris, Grace Kelly, Charlton Heston, Patricia Neal, Maureen Stapleton, Eli Wallach, and Carol Channing. Only the year before, Audrey Hepburn and Kim Stanley were singled out.

One morning, though awake, I was still in bed. Casper answered the phone, then handed the receiver to me. "Ray Stricklyn?" the voice asked. "Yes," I replied, removing the ever-present cigarette from my mouth. "This is Daniel Blum. I'm the editor of the Theatre World publication, and I've called to tell you that you've won one of our annual awards." I was dumfounded; not sure it wasn't a joke. After convincing me that it was legitimate, I thanked him, hanging up the phone. I sat on the edge of the bed, not saying a word. Tears began to roll down my cheek. "What's wrong?" Casper asked. I told him my good news. He too seemed stunned—but not for the same reason.

The next day the winners were announced in the press. Sure enough, a Ray Stricklyn was included for his performance in *The Climate of Eden*. I was in very good company. Some of the others selected? Geraldine Page for her Broadway debut in *Midsummer*; Paul Newman and Eileen Heckart from *Picnic*; Gwen Verdon for *Can-Can*; Richard Kiley for *Misalliance*; Sheree North for *Hazel Flagg*; John Kerr for *Bernardine;* and Rosemary Harris and Penelope Munday for *The Climate of Eden*. I received congratulatory calls from Moss Hart, Edie Van Cleve, Maynard Morris, Paul Bigelow, and yes, even Tennessee Williams. It was a very happy day. Later, Daniel Blum told me that my award was equally for *The Grass Harp*, but in those days, they weren't yet honoring Off Broadway performances.

A few Sundays later, in the afternoon, the awards were presented. I had an evening performance of *The Grass Harp*, so I couldn't celebrate as freely as I felt like doing. Still, I made a big mistake by having three drinks. I wasn't used to drinking during the day, let alone on an empty stomach, plus my general state of euphoria. My head was really whirling. Somehow, I got through the evening performance, running offstage immediately to throw-up in the alley behind the theatre. Right then, I swore I would *never* drink again before a performance. And I didn't.

Jose Ferrer's production of *Stalag 17*, a prisoner-of-war comedy, had been a popular hit, having a lengthy run, with a cast featuring John Ericson, Robert Strauss, Harvey Lembeck and Robert Shawley. An audience favorite was the role of "Veronica," played by Shawley, so nicknamed because his blond hair was always dangling in his face like film star Veronica Lake. Because of the show's popularity, a second road company had been sent out, with the movie actor George Tobias starred in the Robert Strauss role. Tobias was a familiar face from his appearances in dozens of Warner Bros. movies. Shawley was repeating his role as the youngest prisoner. After a few weeks, he decided to leave the cast and gave his notice. Guess who the play's tour director was? None other than Leonard Altobell, my old Irvine Studio teacher. As I'd gotten a little publicity as a result of my Theatre World Award, Altobell called asking me to replace Shawley. I accepted, but only after getting Edie Van Cleve to negotiate special "*and* Ray Stricklyn" billing in the program and ads. I joined the company in the bitter cold of Pittsburgh. First, though, I had to have my light brown hair bleached a white blond. I went to a department store for the coloring, but it was a disaster, with my hair turning green. Finally, it was corrected at another beauty shop, but not before my scalp was festered with sores.

While playing "Veronica" was great fun, there was a major problem. The cast had become bored, and with George Tobias leading the way, they raced through the show, cutting almost an *hour* off the running time! It was ridiculous. In one scene I'm supposed to take a bath onstage in a large tub filled with water. I entered, draped only in a towel (wearing a skimpy jockstrap beneath), and once the soldiers wolf whistles died down, I step into the tub, which is perched on top of a table. When I get out of the tub, they're supposed to chase me around the barracks, trying to strip me of the towel. It was a funny bit. But this cast, being *really* bored, was serious in their intent. One night they succeeded. There I was running around the stage with my ass buck naked (this was before *Hair* made nudity fashionable), much to the audience's shock and delight. When we opened in Chicago, where we'd expected to have a long run, Claudia Cassidy, a very important critic, wrote: "*Stalag 17* came to town last night and was stomped to death." That review was a deathblow. Len Wayland and I were the only ones who didn't get panned.

Back in New York, unbeknownst to me, dear Edie Van Cleve had been negotiating a contract for me to be the resident juvenile at the famed Elitch's Gardens
summer theatre in Denver. It was reputedly the oldest stock theatre in the country and had a prestigious reputation—even Alfred Lunt and Lynn Fontanne had
played there, and Grace Kelly had been there only two summers before (she'd
since had a meteoric rise as a film star). George Sommes was Elitch's artistic
director, which was owned by his wife, who acted in some of the productions,
and she also owned the powerful *Denver Post* newspaper. Edie phoned me in
Chicago to say that Sommes had hired me, sight unseen, for the season. First,
however, I had to get out of my *Stalag 17* contract. No problem there. The play
closed with a resounding thud.

The Elitch season opened with the comedy *Sabrina Fair*. Margot
Stevenson and Laurence Hugo were the company's lead players, so they were
cast in the two main roles (played in the first movie by Audrey Hepburn and
Humphrey Bogart). I was cast in the third lead (the William Holden role). Now,
Margot Stevenson was a lovely woman and a capable actress, but she was way
too mature to be playing the elfin Sabrina. And, as usual, I looked much too
young to be playing opposite her. Our love scenes gave the romantic comedy
a new twist; one I'm sure the playwright would not have sanctioned. Besides
that major problem, my hair was two-toned! Trying to get the bleach out of my
hair when I left *Stalag 17,* I'd gotten a crewcut and had had my hair dyed a
dark brown, trying to cover up the blond. Needless to say, it wasn't too attractive. I'm sure director Sommes had more than second thoughts about having
hired me sight unseen. I had a run-of-the-season contract, but I sometimes
wished he had fired me. The next play was Arthur Miller's *The Crucible*. Not
knowing what to do with me, I was finally cast as one of the old men at the top
of the play. Again, I was very miscast. When I made my entrance, dressed in a black
pilgrim costume, I was directed to doff my hat. When I did, on opening night, the
white powder from my hair ignited in a cloud of white dust. The atomic bomb
explosion seemed minor at the moment. Of course, it elicited a big laugh, definitely not wanted in Mr. Miller's very serious play. After that fiasco, there were no
immediate roles for me, so I spent most of the summer basking in the sun at a
nearby lake.

During one of my sun-tanning days, I happened to notice in the paper that Ann Crowley (whom I'd played with in *Good News* in Houston) was doing a night-club act at a fancy Denver restaurant. I'd seen Ann a few times in New York (when she starred in the musical *Seventeen*) and I'd become quite friendly with her younger sister, Pat Crowley. I had a crush on Pat, who was starring in the *A Date With Judy* television series, and we'd had a few dates. She was soon signed to a Paramount contract and left for Hollywood to co-star with Ginger Rogers, William Holden and Paul Douglas in *Forever Female*. During that period, I'd had an accident, falling in the icy doorway of a Salvation Army shop, breaking my left leg. The shop was across the street from my cold water flat, and I thought I could carry a chest-of-drawers I'd bought for that short distance. Wrong. After a trip to Roosevelt Hospital, I was put in the largest cast you've ever seen; going from my toes up to my crotch. It was also very heavy. Maneuvering up and down the four flights of stairs to my apartment on crutches was not easy. I was in that damned cast for over four months. It was suggested that I sue the Salvation Army for neglect (for not keeping their steps clear of ice and snow). I filed a complaint and promptly forgot about it, knowing that it would be years before it came to small claims court.

Anyway, back in Denver, I arranged for a group from Elitch's to go see Ann's show. There was a hypnotist on the bill with her. During his act, he picked about six people from the audience to join him on stage, where he proceeded to hypnotize us. Yes, I was one of them, obviously the most susceptible. After putting all six of us under, he sensed that I was his best target and he dismissed the others, leaving me on the stage alone. He then proceeded to give me commands, ordering me to do all sorts of wild things. I became Fred Astaire, dancing all over the stage. I was Mario Lanza singing an operatic aria. I'm told I was hilarious, and I'm sure I was! For his finale, the hypnotist placed two chairs about five feet apart. I was told to put my head on one, my feet on the other. Then he commanded that my torso between the two chairs become stiff as a board. Somehow this happened. He then decided to stand on top of my body. This got a big applause. The problem was he didn't know I was just recuperating from a leg fracture. When he stepped on my femur bone, I winced, waking from my trance. Of course, he could have seriously damaged my healing leg. Fortunately, he didn't, though it ached for a few days. I suppose I could have sued him too.

The final play at Elitch's was *My Three Angels*, in which I had a supporting role nearer my own age. Despite all the summer's frustrations, George Sommes and I ended up friendly. That was a surprise. I was afraid that my less than successful summer might have soured Edie Van Cleve on me, but it didn't. My next engagement, also thanks to Edie, was a big improvement. She arranged for me to do three plays in winter stock, at the ritzy Palm Beach Playhouse in West Palm Beach, Florida. This time I was properly cast.

The Palm Beach season opened with Helen Hayes in *Happy Birthday*. It was still playing when I arrived for rehearsals on my first play, so I had the opportunity of meeting "The First Lady of the American Stage," as she was billed. I had been set to play the juvenile lead in *The Vinegar Tree*, a comedy by Paul Osborn. The exciting prospect about that was the show's star—none other than the wonderful Shirley Booth. She'd recently won the Academy Award for *Come Back, Little Sheba*, recreating her Broadway triumph, so it was quite a coup for the management to have signed her. She was great box office. She was also an absolute joy to work with—and play with. Frequently, after a performance, we'd have a late supper at some fancy restaurant. I even found myself dancing with her on a couple of occasions. During one of our "dates" she asked me what other plays I was scheduled to appear in. Next up was *Here Today*, I said, a comedy with Faye Emerson, then *Saint Joan* with Jan Sterling. Sterling had just received a best supporting actress Oscar nomination for her performance in *The High and the Mighty* with John Wayne. I mentioned her nomination, and the actress replied, "Oh, she doesn't stand a chance of winning. All she did was take off her makeup." Booth's comment reminded me of an earlier incident I'd had with Uta Hagen. When I first met Bob Casper he was appearing with Uta in *Saint Joan*. She was considered one of the great actresses of the day. Anyway, one night Casper arranged for me to baby-sit with Uta's young daughter (by her marriage to Jose Ferrer, since divorced). Ferrer had won an Academy Award for his *Cyrano de Bergerac*, now he'd been nominated again for *Moulin Rouge*. When Uta returned home, the little girl said, "Mommy, do you think daddy deserves another Oscar?"

"Hell, no!" Uta quickly answered. "All he did was walk around on his knees for two hours!" So much for Ferrer's Toulouse Lautrec performance.

Shaw's *Saint Joan* was heavy fare for a Palm Beach audience more interested in froth and showing off their latest wardrobes. Going to the theatre was a social happening, the play came second. *Saint Joan* definitely came second as the Easter attraction. I had one good scene as the page with the Dauphin, played by Romney Brent. Then in the long courtroom scene at the end of the play, I doubled as a jurist, covered from head to foot in a hooded black robe. Jan Sterling, who was a joy to be around, was married to film star Paul Douglas. He flew in from the West Coast for our final performance, arriving just before curtain time. He had a wicked sense of humor and decided to surprise Jan. In cahoots with the stage manager, he dressed in one of the robes, with his face hidden, and sat next to me in the jurist box. At the climactic moment, when Joan is fighting for her life, about to be burned at the stake, Douglas revealed his face to Jan, crossing his eyes in the process. The actress, shocked, became almost hysterical, about to turn Mr. Shaw's drama into a riotous comedy. But, being a good actress, she quickly turned her hysterical laughter to sobbing tears. To an audience it looked like an actor's choice on how to play the scene. In reality, it was an actress *saving* the play. A couple of years down the road I'd be co-starring with Mr. Douglas in a Schlitz Playhouse television play called *Honor Thy Father*.

* * * * *

Shortly after I returned to New York, Bob Casper had a call to replace Roddy McDowall in a tour of Shaw's *Misalliance*. That was a good career break for him. I'd been out of town a good deal, now he was leaving. But I was beginning to enjoy the freedom. In my gut, I knew that the relationship was coming to an end. I just didn't know *when*. I wasn't the promiscuous type usually, but I did make an exception with Tony Perkins, whose career was just beginning to take off (he was then starring in *Tea and Sympathy*). We'd met at the Theatre World Awards party and our liaison was one of those spur of the moment attractions when we ran into each other one afternoon in Central Park.

All in all, since moving to New York in 1950, it had been a productive four years. I'd started with a pimple ad, moved on to small parts on television, then a

Broadway play, an Off Broadway play, won an award, toured, did both summer and winter stock. What next, I wondered?

During those years I'd been very good about writing home, penning a letter to mother almost weekly. To my sister, too. She was now happily married to a wonderful husband, Clayton Evans, who was an electrician by trade. They'd had their first daughter, Kathy, who was their pride and joy, with another daughter, Karen, due shortly. The situation with my mother and father had remained stagnant, though improved, as dad wasn't drinking any more. He'd just sit all day long, smoking his pipe or a cigar, reading a paperback Western, rarely speaking. The sad news was that my other childhood friend, Jimmie Wallace, who'd helped raise the church money for my trip to New York, had also died. They were all so young—Billy, J.B., Bill Gideon. Now Jimmie.

* * * * *

The year 1955 would be a turning point in my life. But I didn't know the wheels of change would start spinning that particular day. It was a beautiful autumn morning. After shaving, showering and dressing, I decided to take a stroll through Central Park. The leaves from the trees were spread across the ground as far as I could see. I ambled across a bridge—the same one that had caused the assistant director to yell "Cut!" I stopped to buy a packet of peanuts, then walked to the zoo, where the monkeys eagerly awaited each carefully aimed toss.

"Ray!" Hearing someone calling my name, I turned and saw an actor friend, Michael Rougas, coming toward me. He asked if I'd like to join him for a cup of coffee. After accepting, he said he first had to stop by an agent's office for a quick interview, hoping they'd sign him as a client. I waited in the outer office. It was a new one to me—the Alec Alexander Agency. I was standing near the office's exit door, wearing my jeans and leather jacket, the standard clothing for most young actors, with a cigarette dangling from my mouth. A woman approached, asking if she could help me. "No," I replied, I'm just waiting for a friend." "Are you an actor?" she asked. "Yes." "Do you have representation?" There seemed to be an urgency to her questions. "No one in particular," I said. "Come with me, we're going over to Paramount's office right now!" Who *was* this woman? She was Mrs. Alexander, Helen by name. Before I knew what had happened, we were out the door, hail-ing a taxi. I didn't even have time to tell Michael Rougas I wouldn't be joining him for coffee.

In the cab she explained that the movie director George Seaton was in town casting his next film, *The Proud and the Profane*, which was to star William Holden and Deborah Kerr. There was a second male lead, a young marine that she thought I might be right for. The mere mention of the word marine sent my crazy mind spinning back to my raising the American flag over Iwo Jima with a hard cock pressed against my ass! I was jolted back to reality when the taxi came to a screeching halt.

With no delay, we were ushered into Seaton's office. I was impressed. Whoever this Helen Alexander was, she had enough clout to barge into an important director's office. Seaton was very affable, easy to talk with. He'd filmed *The Country Girl* the year before, winning an Academy Award for Grace Kelly. He said I looked too young for the second lead (he cast Dewey Martin), but would I be interested in doing a very small role; just one brief moment; with Deborah Kerr and Thelma Ritter? He explained the moment—a young shell-shocked marine is being led off a cargo ship. As he comes down the gangplank, he spots Kerr and

In the Virgin Islands for my movie debut in The Proud and the Profane. *Deborah Kerr and Thelma Ritter are to my left.*

Ritter, two nurses. In his delirium he thinks Deborah Kerr is his mother, running toward her, desperately calling "Mother!" Screaming, he is carried off by security guards.

I signed for the movie. I assumed we'd be shooting in Hollywood, but my bit was going to be shot in the Virgin Islands, which sounded even better. On the plane to Puerto Rico, I was joined by two other young actors, Robert Morse and Frank Gorshin, also signed for brief moments. It would be their movie debuts too. During the flight all three of us got tanked on martinis. We were in the Virgin Islands for a week, mostly spent sunbathing at a plush hotel, before our bits were shot. We did it all in one night. I screamed my head off and that was it. I was now a movie actor—sort of. Unbeknownst to me, that flash of screen time was enough for director Seaton to write the Paramount brass that I had an "interesting face that photographed well."

When I returned from location, the Alexanders wanted me to sign an agency contract with them. I found out they had a good reputation, known for representing talented actors. They were particularly excited about one young client, Sal Mineo. He was in the midst of filming an important role in *Rebel Without a Cause*, co-starring with James Dean and Natalie Wood. I was about to sign with the Alexanders when I received an unexpected call from the West Coast. I'd had a series of photographs taken by Roy Schatt (who later attained a certain celebrity with his photos of James Dean). The pictures were quite good, certainly the best I'd yet had taken. Through Schatt, the photographs had come to the attention of Dick Clayton, who was a major agent in Hollywood, working for one of the powerful agencies (similar to MCA). My unexpected caller was Clayton.

He said he was impressed by my photos, also that director George Seaton had mentioned me to him, and he was interested in possibly representing me. He looked forward to meeting me, he said, when he was next in New York. In the meantime, he would like to submit me for a movie about to start shooting. He said it was a wonderful role and could make a star of whoever played it. The film was *Friendly Persuasion*. It was to be directed by the great William Wyler, with Gary Cooper and Dorothy McGuire starring. Wyler wanted an unknown to play the role of Josh, their troubled son who breaks away from the family's pacifist vows to fight for freedom. Clayton said Wyler was sending his associate, Stuart Millar, to New York to checkout the "hot young talent of Broadway and television."

I met with Millar; he gave me a script, saying he'd arrange a reading once Wyler arrived in New York. The meeting took place one Sunday morning in the director's suite at the St. Regis Hotel. They were interviewing a handful of young actors. The initial meeting seemed to go well. Dick Clayton called from the West Coast to tell me that Wyler had narrowed his choice down to three actors: John Kerr, Tony Perkins, *and* Ray Stricklyn. I learned later that he'd originally wanted James Dean for the role, but after *East of Eden*, Dean was no longer interested in playing a supporting role, no matter how good the part might be. Of course, Tony Perkins was the final choice, capturing an Oscar nomination for his performance.

Although Dick Clayton was still interested in signing me, several weeks went by and I didn't hear from him. Meantime, the Alexanders were urging me to sign with them. This was a very flattering position to be in; certainly a new one for me. Alec Alexander asked me to join him for lunch one day, explaining that they were getting so active on the West Coast that they'd decided to close their New York office and relocate in Los Angeles. He wanted me to come with them. Of course he knew of Clayton's interest, but he argued that I could easily get lost in so big an agency; catering mainly to their big star clients. That had crossed my mind too, as I'd seen it happen when I worked at MCA. I explained to Alec that I couldn't afford to move to Los Angeles. He then propositioned me: "If we get you a couple of television jobs, will you seriously consider it then?" I agreed.

True to his word, within days he'd gotten me a part in the *Lamp Unto My Feet* television program. The script dealt with a young girl (played by Nancy Malone, who, incidentally, played the lead in *Time Out for Ginger* when it reached Broadway) who can't make up her mind between three romantic suitors. My rivals for Nancy's affections were Steve McQueen and Robert Loggia. In the final moment, as the boy next door, I won the girl. I'd briefly met McQueen when I was appearing in *The Grass Harp* in Greenwich Village. He used to race his motorcycle in front of the Circle-In-The-Square theatre, making such a racket that the noise frequently would drown out our dialogue inside the theatre. Jose Quintero finally asked him to take his noise elsewhere. No sooner had I finished my stint with Nancy, Steve and Loggia, than Alec came up with another gig, some half-hour television movie that I can't remember the name of. I know it starred Roland Young, the wonderful movie actor who'd played Topper in a delightful series of *Topper* films.

As promised, I signed with the Alexander office, making the scary decision to move to Los Angeles. You get used to whatever way things are, so change can be scary; even depressing. Still, the prospect was also exciting and challenging.

I called Phyllis Gates and Jim Terry in Hollywood, telling them that I would soon be joining them in lotusland. They were delighted. A lot had happened to Phyllis since she'd moved there. A *lot*. First, Jim had gotten her a job with Henry Willson's agency. Because of her "experience" with Maynard Morris at MCA, Willson had hired her. He was a major independent agent, representing handsome actors with odd names like Tab Hunter, Race Gentry and Rock Hudson. Mr. Hudson was fast becoming, if he wasn't already, the most popular star in films. He was in the midst of filming his biggest picture to date, George Stevens' *Giant*, in which he was co-starring with Elizabeth Taylor and James Dean.

During our phone conversation, Phyllis, after swearing me to secrecy, said she was going to *marry* Rock Hudson! After dropping the phone, I said, "Are you serious?" "Yes," she answered, "I've been living with him for several weeks now." Then she came up with the bright idea that I move into her old apartment since she was hardly using it anymore. Sounded like a great idea to me.

Everything was suddenly moving so fast that my head was reeling. My next step was the one I most dreaded—telling Bob Casper that I was moving. He was numb when I broke the news to him. I'd usually been very closed-mouth about my career happenings, so he had no idea that this change had been brewing for several weeks. I'd allowed him to control me during most of our relationship, something I didn't like in myself, but I had allowed it to happen. Now I wanted to break that control. Even so, you don't just walk away without some regrets. In his mind, I think he thought it was just a temporary separation. But I knew the relationship was over.

TAKE THREE

It is easy to remember the date I arrived in Hollywood. October 1, 1955. With Alec, I'd taken the red-eye flight, arriving early that morning at the Los Angeles airport. I was about to embark on a new career, a new life. I was nervous, eager and excited; all the things one feels when starting on a new adventure.

But the excitement was immediately shattered. As we were departing the plane, Helen (Alec's wife), came running toward us, holding up a special edition of *The Los Angeles Times*. The headline screamed: *James Dean Killed in Auto Crash!* The evening before, September 30th, the actor's new Porsche had been demolished on Route 466. His neck broken and twisted, James Dean was dead at the age of twenty-four.

The Alexanders knew Dean because their client, Sal Mineo, had just done two back-to-back movies with him—*Rebel Without A Cause* and *Giant*. My relationship with James Dean was more personal.

We'd first met sometime in 1951. We were just two out-of-work struggling actors making the rounds of the New York casting offices. We were about the same age, similar in height, weight, and coloring. We both wore horn-rimmed glasses and we dressed alike—you know, the jeans and leather jacket. We could have passed for brothers. Inevitably, we were often submitted for the same television and stage roles. And that's how we met, on some casting call, in some forgotten office. Gradually, we began to acknowledge one another—"Hi, how are you?" and go our separate ways. The Cromwell drug store, located in the NBC building was a favorite hangout for actors. We'd linger over a cup of coffee, often because we couldn't afford anything else. Eventually, Jimmy and I started sitting together at the counter or, if we had the money, at a table where we'd wolf down a tuna fish sandwich and a Coca-Cola, discussing what offices we'd been rejected in that day. Occasionally there would be a whoop of joy if one of us landed a television job.

To appease the actors unions, CBS-TV had set up a weekly casting call at one of the local theatres. Once a week, hundreds of actors would show up, grab a number, then wait several hours to be seen by the CBS casting honchos. It was like a cattle call. When your number was called, usually in groups of ten, you'd parade across the stage in front of a large desk where Robert Fryer and Michael Mead were seated. They were the big guys, the ones you wanted to impress. Sometimes their eyes would barely rise above the crotch area, but if you were persistent, and Jimmy and I were, sometimes it paid off. If you kept coming back, week after week, they at least knew you were serious. Of course the jobs, if any, were very small roles on the popular "live" dramatic shows of the day. You certainly weren't going to land a starring role, that's for sure. Most of those, it seemed, were going to Charlton Heston, who was a pet of Robert Fryer's.

One day, however, the CBS-TV casting office called and asked Jimmy and me to test contestant stunts for the popular game show, *Beat the Clock.* We were paid the princely sum of $5 an hour. Granted, it wasn't a part on *Studio One,* but it *was* a job. We tested those stunts for several weeks. It was really quite demeaning. They'd dress us in hot rubber sweat suits, then douse us with torrents of water, or throw pies in our faces. Any outrageous stunt the producers could think up, we gallantly tried them out. Since we were often in the sweat suits for hours on end, we lost a considerable amount of weight; something neither of us needed to do. We were both skinny enough. It was a little more dignified when we did stand-in work for the *What's My Line?* quiz show. It was a much classier program, with the panel, Bennett Cerf, Dorothy Kilgallen and Arlene Francis trying to guess the different contestants' professions. Jimmy and I wouldn't be winning an Emmy that season, but, listen, we were working and grateful for the $5 an hour.

One day Jimmy asked me if I'd cue him on a scene he was working on. He had an audition for a play, *The Scarecrow,* which was being done Off Broadway at the Theatre de Lys with a stellar cast—Eli Wallach, Patricia Neal and Anne Jackson. We met in Central Park and found a secluded spot where we could read the script. But it was a stop-and-start situation, as he was a very poor reader. He'd stumble and stutter on just about every line. Of course a lot of actors are poor at "cold" readings. But he knew the scene, so that couldn't have been an excuse. Maybe it was his way of working. While I was attempting to feed him his lines, he suddenly switched his position, putting his head in my lap. I was startled, quickly looking around to see if anyone was watching. I wasn't one for a public display of affection, particularly between two guys. Before I knew what had happened, he lifted his head from my lap and kissed me firmly on the lips. "Thanks," he said. Needless to say, I was stunned, so answered with an innocuous, "You're welcome." It wasn't that I didn't find him attractive, I did, but he'd caught me so off-guard. If memory serves me, he ended up playing a non-speaking role in *The Scarecrow*. And our intimate moment? It was never mentioned again.

Our individual lots began to improve, slightly. We began doing some featured roles on various television dramas, like *Danger* and *Big Story*—usually playing juvenile delinquents. At least we were no longer wearing rubber suits. Years later, I heard a disturbing story concerning Jimmy. He'd accepted a dinner invitation with an important casting director, who expected sexual favors at the end of the evening. Jimmy had refused. The casting director was so furious that he had the actor's name put on a "blacklist"—not to be hired by any of the network's shows. I don't know the validity of this story, but the casting director's assistant told me this incident, so I believe it was probably true.

Among the stage roles we competed for, often for the same role, were plays like Mary Chase's *Bernardine*, which had two leading juvenile roles, but Johnny Stewart and John Kerr landed those. Another was Elia Kazan's production of Robert Anderson's *Tea and Sympathy*, which every young actor in New York wanted to be in. We were sitting in Kazan's outer office (Karl Malden was assisting him) with about a dozen other types. I was called in first. After a brief interview, I came out, telling Jimmy I'd meet him later at the Cromwell drug store. In about forty-five minutes he showed up, giggling. "Kazan thought I was you!" he said. "He said, 'You were just in here!'" We didn't make the cut on that one either, with John Kerr once again capturing the choice role. Another play was *The Remarkable Mr. Pennypacker*. No luck there either. Ironically, all three plays would figure in my future, but in another medium.

When I was cast in *The Climate of Eden*, I remember dashing to the Cromwell to tell Jimmy my good news. He congratulated me, but I could tell it also depressed him. He sat there, playing with a spoon in his cold cup of coffee, then blurted out, "I'm never going to get a play! I'm getting out of this fucking business!"

However, as fate would have it, he *did* get a play almost immediately. He was signed for a featured role in N. Richard Nash's *See the Jaguar*, toplining Arthur Kennedy and Constance Ford, in which he played a demented kid locked in a cage. Following a brief pre-Broadway tour, it opened at the Cort Theatre on December 3, 1952, but folded after only five performances. It brought him notice, however, and was the start of his climb. The following season he was cast as the homosexual hustler in *The Immoralist* based on Andre Gide's controversial novel. Louis Jourdan, the French film star, and Geraldine Page, fresh from her triumphs in *Summer and Smoke* and *Midsummer*, were the stars. Rumors had been circulating almost immediately that he was clashing with his director, Herman Shumlin, as well as star Jourdan, who reportedly said he "couldn't work with such an undisciplined actor." Jimmy wanted to quit, but Gerry Page pleaded with him to stay, urging him to at least open in the show. He followed the actress's advice, but on opening night he turned in his notice, not even waiting for the reviews to appear. I was one of several actors who read to replace him, but the management opted for an entirely different type, a dark, intense actor named Philip Pine.

Normally, a prestigious production like *The Immoralist* would have been very important to a young actor's career. But I have often wondered if Jimmy knew, when he was threatening to quit the play, that he already had something more exciting lined up? Shortly after he left the play it was announced that Elia Kazan and Warner Bros. had signed him to star in the film version of John Steinbeck's *East of Eden*. Before filming started, Jimmy suggested me for the role of his brother in the movie. As fate would have it, when I was called about an interview, I was suffering with that damnable broken leg and was unable to make the appointment. I know Paul Newman was one of the actors tested. Not that I would have gotten the role, by any means, but it was a considerate gesture on Jimmy's part. Richard Davalos eventually was signed for the role. The rest is film history.

The last time I saw James Dean was in our favorite haunt, the NBC building, where we both had our banking accounts. I was standing in line one morning, waiting to deposit my unemployment check, and Jimmy came in. He was carrying a crumpled brown paper bag. He greeted me with an affectionate hug, then proceeded to open the paper bag. Inside, he said, was ten thousand dollars. "I don't trust Warner Bros.," he giggled, "so I made them pay me in cash." Afterwards, we had lunch. He was on his way to Texas, he said, to start filming *Giant*. As we parted, he hugged me again, saying, "I'll see you in Hollywood." I said I doubted it. "Oh, you'll be there, you'll be there."

That was our final meeting.

* * * * *

As we were leaving the airport, still stunned by the newspaper headline, Alec asked me where I'd be staying. I told him I'd be living in Phyllis Gates' apartment. His ears perked up. "*The* Phyllis Gates?" he asked. "The one going with Rock Hudson?" I nodded. He was silent for a moment, then said a strange thing: "I don't know if that's such a good idea, Ray." I hadn't expected that response, so I asked why? "Well, there's a lot of rumors going on about them and I don't want you getting mixed up in the wrong crowd." I took offense at this, saying, "Phyllis is my best friend. I think I know her better than anyone spreading rumors!" He remained quiet after that.

Her apartment was located on North Fairfax Avenue, just north of Santa Monica Boulevard. It was a small, four-unit building set back from the street. She had the downstairs unit on the right. Living in the apartment to the left was John Smith; a muscular, attractive blond actor who had played a small role in John Wayne's *The High and the Mighty*. The two upstairs apartments were occupied by Steve Drexel, another of Willson's clients, and a middle-aged foreign couple, who seemed out of place in such surroundings. Phyllis was waiting for me when I reached the Fairfax address. Her radiant smile was a welcome sight. She laughed, saying she and Rock had spent the evening before scrubbing the kitchen floor. She invited me to join them for dinner. Since I didn't have a car, or even knew how to drive, she said she'd pick me up.

Rock's house was above the Sunset Strip, up Doheny Drive, on Warbler Place. It was located at the end of a cul-de-sac, with a steep driveway leading up to the garage. The house wasn't large, but the living-room area was quite roomy, so it seemed bigger than it actually was. Of course, after living in a two-room cold water flat for nearly five years, Rock's house seemed like a paradise.

The actor greeted us at the door, wearing a pair of chino slacks, plaid shirt and tennis sneakers. As expected, he was quite tall, and just as handsome as his movies led you to believe. He had a great laugh and made me feel welcome immediately. Phyllis wasted no time in mixing a batch of vodka martinis. And she made the *best* martinis—so smooth. She was also a great cook, whether it be a fancy gourmet dinner or a simple Minnesota farm feast. Rock seemed very down-to-earth, not at all "the movie star." The martinis poured freely and the evening passed much too quickly. They drove me home in his white convertible.

During my first two weeks I saw them almost nightly. Then, one morning, Phyllis arrived at the apartment unannounced. She seemed upset. "Ray, I'm sorry to have to say this, but you're going to have to move for a little while. Something's come up and I'm going to have to move back here for a bit. You can return when the heat is off." It sounded so mysterious.

Later, she explained what was happening. *Confidential* magazine, a tabloid that printed scandalous stories about celebrities, was planning to do an expose on Rock. The magazine had become very popular (like *The Enquirer* would be today, only back then, it was the first and only one, so its impact was much greater. Too, it was a different era and people were more easily shocked).

"I don't want you to get involved," she said. "The press is hounding us, wanting to know *if* and *when* we're getting married, and I don't want them to know I'm living at Rock's." That too, in those days, would have been considered a shocking story. "It wouldn't be wise for you to stay here with me because that would appear odd too." Then she confided that they'd be getting married very soon. "Please don't say *anything* to *anyone*." I found a nearby room and temporarily moved.

Confidential, it seems, was planning a cover story with the bombshell news that Rock Hudson was gay. That would be disastrous to his booming movie career, as he was the "dream man" of many a swooning female fan. Although many Hollywood celebrities were homosexual or bisexual, it was a closely guarded secret. The studio publicity departments worked overtime protecting their valuable properties—the openness of an Ellen DeGeneres and Anne Heche was unthinkable back then. Usually the actors and actresses would have marriages of convenience to offset the rumors. For years gossips had hinted that Cary Grant and Randolph Scott had been lovers. The stories about Greta Garbo and Marlene Dietrich and Tallulah Bankhead were legendary. Tyrone Power and Cesar Romero were suspect at Fox, ditto Van Johnson at MGM. Even Gary Cooper was supposed to have "played around" during his early Hollywood days. There were also recurring rumors about Janet Gaynor and Mary Martin and Claudette Colbert and Joan Crawford and Barbara Stanwyck and Lizabeth Scott. Silent screen star Ramon Novarro, the first *Ben-Hur*, would be brutally murdered by two hustlers in 1968, and back in the 1940's Darryl F. Zanuck wasn't too happy about the close relationship between his two budding young stars, William Eythe and Lon McCallister. Newcomers like Tony Perkins and Tab Hunter would have similar problems, with their individual studios reputedly insisting they stop seeing one another. Certainly the brilliant Montgomery Clift's torment has been well reported, as has Jimmy Dean's bisexuality. The young Sal Mineo would be "coming out" in future years, while British matinee idol, Dirk Bogarde, made his preferences known, as did Michael Redgrave when he admitted he was bisexual. With character types, like Charles Laughton, Clifton Webb, John Gielgud and Noel Coward, it didn't seem to matter as much, since they weren't being presented as romantic heartthrobs. Even so, their known homosexuality was never mentioned in the press. It just wasn't done. But times were changing and, sadly, *Confidential* was leading the way.

Rock's studio, Universal, immediately ordered their publicity department to do everything to stop the story from being printed. He was the studio's most valuable asset. Eventually, a compromise was reached. *Confidential* wouldn't print the story *if* the studio gave them "the dirt" on another player. Not very nice, but we are dealing in sleaze here, and apparently that is what transpired. The story goes that Rory Calhoun, another handsome actor gaining in popularity at Universal, became the sacrifice. He had had a prison record for some misdemeanor when he was younger, so the magazine finally went with that. It wasn't as juicy, perhaps, but in those simpler times, it was still considered a shocker. Of course the magazine played it up much bigger than it actually was. Fortunately, it didn't seem to do much harm to Calhoun's blossoming career. This rumor about Rock, of course, had been the reason that Alec Alexander hadn't wanted me to stay at Phyllis' apartment when I first arrived in Los Angeles.

Soon after, Phyllis and Rock were married in a simple ceremony in Santa Barbara, with only Henry Willson and Pat Devlin, a friend of Phyllis's, on hand.

It was now "safe" for me to move back to the Fairfax apartment. Willson was frequently at the complex because of his clients, John Smith and Steve Drexel. He was particularly pushing Smith. One day he saw me sunbathing and asked Smith who I was. He then started pursuing me, wanting me to become a client, asking me out to dinner, etc. I kept refusing. He had a notorious reputation, especially among young actors whom he'd try to seduce—frequently succeeding. He destroyed more than one young man, believe me. I mentioned to Phyllis that I wished he'd leave me alone. That worked. She told Rock and he put an end to Willson's pursuit. Surprisingly, we remained on sociable terms—for a while.

Rock was working on *Written on the Wind* when they married. The producer, Albert Zugsmith, and his wife, threw a wedding party shortly after the couple returned from Santa Barbara. Of course it was a big social event, but Phyllis was trying to keep the guest list to a minimum. Fortunately, she invited me. But she refused to let Willson invite any of his clients. He particularly wanted John Smith to be included; knowing that there would be a number of important producers and directors in attendance. In Hollywood, business was often conducted at social gatherings.

But she hadn't counted on Henry's ingenuity. Phyllis had suggested I bring a date, but I didn't yet know any girls. Also, I still didn't have a car. John Smith had a stunning girlfriend, Lee Sharon. I'd met her on a number of occasions and he suggested that I ask her. Sounded like a good idea to me. The night of the party she picked me up in her red Thunderbird and off we sped. Henry, of course, would be at the reception.

The Zugsmiths had a lovely home in Studio City and the party was in full swing when we arrived. It was my first Hollywood affair, so I was quite star-struck by the gathering. Rock and Phyllis introduced me to Louella Parsons, the famous gossip columnist. Louella was talking with Susan Hayward, so I lingered nearby when I heard them discussing her new film. "Susan, darling," Louella said, "the word is out that you're absolutely sensational in *I'll Cry Tomorrow.* They're predicting you'll win the Oscar." Very grandly, Miss Hayward replied, "Yes, it's a role that comes along, if you're lucky, once in every ten years." (She almost won the Oscar too, but Anna Magnani beat her in the homestretch).

I glanced around the room. I saw Robert Stack and Dorothy Malone, who were two of Rock's co-stars in *Written on the Wind* (both would capture Oscar nominations too, with Miss Malone winning). I noticed Yvonne DeCarlo and her new stuntman husband. I saw George Nader, who was Rock's best friend, and getting a big publicity buildup at Universal. If memory serves me right, Jane Wyman and Barbara Rush were there also (they had been Rock's co-players in *Magnificent Obsession*). Then the front doorbell rang, and in walked Humphrey Bogart and Lauren Bacall (she was Rock's leading lady in *Written on the Wind*). All eyes were suddenly on them. Bogart looked quite frail; suffering from the cancer that would soon take his life. Everyone was clustered around them, especially Miss Louella, paying homage to the ailing actor. He tired easily, though, and didn't stay at the soiree too long. He suggested that Bacall stay if she wanted, which she did. Rock said he would drive her home.

The evening was winding down when suddenly there was another doorbell ring. The Zugsmiths opened the door. Who was standing there? John Smith. He introduced himself, saying he was there to pick up his girlfriend, Lee Sharon. Aha! That was Mr. Willson's plan all along. Very smart. Phyllis was noticeably upset, but there was little she could do. Immediately, Henry was taking the handsome young actor all over the room, introducing him to the "right" people.

Of course, I wasn't really that disappointed, since Rock and Phyllis would now drive me home too—with Lauren Bacall, yet. The four of us piled into Rock's convertible and headed for the plush Holmby Hills, where the Bogarts had their palatial estate. We'd all had several drinks, so we were feeling no pain, laughing and screaming all the way to Beverly Hills. As we passed different celebrities' homes, Bacall would make some caustic comment: "Oh, Lana Turner lives there! I wonder who's sleeping over tonight?" . . . "Poor Alan Ladd, he's so miserable" . . . "Miss goody-two-shoes lives there," she said, referring to June Allyson. For a moment things got serious when Rock said he didn't want to make his next scheduled picture, which was to co-star Miss Allyson. "Don't worry," Bacall said, laughingly, "I'll speak to the head of the studio and tell them to put that Indian in it instead" (she was referring to Jeff Chandler). When *Stranger In My Arms* was finally made, three years later, indeed it did co-star Allyson and Chandler. Judy Garland and Sid Luft lived next door to the Bogarts. As we passed their house, the actress said, "That Sid Luft is something else! He's so desperate to be a member of Bogie's rat pack that he's threatening to dig a tunnel under our fence!" As we pulled into her driveway she invited us in for a nightcap. Of course I was eager to accept, but Rock begged off. Still, it was quite a night.

Christmas of 1955 was approaching. Phyllis asked me if I'd like to go shopping in Beverly Hills. We were on Rodeo Drive, entering all the fancy shops, when a very handsome young man hollered, "Hey, Phyllis!" They hugged, obviously were quite friendly, and she introduced me to Craig Hill. I recognized him, of course, as he'd been under contract at 20th Century Fox and had appeared in a number of films. From the moment he made his debut in a bathing suit, pursuing Jeanne Crain in *Cheaper by the Dozen*, the female fans had begun to swoon (and no doubt a few guys too). It was a small role, but his masculine good looks, and the fans' reaction to him, caused the studio to sign him to a term contract. At the time, Miss Louella had written in her column that he received more fan mail than all of the new male players; even above Rock. Though Fox used him steadily for a while, he never got that one role that would catapult him to major stardom. He hadn't lost his blond good looks, however. Since he was a good friend of Rock's, Phyllis invited him to stop by over the holidays.

Not long after our Rodeo Drive meeting, Phyllis invited me to dinner. Since I still didn't drive, she said Craig Hill would be picking me up. This could be the start of something, my subconscious kept telling me. The subconscious was right. From that evening on, we became inseparable. It was the beginning of a very happy period—a wonderful way to start the New Year.

* * * * *

Shortly after my arrival in Los Angeles, I made my first visit to a movie studio. It was the old Columbia lot on Gower Street in the heart of Hollywood. Alec had arranged for me to meet the casting people. The Columbia lot was small compared to the acreage surrounding the other studios, like MGM, 20th Century Fox and Warner Bros. But on that first visit, Columbia seemed massive enough for me.

After my appointment, Alec suggested we walk over to the soundstage where *Storm Center* was shooting. He had a child client, Kevin Coughlin, in the cast. Bette Davis was starring in the film, supported by Brian Keith and Kim Hunter. I couldn't believe that I might actually *see* Bette Davis! *But there she was.* While Alec was visiting with young Kevin in his dressing room, I stood on the sidelines watching Davis and Brian Keith rehearse a scene with the director, Daniel Taradash. There seemed to be a disagreement over how the scene should be played. Not surprisingly, they did it her way.

For years, of course, Bette Davis had been the undisputed Queen of Hollywood. Who could forget her string of brilliant performances in such films as *Dark Victory, The Letter, Now, Voyager, The Little Foxes* and *All About Eve*? By 1955, however, she, like many of her contemporaries, was finding it difficult to find strong roles in good films. *Storm Center,* released in 1956, would not be a box office success, though it was a valiant effort. Little did I realize, standing on the sidelines, that I would be in Bette Davis' next picture.

* * * * *

With the release of *Rebel Without a Cause*, Sal Mineo suddenly became a "hot" property. Jimmy Dean's untimely death had given the film a growing cult following. Sal had received a best supporting actor nomination, which made Alec very happy, as it gave him increasing bargaining power. Sal was about to start a new film *Crime in the Streets*; a hard-hitting juvenile delinquent story based on an extended Reginald Rose television script. John Cassavetes, in his film debut, and James Whitmore top-starred. The psychological drama also had several featured roles, members of Cassavetes' gang. I was cast as one of them. Mark Rydell, also fresh from New York, was another (you know him better today as the fine director of such films as Bette Midler's *The Rose* and the Hepburn-Fonda starrer, *On Golden Pond*). While the gang's supporting roles didn't offer much opportunity to individually shine, they did keep us on the payroll for the entire shoot. It was a definite step up from my debut in *The Proud and the Profane*.

Good fortune, combined with good luck, started to come my way almost immediately. No sooner had I completed *Crime in the Streets* than I was promptly cast in a trio of MGM films. The first was *Somebody Up There Likes Me*, based on the life of prizefighter Rocky Graziano. It was a strong script with a highly regarded director, Robert Wise (who went on to win Oscars for his direction of *West Side Story* and *The Sound of Music*). The film had originally been slated for James Dean. Now Paul Newman, fresh from his Broadway appearance in *The Desperate Hours*, was set to star. After the debacle of his film debut in *The Silver Chalice*, Newman thought his film career was over before it started, so he was eager to accept the role, as it offered an opportunity for a solid, in-depth characterization. I had met Paul in New York. Surprisingly, not through Maynard Morris at MCA. He was a friend of Bob Casper's. When he was doing *The Desperate Hours* he came over to our apartment one night following a performance. He was in a stew. Prior to the play's opening, Maynard had a clause inserted in his contract guaranteeing that he would be upped to star billing, above the title, with Karl Malden and Nancy Coleman. Maynard was anticipating rave reviews for the actor, and it would have been a good publicity ploy—"a new star is born." While the reviews were certainly very favorable, Paul didn't feel that he'd received strong enough notices to warrant putting his name above the title. Maynard's contract won out, however.

In *Somebody Up There Likes Me* I had only one scene, but it was with Paul. I played his GI buddy who he tries to coerce into going AWOL with him. My character refuses, telling him off. Pier Angeli was cast as his love interest, with Eileen Heckart, Sal Mineo and Everett Sloane in featured roles. Also appearing in very small roles were Steve McQueen and Robert Loggia (remember we'd competed for Nancy Malone's affections on *Lamp Unto My Feet*), and Dean Jones had a bit, as did Mart Crowley (who went on to write the Off Broadway sensation, *Boys In the Band*). When the picture was released it was a hit, both critically and at the box office. It made Paul Newman a major star, which he has remained to this day.

While the Graziano bio was filming, MGM was prepping *The Rack* as Newman's next vehicle. It, like *Crime In the Streets*, was another television-to-movie adaptation, with Stewart Stern reworking the Rod Serling original. MGM, with director Arnold Laven, had lined up a strong co-starring cast: Walter Pidgeon, Edmond O'Brien, Wendell Corey, Lee Marvin and Anne Francis. An actress named Cloris Leachman was also cast in a small role. Once again, I had only one scene, this time with Walter Pidgeon. It was the opening scene in the script and I played a young army drill sergeant, shouting out commands to his troop. Colonel Pidgeon arrived and we exchanged a few words. It was a totally superfluous moment and was cut from the completed film. My first experience on the cutting room floor.

While filming my moment in *The Rack*, MGM casting told me to drop by director Richard Brooks' office. T*he Blackboard Jungle*, with Glenn Ford and Sidney Poitier, had recently been released and was a big box-office winner, making Brooks the hottest director on the lot. His next assignment was *The Catered Affair*, yet another small screen to big screen transfer. Gore Vidal had adapted Paddy Chayefsky's acclaimed television script and Bette Davis had been signed to star, making her first appearance in an MGM film. Set to star with Davis as members of the Hurley family were Ernest Borgnine, Debbie Reynolds and Barry Fitzgerald, with a new Australian actor, Rod Taylor, cast as Debbie's boyfriend. The other member of the Hurley household was the younger son, Eddie, who was about to be drafted. It wasn't a large role, but one that would pop up throughout the film. so whoever got the role would be on the picture from start to finish. That's always good, financially, anyway. During our meeting, Brooks also explained that he'd demanded a week's rehearsal for the family members— something rarely done in those days (or these, for that matter). He didn't read me for the role, but after talking for a while, he said, "Yes, you could be Debbie's brother. You're cast." As I was happily leaving his office, he added, "The only problem is you're prettier than Debbie!"

When I arrived at the studio for the first day of rehearsal, Hank Moonjean, the assistant director, showed me to my dressing room. I was surprised to find an elegantly wrapped basket of fruit, as well as an expensive bottle of Scotch on my dressing-room table. Attached to the basket was a note from Dore Schary, the head of the studio, welcoming me to MGM. That's the first time I'd had that kind of treatment, so I was thrilled.

Mr. Brooks had a hellish reputation for being rough on certain actors. I was told it was usually the youngest cast member who became his "whipping boy." I was sure I was in for it. Fortunately, I didn't become the target of Brooks' wrath. That dubious distinction fell on the shoulders of poor Debbie Reynolds.

A jovial moment on the set of The Catered Affair. *Debbie Reynolds and Ernest Borgnine played my sister and father.*

He hadn't wanted to cast her. Prior to this, she'd mostly done musicals and light comedies, but this was a dramatic role, and Brooks didn't think she could handle it. But she was becoming so popular that Dore Schary had insisted he use her. She was dating Eddie Fisher at the time, and they were the darlings of the fan magazines. Eddie was the hot singing sensation of the moment, and every day, it seemed, the trade papers would headline some fabulous new million-dollar-deal he'd made with a network or recording company. In his case, both. Shortly after we started filming, they announced their engagement.

The week's rehearsal was a wonderful bonding time for the cast. We really began to feel like a middle-class Bronx family. Fireworks had been expected between Bette Davis and Brooks—each very definite in their way, each known for demanding control, and each quite volatile. But it turned into a love match of mutual respect and trust. Bette was capable of a few salty expressions; but Brooks' tongue was a master at using every four-letter word in the book. Davis needed a strong director, like she'd had with William Wyler, and she found him in Richard Brooks.

Each day, however, the director found some way to needle Debbie. Referring to all the trade articles, he'd make some barbed remark about Eddie Fisher's money. She tried to laugh it off. But one day was particularly disturbing. Eddie had just given her a huge, obviously very expensive, engagement ring. This particular day she forgot to take it off before the camera rolled. Suddenly, Brooks spotted the sparkling diamond; hardly a suitable prop for a poor Bronx family. "Cut!" he shouted. He then proceeded to call her every foul name in the book, screaming that he hadn't wanted her in the picture, that she was a lousy actress. It was brutal. Hank Moonjean called lunch. None too soon.

Debbie and I frequently ate together in the MGM commissary, as we did on this eventful day. Normally, she seemed sweet and down to earth, eagerly talking about her wedding plans. But not today. When she joined me it was obvious that she'd been crying. During lunch she said how distressed she'd been by Brooks' treatment. She even called her friend Elizabeth Taylor, who was working on a nearby soundstage, telling her what had happened on the set. Elizabeth apparently tried to calm her, saying that the same thing had happened to her when she made *The Last Time I Saw Paris,* which Brooks had directed. Of course that film was before *The Blackboard Jungle* and he didn't have as much clout then. It seems Miss Taylor had arrived on the set, ready to do her big death scene. The only problem being that she was heavily made up and looking absolutely gorgeous. Brooks took one look at her and started screaming obscenities: "You're supposed to be dying, for chrissakes! You've been ill for weeks! You look like you're ready for a fucking premiere!" At which point he ran his thumb across the actress' mouth, smearing her lipstick. "And get rid of that fucking lipstick! Your mouth looks like a bloody cunt!" Understandably in tears, the actress ran from the set, locking herself in her dressing room, refusing to return to work. "Not until that bastard apologizes!" she screamed at the assistant director. "You tell him I'm more important than he is, and if he doesn't apologize, I'll have him fired off the picture!" The film was eventually finished, so draw your own conclusion. A few years later, however, Miss Taylor was capable of matching the director's colorful vocabulary and they became very good friends when he guided her to an Oscar nominated performance in *Cat on a Hot Tin Roof.* Whether Dore Schary spoke to Brooks about his treatment of Debbie, I don't know, but for the remainder of the shoot there were no further unpleasant situations.

While the movie was shooting, Ernest Borgnine, who was of Italian descent, had been nominated for an Academy Award for his performance as *Marty.* Indeed, he won the best actor trophy, with the fiery Italian Anna Magnani taking home the actress award for *The Rose Tattoo.* Borgnine had a late set call the morning after the ceremony, so Bette had a big sign printed up and posted on his dressing room door: "Italians Go Home!"

The final day of shooting there was the traditional wrap party. As usual, Debbie was the most energetic one, handing out gag gifts to everyone. She gave Davis a ratty old fur stole; she gave me a draft card; and, with her wicked sense of humor, she got even with Brooks by giving him a pair of earmuffs, "So you won't have to listen to yourself," the card said. She also gave him a bank savings book, referring to all his cracks about Eddie's money.

Although I didn't get to know Miss Davis well during the filming, she was always very cordial and wished me "the best" when we said our good-byes. For me, it had been a glorious seven weeks, honored to have been part of a prestigious project. When the film was released (1956) it received a mixed critical reception, with some critics preferring Thelma Ritter's television performance. Miss Davis, however, frequently said on talk shows that it was one of her favorite performances. As for Miss Reynolds, well, she got the best reviews of her career. That must have given her quite a bit of satisfaction. As for me, after three MGM films in a row (if you can count *The Rack*), there was talk I might get a studio contract. It didn't happen.

Although I'd only been in Hollywood a few months, I had appeared in four films in a row, plus *The Proud and the Profane*, and all were released in 1956. Granted, the roles were very small, but the future was looking brighter. And, most importantly, I was earning a living. I'd even managed to buy my first car—a white Ford convertible with red interior—purchased while I was making *The Catered Affair*. Craig Hill taught me to drive over the treacherous curves of Laurel Canyon Boulevard. And I became a good driver too.

Soon I'd be offered another MGM film. This one I really wanted to be a part of—the film version of Robert Anderson's *Tea and Sympathy*. Deborah Kerr and John Kerr (no relation), along with Leif Erickson, were repeating their Broadway roles, an oddity in itself. Elia Kazan wouldn't be directing as he'd done for the stage, but Vincente Minnelli would be. I met with Minnelli and he asked me to play one of the college students. Again, it was a small role, but one that appeared now and then, so it would be several weeks work.

However, something bigger was brewing down the road at 20th Century Fox. Director Delmer Daves was prepping a CinemaScope Technicolored Western called *The Last Wagon*. Richard Widmark was to star, with the young British actress Joan Collins announced as his leading lady. There were also four other leading roles, two males, two females, and the studio wanted to use "fresh faces." After meeting with Daves a couple of times, I was asked to screen test for the role of Clint. Barry Coe, a very handsome young actor, would also be testing for the part. The other male role had been narrowed down to either Nick Adams or Michael Landon. The day of the tests, we all met in the wardrobe department to get suitable western attire. Miss Collins happened to be there, preparing to do a wardrobe test. She was bitching, however, saying she didn't want to do the movie as her British accent wouldn't be appropriate in the Arizona locale. Since we weren't competing for the same role, Michael Landon and I became friendly during the test process.

Following the usual waiting period, which is always hell for an actor, my agent called with the good news that I'd won the role. Plus, he said, the studio wanted to take an option for a possible studio contract. Unfortunately, the shooting schedule on *The Last Wagon* would conflict with *Tea and Sympathy*. I'd have to make a decision between the two. This was a new and pleasant situation to be in, though frustrating that I couldn't do both. But there was really no decision to make. The Fox film offered me far better opportunity, being my first leading role, plus the possibility of a studio contract.

The film was to be shot almost entirely on location in Sedona, Arizona. Susan Kohner and Stephanie Griffin were the "fresh faces" signed for the girls' roles, with Tommy Rettig (of *Lassie* fame) also set for a featured role. Joan Collins, however, had gotten her wish and had been withdrawn from the cast, with Felicia Farr on loanout from Columbia replacing her. Oh yes, Nick Adams was selected over Michael Landon. I was disappointed by that decision.

Meanwhile, on the personal front, Craig Hill had been signed to do *Tammy and the Bachelor* at Universal, competing with Leslie Nielsen for Debbie Reynolds' affection. Good. We were both working.

For seven weeks we toiled in the blazing Arizona sun. The hot, sticky red clay clung to your clothes and body. Even after a shower, you never felt like you'd removed all the dirt and grime. We were all housed in various cabins at a lodge near the location sites. With dozens of crew people, plus the cast, the living quarters were at a premium. This forced Nick Adams and I to share a cabin, which neither one of us was too happy about, but we managed to stay out of each other's way, most of the time. One evening though, I returned to the cabin to find him using my typewriter. He said he was writing a fan magazine article on his friendship with Jimmy Dean (they'd worked together on *Rebel Without a Cause*). I too had been approached about doing such an article, but had turned down the request. It just seemed too private, too personal, and I took offense at Nick's doing it. I thought he was just using Jimmy's death to further his own career. I didn't confront him about it. After all, it was his own business, but it altered my feelings about him. I also found him a little too cocky for my taste.

In the evenings, following a long day of shooting, there was very little to do to entertain ourselves. Occasionally, the studio would send up a copy of a new film and there would be a screening, but usually we were on our own in a very remote area. Susan Kohner and I, after dinner, would frequently take long walks in the Arizona desert. It was breathtakingly beautiful in the early evening. We became quite fond of one another. She was obviously a young lady of breeding and class. She also came from a very protective family; her father being Paul Kohner, one of the best agents in the business. His prestigious client list included directors John Huston and Ingmar Bergman, as well as Lana Turner. In fact, he handled almost every major foreign star or director who arrived in Hollywood, it seemed. Susan's mother had been a Mexican film actress, Lupita Tovar, but she had retired once she married.

Despite my happy relationship with Craig, I still had my sexual confusions, and I found myself very attracted to Susan. Though we exchanged a few kisses, the friendship was quite innocent. Of course, long locations often bring about temporary liaisons. Certainly Nick and Stephanie Griffin, a beautiful young blonde actress making her film debut, seemed more than just friendly. And Richard Widmark was very attentive to Felicia Farr. I don't know if the relationship went beyond that. I liked her a lot and she had a great sense of humor. Later, of course, she married Jack Lemmon (and *stayed* married too).

Finally, we returned to Fox to complete a long courtroom scene. I preferred shooting at the studio, where things seemed to be more in control and you didn't have to fight the elements. It was a joy to finally be rid of the red clay.

In *The Last Wagon*, Widmark continued his gallery of tough roles. He played a man who had just murdered three brothers in revenge for his wife's death. He is arrested and chained to a wagon train. When Indians attack the procession, there are no survivors except a group of young people (that was us), and Widmark, who had been left for dead. My character frees him and he takes control of the group and is responsible for leading us safely back to the nearest fort. As one critic wrote: "*The Last Wagon'* is a suspenseful and action-packed Western. Its cast is

Above: Craig Hill, my first Hollywood friend
Above right: Yes, that's Joan Collins. I had quite an infatuation
Right: Publicity shot from The Last Wagon, *my first leading role.*

With Richard Widmark and Felicia Farr in a tense moment from The Last Wagon.

made up largely of talented newcomers, and it is to director Daves' credit that the picture plays so well. The film is tough and taut throughout."

After viewing some of the rushes, Tommy Rettig's mother said to me, "In some of those close-ups you remind me of a young Gregory Peck." This was a new comparison, but I was certainly flattered. Nearer the film's 1956 release, the Fox publicity department started the buildup—a common one asking—"Is Ray Stricklyn a new James Dean?" That sort of publicity, of course, was put out about almost every young actor opening in a new film. There would be many would-be Jimmy Deans, but no one really came close to creating the excitement he'd caused in just three major film roles.

Despite *The Last Wagon* being a commercial hit, Fox did not pick up my option. I was very disappointed.

* * * * *

Craig Hill had a small apartment in Brentwood, not too far from close friends of his, Bill Moran and Jack Owens. Bill was a wealthy oilman, with a beautiful estate and an elegant yacht moored in Newport. Jack was a would-be writer. They'd been lovers, but the relationship was pretty stormy, and now they were just sharing the house, with Jack more or less running the establishment. We spent a good deal of time with them, particularly with Jack, who cooked wonderful dinners (or the maid did), with the booze poured much too freely. Jack was also an alcoholic. Every weekend there would be all-day pool parties, with luxurious luncheons and dinners. Craig was a good swimmer and helped me become proficient in the pool, although a Johnny Weissmuller or Esther Williams I wasn't. Other friends would also be there and there would be games of lawn croquet, etc. I was fairly adept at that. They were fun, relaxing weekends.

Craig and I discussed moving in together, but the 1950s were still a very homophobic time in Hollywood and, because of our individual careers, we decided it best to keep separate apartments. Even when we'd dine out, which was frequent, we were careful not to go to popular restaurants, choosing instead out-of-the-way steak houses near the Santa Monica beach. With Phyllis and Rock, we spent a good deal of time at the home of George Nader and his friend, Mark Miller. They were Rock's closest friends. Miller, like Jack Owens, was also a would-be writer, then working on a modern version of Chekhov's *The Sea Gull*. Nader was becoming quite popular as an actor, particularly in the fan magazines. His layouts were usually on the beach or at poolside to show off his very muscular body. Universal was giving him a big "push." Often, when we'd dine there, George would retire early. Perhaps he was studying a script, but he appeared to be more of a health nut, taking proper care of himself and not drinking as much as the rest of us.

After I finished *The Last Wagon*, I started doing quite a lot of television. Frequently I'd get parts that Sal Mineo had rejected. His film career was progressing very steadily, and he didn't want to appear on the small screen. Although Sal was considerably younger than I, and we didn't look a bit alike, I could still play teenagers, so Alec would usually suggest me if Sal didn't want to do a particular show. More often than not, I was cast. Among the routine series I appeared on, always in leading roles, were *Dr. Christian* with Macdonald Carey; *The Millionaire*, on which I played opposite a young blonde named Barbara Eden (long before she showed her navel on *I Dream of Jeannie)*; a Ford Theatre episode featured me with the wonderful character actor Charles Bickford. I guest-starred on a *Matinee Theatre* with Betty Lynn and James Lydon, did a *Father Knows Best* episode with Robert Young and Jane Wyatt, as well as *The Danny Thomas Show*. For Fox, I did several segments of their *Broken Arrow* series. In one script, I was Nochise, son of Cochise, playing Michael Ansara's offspring. They put me in redskin makeup with a long dark wig. I looked like Dorothy Lamour in one of her sarong movies. On a *Navy Log* episode, I shared the screen with Chuck Connors. Another series I did was *Markham*, starring in a segment entitled *The Nephew*. It toplined former Oscar winner Ray Milland. The producers said the character would become a running role, but the series was canceled before that became a reality. I didn't tell Mr. Milland that I had *almost* been an extra in his film, *The Thief*. When I did Rod Cameron's series, *State Trooper*, I was having trouble "matching" my shots. If you did a certain piece of business, like lighting a cigarette or putting down a cup of coffee, you'd always have to match doing the same thing, at the exact same time, when the scene was repeated from a different angle. I was having difficulties one day, and the script girl, whose job it was to make sure the actors matched, suggested that I keep my hands in my pockets all the time, then I wouldn't have to worry. "That's what Rod Cameron does," she told me. Yes, I thought to myself, and that's why he's such a stiff actor.

* * * * *

It was Christmas time once again. I'd been in Hollywood a year and three months. I'd known Craig for a year now and I wanted to give him a nice gift. I decided on a new stereo. One evening just Jack Owens and I were having dinner at the Brentwood house and, while savoring our after-dinner drinks, which we didn't need, I happened to mention that I'd bought the stereo as a surprise gift. Jack, who was getting pretty drunk, suddenly became very quiet. Finally, his speech blurred, he said, "Ray, I don't think you should give Craig such an expensive gift." "Why not?" I asked. He hesitated for quite a long time, then blurted out: "He's having an affair with someone else." I sat there stunned, not wanting to believe what I'd just heard. "He's seeing an actor named Bill Lundmark," Jack continued. "They've been here for dinner a couple of times." Lundmark was a

No, it's not Dorothy Lamour. It's me as Nochise, son of Cochise, in a Broken Arrow *segment.*

handsome blond actor. I knew who he was as we'd occasionally competed for the same roles.

Craig and I had been together exactly one year. Not a long time, perhaps, but long enough to have made a deep impact. Still, I didn't want to believe Jack's story was true. Craig hadn't told me himself, so I kept hoping the situation would resolve itself. I didn't confront him, because I didn't want to hear the truth. On Christmas day I delivered the stereo to his apartment. Of course, he seemed pleased by the gift. I don't recall what he gave me—a sweater? A book? We had a drink to "celebrate" the holiday. The alcohol, of course, loosened his tongue and he finally told me about Lundmark. He said he didn't know if it was a serious relationship, but he wanted to give it a try. And that was that. For him.

For me, however, it was a different story. I allowed myself to be badly hurt. I felt betrayed. Nothing thus far in my personal life had hit me so hard. Phyllis, of course, was sympathetic, but that didn't stop the ache. The depression was debilitating, made more so by my solitary drinking. I even turned down a couple of television jobs.

* * * * *

During this wounded time, I ran into an acquaintance from New York, Paul Marlin. We exchanged phone numbers. One day he called, asking if he could drop by—he was with someone he wanted me to meet. Reluctantly, I agreed.

The someone turned out to be an Englishman named Edward James. He was in his fifties, I guessed, with a little goatee sprouting from his chin. His clothes were ill matched and slightly rumpled. His fingernails also could have used a trim. He was a writer, I was told. After exchanging a few pleasantries, Paul asked the question he'd really come to ask: "Ray, I know your career is going well, but do you still type?" It reminded me of an incident a few years earlier at Riis Park in New York, a popular sunbathing beach. I was standing in the hot dog line, waiting to give my order, when someone tapped me on the shoulder. "I've been looking for you," the voice said. I turned to find William Inge, the playwright of *Picnic* and *Come Back, Little Sheba* fame, standing behind me. Aha, I thought, he's written a new play and I'm perfect for the role! Instead, he asked, "Do you still type?" He needed someone to type script revisions and Tennessee had told him about me. Trying to conceal my disappointment, I replied in the negative.

I said the same to Paul and Mr. James. Paul laughed, adding, "I didn't think so, but thought I would ask. Edward needs someone to help him for a couple of days." They invited me to join them for dinner and I accepted. There *was* something fascinating about James. During dinner the subject came up again. Before the evening was over, I'd volunteered to assist him. Actually, for some odd reason, I loved typing. Besides, I wasn't doing anything else, except sitting at home feeling sorry for myself. "I'm staying at the Bel Air Hotel," James said.

The next day, around noon, I arrived at the hotel. The Bel Air was, and is, a very exclusive home-away-from-home, catering to the wealthy and a favorite spot for movie people. Its setting was also unique, almost like being in the country, with beautiful flowers and foliage surrounding the grounds. There was also a lake with real swans floating by. I found James' suite, in a more secluded section of the grounds, and rang the doorbell. There was no answer, so I rang again. Finally, he opened the door. He was on the phone, dressed in a lounging robe. While he was chatting away, I noticed water pouring out from under the bathroom door. I quickly opened the door and found water overflowing from the sink. I hastily turned off the faucet, and as the water began to drain from the sink I noticed about a half-dozen yellow pencils floating around. Odd, I thought. I grabbed several towels and began sopping up the wet floor. Finally off the phone, James giggled, "Oh, dear, what a mess! I was sterilizing my pencils." He said this as though it was a perfectly normal thing to do. Not only did he clean his pencils before using them; he also wiped the typewriter keys with a cleansing fluid before I used it. This was certainly going to be unlike any previous typing job I'd had, I said to myself. Before starting, however, he ordered some food and soft drinks from room service.

It was a very brief typing session, an hour maybe, if that. He was working on a book of poetry, but his interest soon waned. "My creative juices aren't flowing," he said, but not before noticing that my fingers moved rapidly across the Remington Rand keyboard. He asked if I'd like to continue tomorrow. By now this odd character intrigued me, so I agreed. I hadn't planned on him paying me, thinking I was doing it as a favor, but as I left he insisted I take the bills he was offering. On my way to my car, I counted the assorted denominations—he'd given me over a hundred dollars. Not bad, I thought, for less than an hour's work.

Edward James became a quite fascinating diversion. Though he could drive (badly), he didn't like to, and usually took taxis. When I was available, I would drive him around. I called Paul Marlin, laughingly asking, "What have you gotten me into?" He then proceeded to give me the preposterous details.

Edward was an English millionaire, Paul said, and reputed to be the illegitimate son of the royal family. He was given a huge trust fund to keep this indiscretion silent. He spent most of his time traveling; though he had a coffee plantation in the wilds of Mexico, where he was in the process of building a large house. He also had two homes in Los Angeles, but never stayed in either of them, nor did he rent them out. One was just past Malibu at the beach, in Trancas, the other was an old house in the Hollywood hills, a section called Whitley Terrace. In the 1920s and '30s it had been a favorite location for many movie stars. He had bought the Hollywood house as a wedding gift when he married a well-known dancer named Tilly Losch (last seen, briefly, as Jennifer Jones' gypsy mother in *Duel in the Sun*). The marriage was quite brief, however, and was annulled. It seems on their wedding night, he'd crawled into bed with Miss Losch (or Mrs. James) only to have her scream, "Out! I only married you for your money, you damned pervert!" Though he had furnished the house, after the disastrous wedding night he never went near it again, if he could avoid it.

Edward James was also quite well known for supporting the arts. He financed many a struggling artist, one being Salvador Dali, who went on to great success. He also backed plays and ballets. He was very instrumental in the early European careers of Kurt Weill, Lotte Lenya and Bertolt Brecht, as well as a young ballerina named Vera Zorina. With much fanfare, Zorina was signed by Paramount Pictures and given the sought-after lead opposite Gary Cooper in Ernest Hemingway's *For Whom the Bell Tolls*. After a few days of shooting, however, her inexperience as an actress was too evident and she was replaced with Ingrid Bergman. James seemed to know everybody, at least in the art and literary world. Eventually, I would join him in visits with such esteemed artists as composer Igor Stravinsky, and writers like Aldous Huxley, Christopher Isherwood and Gavin Lambert. A heady crowd, to be sure. Lambert had even written a delicious novel, *Norman's Letter*, loosely based on James' exotic antics.

Although the subject was never discussed, I assumed Edward was a homosexual. In fact, he probably was asexual. He enjoyed the company of attractive young men, but never once did I hear of him making a pass or seducing anyone. Over the weeks, he obviously liked me and came to trust me. One day, shortly before he took off for Mexico, he asked me if I would like to live in the Hollywood hills house? Rather than leave it empty, he said he'd feel better if someone was staying there. Though he hated entering the property, he volunteered to show it to me.

The house was located on Milner Road, up a very winding road off Highland Avenue. The exterior of the house didn't look too imposing, in fact, it looked rather small. But, once you'd entered from the street level, the structure went *down* the hill, three floors below. The entrance floor consisted of three bedrooms and three baths. One bedroom door was locked. *That*, he said, was to have been his bridal suite. He refused to open that door (my God, I thought, Tilly Losch has probably rotted away in that room!). From the upper hall you went down a staircase, which had a trap door in case you wanted to shut it off. Upon reaching the second floor below, you went down a few steps into a huge living room. At the far end of the room was a massive fireplace, one you could almost stand in (similar to the one Orson Welles used in *Citizen Kane*). The room was furnished with large, oversized pieces, all custom-built. Two mammoth sofas could have easily slept a half dozen people. You felt positively dwarfed when you sat on them. Off the living room were French doors leading to an enclosed, high concrete walled patio. At the other end of the living room, going up a few steps, was the dining room and off from that, the kitchen. A steep, dangerous staircase in the kitchen area took you to the third floor below. There was a small apartment down there, likely meant to be maid's quarters.

Actually, since he didn't live there, he was using the house as a storage space for his priceless art. The walls were covered with original paintings, many by Salvador Dali. They were worth a fortune. After I'd been living there for a while, *Life* magazine came to the house to shoot a pictorial layout of the Dali paintings.

As tempting as Edward's offer was, I didn't know if I wanted to live there. It seemed spooky. I wouldn't have been surprised if Gloria Swanson and Erich von Stroheim suddenly appeared. I mulled his offer over for a couple of days, certainly there were many pros for accepting—there wouldn't be any rent, a decided plus, and I could at least *pretend* I was a movie star in such surroundings. Finally, I told him I would do it, *if* I could have a roommate. He agreed. And so, Jim Terry and I moved in.

* * * * *

All this activity diverted me, for a while, from the loss of not having Craig in my life anymore. But I was still hurting. I was depressed a good deal of the time, which only accelerated my drinking. My days were usually okay, but as the evenings rolled in, waves of self-pity washed over me. I felt like I was drowning.

One evening an actor friend of Jim's was visiting. We were in the living room, alone, sitting on one of the giant sofas. After a couple of drinks, I poured my broken heart out to him. He could tell I was in considerable anguish. Being in the midst of therapy himself, Paul recognized that I needed help. He suggested I see his therapist. Though I knew he was right, I kept resisting his efforts. Finally, he became quite upset, saying, "Ray, it's like you're drowning and someone is offering you a helping hand and you won't take it!"

During the course of my verbal vomiting, I had told him how unhappy I was being homosexual. Just saying the word nauseated me. I hated putting labels on human feelings. In the past, being with a member of my own sex hadn't seemed a problem, in fact I rarely thought about it one way or the other. I was so wrapped up in my career that my sexual orientation was way down on my list of priorities. But the breakup with Craig had caught me off-guard and I was very vulnerable, telling myself I never wanted to be with a man again. Paul then confessed that he, too, was having similar feelings, which is why he was in the midst of therapy with a woman named Liz. He swore it was working for him (and perhaps it did. He later married her).

And so I began my twice weekly, hour-long sessions. I would exorcise my adolescent demons, I told myself. I would be a *man*. I would be *straight*, so help me God!

Cary Grant had recently made headline news when he admitted he'd been taking LSD, a powerful, mind-altering drug, under the supervision of his psychiatrist. After I'd had several hours of sessions with Liz, she didn't feel we were making enough headway in breaking down my defenses. LSD was supposed to be a shortcut through the muck and mire. She recommended that we try the treatment.

It was a painful experience. Not physically so much, but mentally. After the drug would take effect, you would regress to your childhood, dredging up every subconscious thought you'd ever had, even before childhood. I was back in my mother's womb, frightened to emerge in a world where I thought I wasn't wanted. Sometimes the memories would be so sharp and painful that I would repeatedly bang my head against the office wall. During these sessions, Liz always had an assistant with her, just in case of such emergencies. This protection was a necessity too, because Liz was in a wheelchair, crippled since birth with polio. The drug brought back all my childhood rage against my father. I recalled the cutting of my blond curls, my fear of women. *Women can cause trouble*, my mother had warned. The female body was *dirty* and *disgusting* my homeroom teacher had screamed.

Once an LSD session had ended, it would take at least an hour for the drug to wear off, so I'd stay on one of Liz's couches until I was able to drive home. After several weeks, I seemed to be making considerable progress. Strangely enough, after banging my head and purging my soul, I was beginning to feel cleansed, rejuvenated, as if a giant weight had been lifted from the pit of my stomach. Though I was still hit with moments of depression, they were less frequent. Too, I had started attending the Hollywood Church of Religious Science, a branch of the Science of Mind philosophy. Everything was in your *thinking* it taught—the good and the bad, the negative and the positive. We each perpetuate our own condition we were told by Dr. Robert Bitzer, that is why we go from bad to worse or from success to greater success. Bitzer's teachings were helping me a lot, even more that the therapy sessions, I came to believe. And so, I stopped seeing Liz.

Now it was time to put Dr. Bitzer's words into action. It was time to return to work—*ah, work!*—the loveliest of all four-letter words. It was time to go from success to greater success.

The television roles were getting better. Co-starring with Ida Lupino in That Woman, *an episode for 4-Star Playhouse*

TAKE FOUR

With a new attitude, and free from the deep depression I'd been suffering, I plunged into a renewed enthusiasm for work. *That* was the most important thing, that was why I'd come to Hollywood, to pursue my drive for success, to *be* somebody, to make a name for myself.

Besides attending Dr. Bitzer's weekly Sunday sermons at the Hollywood Church of Religious Science, I also enrolled in his special Wednesday night classes. Jim and Phyllis often attended with me. You left feeling good about yourself, positive in your outlook, knowing a bright future was on the horizon. Many actors attended the classes, and it was here I first met Mary McCarty, a Broadway musical comedy performer. I'd seen her years before, when she co-starred with Eddie Albert and Allyn Ann McLerie in Irving Berlin's *Miss Liberty*. Mary was usually with actress Margaret Lindsay, who appeared in scores of Warner Bros. movies in the late '30s and '40s (most notably, perhaps, as Bette Davis' rival for Henry Fonda's affections in *Jezebel*). I was later to discover that they'd been lovers for a long time, though now were just "good friends." In the years ahead, Mary would find renewed success as a leading player in Stephen Sondheim's brilliant musical *Follies*, as well as Bob Fosse's original Broadway production of *Chicago*, then as a regular on the hit television series, *Trapper John*, with Gregory Harrison.

I attributed my new positive attitude, thanks to Dr. Bitzer's teachings, for the sudden upswing in my television career. The shows I would be doing were classier, with stronger roles, with bigger stars. A few segments stand out. One favorite was a 4-Star Playhouse episode called *That Woman*, with Ida Lupino as the star. The 4-Star Playhouse was an anthology series produced by film stars Charles Boyer, David Niven, Gig Young and Miss Lupino. Each week they'd alternate in different stories.

Ida Lupino, of course, had had a long career, particularly shining when she signed with Warner Bros. and gave many notable performances, such as *They Drive By Night*, which she did with George Raft, Ann Sheridan and Humphrey

Bogart; *High Sierra*, which made Bogart a big star, and *The Hard Way*, for which she was named best actress by the New York Film Critics. Yet even with her often dynamic performances, she was usually second choice to Bette Davis in getting the plum assignments.

That Woman was the tale of a mentally disturbed woman who returns to a farmhouse to recuperate and becomes infatuated with a young lad (me) who lives on the farm. He is equally fascinated by her. Their relationship, and growing fondness for one another, was the crux of the teleplay. The townspeople, however, become alarmed, thinking she had seduced the boy. Lupino was very fond of young talent (later producing/directing her own films which featured promising young players) and she took a strong liking to me. After almost every scene, she'd say to the cameraman, "Now get a good close-up of Ray." She kept insisting on this until he finally said, "Ida, *you're* the star." I was never better or more lovingly photographed in my life.

Another strong role was on Lee Marvin's series, *M-Squad.* In an episode entitled *The Second Best Killer,* I played a real psycho. In the script, Marvin had captured me, handcuffing me to an about-to-explode boiler, threatening not to release me until I'd confessed to a killing. It was basically a two-character piece, an exhausting shoot, with lots of high dramatics on my part. The evening we finished shooting, a rather bizarre incident took place. Marvin, with his stand-in, invited me to join them in his dressing room for a drink. After we'd downed a couple (he had quite a reputation as a womanizing boozer), the actor excused himself to go to the john. When he returned, he had a huge dildo sticking out of his jacket pocket. With this big phallic cock staring me in the face, I didn't know how to react. Was it a joke? Was he trying to shock me? Was he trying to turn me on? I didn't stick around to find out. But it was weird.

Shortly after that I had another call from Revue Productions, the television arm at Universal Studios. I was cast in a Schlitz Playhouse segment called *For Better, For Worse.* The Schlitz Playhouse, like 4-Star Playhouse, lured big stars to the small screen. This one was special, however, because it would mark Bette Davis' television debut. She had casting approval and when my name was brought up, she remembered me from *The Catered Affair* and okayed me for the role of her stepson. In the teleplay she was a former actress, now married to my wealthy father (played by the distinguished John Williams). Her character had a serious flaw, however, being a pathological liar. Following a party scene, we leave together. Driving home we're involved in a terrible accident and someone is killed. Though I had been driving, she takes the blame to protect me and is charged with manslaughter. In the end, of course, the truth is revealed. It was melodramatic, but it offered me a good opportunity and, more importantly, I was playing opposite Bette Davis! I couldn't believe it. Dwight Taylor, the son of the great Laurette (*The Glass Menagerie*) Taylor, incidentally, wrote the script.

On the final night of shooting, only Bette and I were working. Director John Brahm was lining up the last shot, a scene where we're parked in a Thunderbird convertible having a serious conversation. It was approaching 10 P.M., it had been a long day, and everyone was anxious to complete the final shot, and go home. Everyone but me that is. I didn't want this magical experience to end. Finally, Brahm called the last "print it."

The actress asked me if I'd like to have a drink, so I followed her into her dressing room, where her sister, Barbara, was already packing her belongings. Bette offered me a Scotch—not my drink of choice, but I wasn't about to refuse. She complimented me on my performance, then mentioned how fond she'd been of me during *The Catered Affair*. (I wondered if that was because she always saw me standing behind the camera watching her admiringly?) We had a second drink. Suddenly we heard a crew member holler, "We're closing up, Miss Davis!" It was time to go. I said my goodbye, gently kissing her on the cheek.

It was pouring down rain outside. As I'm driving down a studio street, I saw another car approaching me. It was Bette and Barbara. She honked her horn, rolled down her window, and yelled, "I'm having a dinner party tomorrow night in Newport Beach (where she was renting a house). Why don't you come spend the weekend? You can be Barbara's daughter's date," she laughed.

The next morning, Saturday, I left early for the long drive to Newport. The house was right on the beach in a secluded, gated area, obviously a very expensive section. She introduced me to her two children, B.D., her daughter, and to little Michael, her adopted four-year old son. "Gary is working," she said, "so he won't be joining us." Gary, of course, was her husband, Gary Merrill, the actor she'd fallen in love with when they made *All About Eve* in 1950.

I couldn't believe I was actually playing opposite Bette Davis (with John Williams) in For Better, For Worse, *a Schlitz Playhouse episode.*

The dinner party turned out to be a small affair for her doctor and his wife. She'd rented a private room in a Mexican restaurant for the occasion and, after dinner, we drove Barbara and her daughter to their nearby quarters, then we returned to the beach house. While she was changing into a dressing gown, I made her a Scotch and myself a vodka on the rocks. From her bedroom, she hollered, "Ray, start a fire!" When she returned, she stretched out on the couch, facing the burning embers and proceeded to tell me that Gary was rehearsing a Playhouse 90 television script, which is why he wasn't there for the weekend. "Turn on the television, I want to watch the news." An old 1939 Warner Bros. movie, *Dust Be My Destiny*, with John Garfield and Priscilla Lane, was just ending. As the credits were rolling by, she sighed, rather sadly I thought. "Half my life just went by on that screen," she said, referring to the names of the cameraman, the lighting man, the costumer, and the makeup man. "I worked with them all." She handed me her glass, ready for one more Scotch. As I was putting ice in her drink, she asked, "What did you think of John Garfield?" I said I liked him very much. "I didn't think too much of him," she returned. "Overrated." The news then came on. I moved to the floor, beside the couch. It reminded me of a scene from Shaw's play, *Candida*, the one I'd so much wanted to do after I graduated from the Irvine Studio. At last, here I was, playing Marchbanks to Bette Davis' Candida! It was raining outside and the fire was making a delicious crackling sound. Indeed, it was a very romantic setting. I felt a strong urge to touch her. Something told me that she wouldn't have minded.

Sunday morning, with the children, we sat out on the beach reading the morning *Times*, working the crossword puzzle, drinking Bloody Marys. It was a lovely morning. She said Barbara and her daughter would be coming for dinner.

We had finished our meals, were having after-dinner drinks, when, suddenly, the headlights of a car flashed through the window. "Oh, God," Bette said, "*he's* home!" Gary greeted her with an impish grin, kissed her on the cheek, saying, "We finished rehearsal earlier than anticipated, so I thought I would surprise you." He had. He seemed in a jolly mood. While Barbara was fixing him a drink, he began talking about the Playhouse 90 rehearsal. "Claire Trevor's going to be absolutely sensational," he said, "she'll probably win an Emmy." I could tell this bit of information didn't set too well with Miss Davis. She poured herself another drink;

a stiff one. Bette, you see, had originally been announced to play opposite Gary on the show, but for some reason, had backed out of doing it. Probably because the Playhouse 90 shows were done "live."

They were both heavy drinkers, though she seemed to hold her's better than Mr. Merrill. The evening was beginning to turn chilly, and not just from the weather. From out of nowhere, Gary suddenly said, "Shit! I wish I were Gregory Peck and could afford to do only one good film a year!" They were off. "For chrissakes," Bette retorted, "you're lazy! And if you're going to pick an actor to be like, at least pick a good one!" Barbara, having witnessed these scenes many times, suggested we "children" watch television in another room. I didn't like being relegated to the adolescent category, but I dutifully obeyed. However, I kept my ear to the half-opened door in case something exciting happened.

Bette explained my presence by saying that I'd been the date of Barbara's daughter. That seemed sufficient to Gary. The next morning he asked me if I'd like to go sailing with him and young Michael. I begged off, saying I had to start the drive back to Los Angeles. After they'd gone, Bette thanked me for not joining them. "I didn't want to be alone," she added. We sat on the beach for a while, mostly in silence. I could sense the marriage was no longer made in heaven. She said they would be heading back to Maine, where they lived, as soon as Gary finished working.

Some months later, she was back in Hollywood doing another television show; this time playing a favorite character of hers, Mary Todd Lincoln. That morning *Los Angeles Times* had a front-page story saying the Merrills were divorcing. I drove over to Columbia, where she was filming, and she greeted me warmly. But once in her dressing room, she broke down, starting to cry. This was a side of Bette Davis I had never expected to see. She always seemed so strong. "My whole life is shattered," she wept. "One more divorce, at my age. I don't know if I can handle it." Of course she could and did. But she would never marry again.

She was staying in the penthouse apartment at the Chateau Marmont, a hotel just off the Sunset Strip. She asked me if I would escort her to a small dinner party she was having at the Ambassador Hotel, where Sammy Davis Jr. was performing his sensational nightclub act. Paul Henreid and his wife would be joining us. Henreid, of course, was the European actor who'd co-starred with Bette in

Now, Voyager, creating a memorable movie moment when he lit two cigarettes at once, then handed her one. Bette looked fabulous when I arrived at the Chateau. She was wearing a black evening gown, with a full-length white ermine coat draped over her shoulders. All through dinner, fans kept disturbing her, interrupting for autographs. She graciously signed a few, but quickly tired of the inconsideration and refused to sign any more. At the end of Sammy Davis' show, he introduced her from the stage. She received a standing ovation. "Get me out of here!" she whispered. It was like a scene from one of her movies as she stormed through the crowded club, dragging her white ermine fur behind her. Outside, of course, we had the task of waiting for her limo. Again, fans pestered her for autographs. She refused, coldly turning her back on them. Barry Sullivan, who had played opposite her in *Payment on Demand*, was also waiting for his car and they had a brief, but very friendly reunion. The next day she returned to Maine.

A considerable amount of time passed before she returned again. This time she'd rented a house in Brentwood, but her stay was marred by a bad accident. Not knowing the layout of the house too well, she'd opened a door off the hall, falling down a steep flight of stairs and badly hurting her back. When I visited her, she was in bed, in traction, and in a considerable amount of pain. She was particularly upset, she said, because she'd been offered the lead in a new Broadway play, *Look Homeward, Angel*, which had a beautiful script by Ketti Frings. The accident prevented her from accepting the offer, which eventually turned out to be a major dramatic hit for Jo Van Fleet and Tony Perkins. It would be several years before our paths would cross again.

In author Lawrence Quirk's 1990 biography, *Fasten Your Seat Belts: The Passionate Life of Bette Davis*, he devoted several pages to my relationship with Miss Davis. I was surprised, however, to read one section. Publicist Jerry Asher, who had known Bette quite well, told Quirk that he felt Davis had been in love with me for a while. He told Quirk, and I quote: "When they met, she was pushing fifty and he was in his twenties. He seems to have been the first in a line of young men half her age with whom she was destined to fall in love with, never happily. Ray was a gentleman with her, compared to the way some of the other pups treated her. I think she was trying to recapture some of her own lost youth by osmosis with these young men."

* * * * *

When Rock Hudson was signed to star with Jennifer Jones in David O. Selznick's lavish remake of Ernest Hemingway's *A Farewell to Arms*, there was a squabble over who would get top billing. Selznick, of course, as the producer and husband of Miss Jones, assumed it would go to his wife. Henry Willson, however, insisted that Rock's popularity entitled him to the top position. They were at a standstill in contract negotiations. Finally, the very canny Mr. Willson made Selznick a bet. "If Rock gets a best actor Oscar nomination for *Giant*, then he should have his name first." Selznick reluctantly agreed, but it seemed like a safe wager. After all, Rock wasn't known for his great acting ability. But he *did* get the nomination (along with James Dean for the same movie) and Willson won the bet.

The long Italian location on *A Farewell to Arms* helped end the marriage of Phyllis and Rock. While he was away, Phyllis became very ill with infectious hepatitis. For a while, it didn't look like she'd recover. She had around the clock nurses and intravenous feeding because she couldn't hold anything on her stomach. She was also on tranquilizers to combat severe depression. Rock had talked long-distance with her doctor when she'd first gone into the hospital but, since then, had no direct contact with her. This, of course, depressed her even further. Her doctor was furious, finally reaching Rock in Rome, demanding to know *why* he hadn't called. The actor's lame excuse was he'd just been "too busy" on the movie. What he didn't add was that he was also having an affair with a handsome young Italian actor.

Once Phyllis was released from the hospital, she couldn't stay in the Warbler Place house because heavy construction was going on next door and the noise was deafening. She rented a beach house in Malibu and I spent many a day and night there, keeping her company, running errands, generally assisting her. One evening, Anna Kashfi, who'd appeared with Rock in *Battle Hymn*, came out for dinner. She was quite lovely, with dark olive skin and long dark hair. She was engaged to Marlon Brando and, over dinner, the two discussed the pros and cons of being married to a famous celebrity. I'm afraid Phyllis wasn't too encouraging. Anna and I had one too many martinis and became quite cozy in front of the fireplace, ending up in an impassioned embrace. The situation didn't go any further, but I *was* trying (I was going straight, remember?). As has been well documented elsewhere, the Kashfi-Brando marriage was a disaster.

Many in Hollywood thought Phyllis and Rock's marriage had been one of convenience, to cover up his homosexuality. While that may have been his (and Henry Willson's) motive, I believe Phyllis was really in love with him. I know she was completely faithful during the marriage. Shortly after his return from Rome, she filed for divorce and a bitter alimony battle ensued. The union lasted just a little over two years.

During one of my nights at the Malibu house, Phyllis had told me about the dreaded *Confidential* magazine article. It seems there had been a gang bang at Willson's house (not an infrequent happening, by the way) involving Rock and other young men. One of them talked to the magazine about it. Phyllis had always thought Universal's publicity department had killed the story but, during the messy divorce battle, she heard that Willson had hired a gangster to dissuade the *Confidential* editor from publishing the expose. "I don't know if that's absolutely true," she said, "but I know Henry was capable of such a thing; he'd fight like a tigress to protect his prized client." Phyllis was still in denial, not wanting to believe that Rock would allow himself to be dragged into such a sordid affair. Or would he? The question remained unanswered. Regarding Henry Willson's "gang bangs," I attended one once. Of course, I thought I was just going to a party, not knowing how the evening would evolve. There were dozens of the most attractive young men in Hollywood in attendance, including, to my surprise, several well-known, supposedly "straight" movie actors. Now I was no goody-two-shoes, to be sure, but I was definitely not into group sex and left when I realized where the evening was headed. This Texas boy was still a square in some regards.

* * * * *

Alec Alexander phoned and said I had an interview for a new movie, a United Artists effort called *The Return of Dracula*. The role was the young hero who saves the heroine from Dracula's fangs, driving a stake through his evil heart in the final reel. I met with the producers, Jules Levy and Arthur Gardner, as well as the director, Paul Landres. My audition consisted of whether I could lift the leading lady, Norma Eberhardt. Sounds easy, and since Miss Eberhardt was at the meeting, I proceeded to do this manly request. I passed this odd test and was signed for the film. Francis Lederer, who had been a star in the 1930s and '40s, was returning to the screen in the title role. Norma was an attractive blonde with a very distinctive feature—she had one blue eye, one brown. This caused a little concern for the cameraman, but he shot her in profile as often as he could. During the film's finale, the cave scene where Norma has fainted, my audition didn't work too well. With her supposedly in a dead faint, I had great difficulty in picking her up, with almost every take being pretty clumsy. The editor finally pieced that one together. Norma and I became quite friendly during the filming and she'd frequently come over to Milner Road for dinner with Jim and me. One night, we'd had too much to drink, and she stayed over. We ended up in my bed, but after playing around a little, the booze took over and we both passed out (*yes! I was still trying!*). Over the years, *The Return of Dracula* (sometimes listed as *Curse of Dracula*) has developed a cult following. There always seems to be a curiosity about old Count Dracula. And Norma Eberhardt? Shortly after we completed the film, she married the French film actor, Claude Dauphin.

* * * * *

As the hero in The Return of Dracula *with Norma Eberhardt*

During this period, Craig Hill and Bill Lundmark had continued their relationship. Eventually, they shared the same apartment and were together a number of years. Craig's career had a sudden boost when he signed to co-star with Kenneth Tobey in the syndicated series, *Whirlybirds*. His female fans were swooning once again. One day Alec called and said I'd been asked to guest-star in a segment entitled "Hideout." At first I thought I wouldn't accept, but I was curious to see Craig again and changed my mind. I must admit there was a twinge of remembrance of what once-had-been, and he was very considerate during the filming. But I was glad when the shoot was over, as it was dredging up memories I didn't want to cope with. We would meet again, though. And again.

* * * * *

The phone kept ringing and ringing. I was in the shower and couldn't answer it in time. A few minutes later it rang again. It was Alec. He sounded urgent: "Where were you? I've been trying to reach you. You've got an eleven A.M. interview at 20th Century Fox." He hung up before I got any particulars.

When I arrived at the studio's casting office, it was jammed with young actors. I spotted Robert Morse in the crowd. I hadn't seen him since our debut bits in *The Proud and the Profane* in the Virgin Islands, though I knew his career was on the rise, having scored in the Broadway production of Thornton Wilder's *The Matchmaker* with the deliciously eccentric Ruth Gordon. The show had recently played Los Angeles and he'd been absolutely delightful in it. Before too much longer he would reach stardom in *How to Succeed In Business Without Really Trying,* but that was still in his future. We had a few laughs while waiting to be called into Michael Garrison's casting office.

When my turn eventually came, Garrison introduced me to the white-haired gentleman sitting next to him. It was producer Charles Brackett. I remember being quite impressed, as he was one of the most respected and successful producers in the business. With Billy Wilder as his director, he'd had tremendous critical and box-office hits with *The Lost Weekend*, which had won the best picture Oscar in 1945, and, for my money, one of the great films of all time, *Sunset Boulevard*, in 1950. Now he'd left Paramount and had signed a new contract with Fox. His next picture, and the reason I was there, was to be *Ten North Frederick*, based on a best-selling novel by John O'Hara. They said there was a choice role in the script, written and to be directed by Philip Dunne. The part was the cynical young son, Joby Chapin, who has a serious drinking problem. Brackett asked me where I was from. "Texas," I replied, thinking nothing of my honest answer. Garrison handed me a scene from the script and suggested I go in another office and look it over. They also told me that Spencer Tracy would be starring in the film. Now I was *really* impressed.

About twenty minutes later, I re-entered Garrison's office. The scene was a very dramatic one, with Joby, fighting a hangover, telling off his mother in a heated moment. When I finished, both men were very complimentary.

I felt the interview and reading had gone well, and using all my Dr. Bitzer positive thinking training, I sailed out of the office. As I was exiting the building, an assistant from Alec's office was just arriving. "How'd the interview go?" he asked. I cheerfully responded with, "I'm going to get this role!" Being a dour type, he said, "I doubt it, they'll probably give it to Robert Wagner." Fuck you, I thought.

Just as I was about to get in my car, I noticed Craig Hill and Bill Lundmark drive up. Bill got out and dashed into the casting building. He must be seeing Brackett and Garrison too, I reasoned. Craig, obviously waiting for him, lit a cigarette and started to read a copy of *Daily Variety*. I started to walk over to his car, but then I changed my mind. I was feeling too good to possibly ruin my mood. Instead, I drove off the Pico lot and headed east, home to Milner Road.

A few days later I had a call from Garrison. "Ray, Brackett wants to see you again. You'll also be meeting the director, Philip Dunne." There was a slight pause, then he added, "By the way, if Brackett asks you again where you're from, *please* say New York. The character is from a sophisticated Pennsylvania family and he was concerned about your being from Texas."

Again, the interview seemed to go well. Brackett didn't ask me about my origins, so that was a relief, and Dunne seemed a very easy-going gentleman. I knew he'd had an Oscar nomination for his script on *How Green Was My Valley*, which went on to win the best picture prize in 1941.

Yet another week went by and, again, I received a call from Mike Garrison. This time he said, "Brackett and Dunne want to screen test you, but first they want you to meet Spencer Tracy, as he has casting approval. If he okays you, then we'll go ahead with the test." Now I was really nervous. On the appointed day, there *he* was, Spencer Tracy in the flesh. He seemed quite pleasant, though he didn't ask me one thing about acting or my background, spending most of the interview explaining why he'd decided not to do *The Diary of Anne Frank*, which was upcoming on the studio's production slate.

I guess I passed muster with Mr. Tracy, for soon I was testing. I did my scene with a young contract actress named Rachel Stephens, playing my sister (she would later play a small role in the picture). I know Robert Morse tested, but I didn't meet any of the others, nor did I see Robert Wagner.

Screen tests at Fox weren't new to me. Besides *The Last Wagon*, which proved successful, I tested for a leading role in *Bernardine* (the Mary Chase play that Jimmy Dean and I had been rejected for in New York). In that one, my test was with Janet Gaynor and Dean Jagger, who played the parents in the comedy. For a while, it looked like I was going to land the role, but it finally went to Dick Sargent. I'd also tested for the title role in the *Dobie Gillis* television series (with Tuesday Weld, yet), but Dwayne Hickman won that one. And, more recently, I'd lost an important role in *Peyton Place* to Russ Tamblyn, who went on to garner an Oscar nomination.

With the *Ten North Frederick* test completed, now came the dreaded waiting period. A couple of weeks went by and still no answer, so I'd about given up on the project, badly disappointed of course. I was still working on *The Return of Dracula* at the time. While waiting for my set call, I read in *The Hollywood Reporter*, a trade paper, that Spencer Tracy was out of the picture and the studio was seeking another major star to replace him. The picture had been temporarily postponed. Aha, I thought, perhaps that's why no decision has been reached about me.

One evening we were doing some night scenes for *Dracula* on a residential street (which just happened to be down the road from Liz's home, my former therapist). I was off camera and saw Dick Clayton walking toward me. Clayton, you may recall, was the agent who had submitted me almost three years earlier for *Friendly Persuasion*. I had finally met him when I first arrived in Hollywood. By that time he was representing Tab Hunter, who was the current fan magazine favorite, being an absolute knockout in the looks department, and getting a big buildup at Warner Bros.. Dick said Tab wanted to meet me. Well, I wanted to meet Tab Hunter, too. We met, had sex, and that was it. Almost that fast, too. Certainly not a very satisfying encounter, all rather cold and matter-of-fact. We lusted a second time, but there was little improvement. Other than our incompatibility, he seemed a very nice guy.

Above: My big dramatic moment at the climax of Ten North Frederick. *It would bring me a Golden Globe nomination.*
Below: With Gary Cooper and Geraldine Fitzgerald in a scene from Ten North Frederick

A sobering moment with Diane Varsi in Ten North Frederick. *We were very close during filming.*

But I digress. Back to the most important moment, thus far, in my movie career. Dick Clayton approached me on the *Dracula* location, saying, "Congratulations." "For what?" I asked. "I've just heard you've been cast in *Ten North Frederick*." "WHAT?!!" I asked. He repeated his news. "Well, I certainly haven't heard about it," I answered. "You will," he returned. "I got it from a very high up source at Fox."

And that's how I learned I'd won the role of Joby Chapin.

* * * * *

Ten North Frederick had a complex plot, telling the story of a wealthy businessman, who is goaded into politics by his ambitious wife, and who donates a large sum to a conniving politician in order to win a nomination. He finds no pleasure in politics, just as he has found little satisfaction in his family life, but he falls in love with a beautiful young girl and for a while enjoys the only loving relationship he has ever known. But he realizes the vast age difference and gives her up. Not long afterwards he learns he is suffering from a terminal illness and reconciles with his family. His teenage children, Ann and Joby, complicate the situation considerably.

With Spencer Tracy out of the film, the studio signed another super star to replace him. Gary Cooper. For years Cooper had been one of the major stars in the industry, consistently ranking among the "top ten" at the box office in the yearly exhibitor polls. Like Tracy, he, too, had twice won the best actor Oscar trophy. For the role of the ambitious bitch wife, Brackett was bringing the noted actress Geraldine Fitzgerald back to the screen. She had particularly scored in her first two films, the 1939 releases, *Dark Victory* with Bette Davis, and *Wuthering Heights,* opposite Laurence Olivier (receiving a best supporting actress nomination for the latter). For the role of the young woman, the beauteous model Suzy Parker was signed. This was only her second movie. And for the important roles of the daughter and son, a young actress named Diane Varsi and yours truly were cast. Varsi had just completed her debut film, the much-anticipated *Peyton Place*, so she was considered a potentially hot new personality. Stuart Whitman, another comparatively new actor, was cast as her musician lover.

As often happens in making a film, they started at the end. My big moment, when the drunken son comes careening down the stairs following his father's funeral, accusing the mother of having killed him, was going to be my initiation scene. Not an ideal way to start, as you haven't really adjusted to the other actors, the set, the crew. The day before I was to start, I was on the set, and Miss Fitzgerald asked me if I'd ever been drunk before. Did I know what it felt like to have a hangover? I lied and said no. She suggested I have a few and see what it felt like. I didn't take her advice. I already knew that mixing alcohol and work wasn't for me.

The next day it was time for my scene. There was a crowd of featured actors (wonderful character players like Tom Tully, Philip Ober, and John Emery), as well as about two dozen extras milling around at the bottom of the staircase. I came down the stairs as my sister (Varsi) tried to stop me. As I reached the last step, I confronted my mother (Fitzgerald). In a very dramatic finale she slapped me—hard. When I finished the scene I was stunned to hear the outbreak of applause. I looked up to see Mr. Cooper leading the crew and cast in saluting my efforts. What a wonderful moment that was! The next day when I arrived on the set, Charles Brackett had placed a new leather chair outside my dressing-room door—with my name printed boldly on the back.

I became particularly close with Diane Varsi. She was a rebel, even then, and wasn't ready for the onslaught of attention that would be forced on her when *Peyton Place* was released, which happened while we were shooting. Though very young, she had a young baby and was getting a divorce. I used to drive her to her apartment on our lunch hour so she could play with the baby. Stuart Whitman, who was playing her lover in *Ten North Frederick*, was a nice guy, a real sturdy, macho type, but she complained to me that he was all over her during their love scenes, indicating that he wanted to continue their tryst off-screen. Then she added, "You'd be far more a threat than he would be." I took that as a compliment, though I didn't know quite what to say. The Oscar nominations were announced while we were filming. To her surprise, she'd received a best supporting actress nod for her *Peyton Place* performance. We were joking around one day, trying to decide what she should say if she won. She came up with: "I'd like to thank all the people who got out of my life to make this possible." I had a feeling she meant it, too. However, she lost the statuette to the Japanese actress,

Miyoshi Umeki (*Sayonara*). She also enjoyed going against whatever the Fox publicity department wanted her to do. Perhaps she was trying to be a female Brando or Dean, but it seemed sincere. She really didn't like the attention. Instead of driving a conventional car, she'd drive through the studio gates in an old, beat-up truck. As we became closer, she confided in me that she was having an affair with a beautiful blonde starlet. Somehow that didn't particularly surprise me. She was also running around with Tab Hunter and his crowd.

Though I only had about four brief scenes with Gary Cooper in *Ten North Frederick*, he couldn't have been nicer. My final line in the film, after his death, was: "He was a gentleman in a world that no longer respects gentlemen." I had no trouble reading that line. It fit Cooper perfectly. I would often watch him shooting his scenes, though. He was particularly helpful with Suzy Parker. She was inexperienced as an actress and they would meticulously shoot their scenes over and over, but he never once complained. And Suzy? Well, she was even more beautiful in person. She also seemed to have a powerful friend in the upper ranks at Fox. Some guessed it might be Buddy Adler, the head of the studio, but that was just a rumor. She *did* seem to know a lot of "inside" information, though. For instance, she came on the set one day and spilled the unknown news that Fox was going to sell off the studio's property. It didn't happen for a while, but it *did* happen, and the old back lot became Century City.

During the filming I also became friendly with Geraldine Fitzgerald. The Irish-born actress was now living in New York, concentrating more on a stage career, but she seemed pleased to be doing a movie again. I'd occasionally drive her home from work and she'd tell me about her "old days" in Hollywood. She was a particularly good friend of Bette Davis. Bette had told her to hold out for stronger roles and scripts, as she had done. It worked for Miss Davis; it didn't work for Miss Fitzgerald. She made a major misjudgment, she said, when she turned down the female lead opposite Humphrey Bogart in *The Maltese Falcon*, which, of course, became a classic film, aided considerably by Mary Astor's chilling performance.

Like they had done on *The Last Wagon*, Fox had taken an option on me when I signed my *Frederick* contract. That time they didn't pick it up, *this* time they did. I was now a 20th Century Fox contract actor and thrilled to be one.

When the film had a "sneak preview" in Hollywood, the reaction was quite favorable to my performance. Louella Parsons even headlined her *Herald-Examiner* column with a story about the preview-card reaction. She wrote: "Those who have seen the new young player Ray Stricklyn in *10 North Frederick* are sure he will be our next important newcomer on the screen. He could be the next Montgomery Clift." From her mouth to . . .

Prior to the film's release, Fox held a private screening at the studio. I escorted Gary Cooper's charming teenage daughter, Maria. Robert Wagner and Natalie Wood sat directly in front of us. I kept wondering if he'd really been considered for Joby? I also noticed George Sanders and Zsa Zsa Gabor in the screening room, as well as studio executives and, of course, the cast and crew. I remember going to the bathroom and the man standing next to me at the urinal said, "I enjoyed your work very much." I responded with, "And I've enjoyed yours for years." He seemed surprised that I knew who he was, particularly when I praised one of his earlier musical scores for *Hangover Square* (a Linda Darnell movie). He was the great film composer, Bernard Herrmann.

Fox scheduled the movie's 1958 premiere in Santa Barbara, a beautiful community about two hours from Los Angeles. They chartered a special train to take the cast and other celebrities to the screening. I was so proud to be a part of it that I wanted my mother to fly out and share the experience. It was her first trip to California. At last, in some small way, I could repay her for some of the sacrifices she'd made in my behalf. Also, she could return to Houston and tell Uncle Elliott that I wasn't the bum he had predicted I would be. When she arrived, she was flabbergasted by the size of the Milner Road house. I'd also asked the Fox wardrobe department if they'd loan her a fur stole to wear to the premiere. They happily supplied a gray mink. She was thrilled.

My date for the junket was a new young actress Fox had recently signed, Diane Baker. Diane was a lovely brunette, about eighteen years old. She wasn't flashy looking, but she had a sweetness that was most ingratiating. You know, the kind of girl you'd take home to mother. I did, as a matter of fact. Mother approved of her too—no Michelle Condre here, she was quick to remind me. I'd first met her when she was testing for her studio contract and she'd come on the set of *Ten North Frederick* with her scene partner, a handsome young actor named Robert

Osborne. Bob would become a lifelong friend. When he gave up his acting career, he became a columnist for *The Hollywood Reporter* trade paper (a position he still holds today), as well as the official biographer for the Academy of Motion Picture Arts & Sciences, writing a beautiful coffee-table book on the history of the Academy Awards. Today he is prominently featured on the Turner Classic Movies channel introducing their catalog of outstanding old films.

Anyway, on the appointed afternoon, the chartered train took off for Santa Barbara. The studio had arranged for the beautiful actress Maureen O'Hara to be host for the evening. Tab Hunter was on the train, as Diane Varsi's date, as well as other cast members, Suzy Parker and Stuart Whitman, and a blonde tootsie named Barbara Nichols (well, she played a tootsie in the movie). Other celebs on board included Yvonne DeCarlo, Richard Egan, Tom Tryon, Nick Adams, Venetia Stevenson and Forrest Tucker.

Following the premiere, there was an elegant supper-dance held at the Montecito Country Club. Mother was in another world, literally. But she was *really* in another world on the train ride back to Los Angeles. It was after 1 A.M.

when we boarded the Southern Pacific. Mother and Diane were tired, so they both stretched out in separate chairs in the darkened car, attempting to sleep. I, however, joined the festivities in the club car, where everyone was singing and having a merry time, particularly Barbara Nichols, who was doing some sort of hoochee-coochee dance.

Sitting across the aisle from mother, unbeknownst to her, were Forrest Tucker and Ken Scott, another new actor at the studio. Tucker, who had long been in movies, was now enjoying

With Maureen O'Hara, Venetia Stevenson and Tab Hunter prior to Ten North Frederick *premiere.*

a new success with his popular television series, 'F'Troop, which happened to be one of mother's favorites. She'd pulled her gray mink stole over her head and had dozed off. Tucker went to the bar to get another drink and, upon his return, he noticed mother's legs sticking out in the aisle. Being a playful male, he gently ran his fingers up her leg. She stirred, the mink falling from her covered face. Tucker, upon seeing it was a little gray-haired lady, quickly retreated to his seat across the aisle. But the plot thickens. A young male movie fan, obviously gay, had sneaked on the train and, apparently, was a big admirer of Mr. Tucker's. He kept standing in the aisle staring at the actor. Finally, the half-inebriated Tucker said, "All right, I know what you want!" At which point he unzipped his pants, whipping out his cock. "See," he said, "it's as big as has been rumored." Diane in the meantime had awakened and saw what was happening, as had my mother. Diane came dashing to the bar area, "Ray, you've got to move your mother! It's getting pretty rough back there!"

I hurried to mother's aid—"I think you'd better move," I whispered. "Oh no, dear, I'm having a perfectly fascinating time." Hmmm. Forrest Tucker quickly became my mother's favorite actor. When she returned to Houston, Mary Ann said all she'd talk about was Forrest Tucker. It got so bad that even my father refused to watch 'F'Troop. That's probably as close as they ever got to a divorce court.

Now, as far as I know, Forrest Tucker was as straight as they come. But he was also well aware of his assets. When he was touring with *The Music Man*, a legendary theatre story goes that when the show first started, he called all the male dancing gypsies into his dressing room. He reportedly said to them, "I know all the whispering behind my back, so let's get it out in the open right now, so you can concentrate on your work." He proceeded to show them his penis, then quietly put it back in his trousers and resumed putting on his makeup. The boys left satisfied and the whispering stopped.

* * * * *

While waiting for my next assignment, I met with director George Stevens about *The Diary of Anne Frank*. It was going to be a major production, based on the hit Broadway play. Of course Stevens was one of the very finest directors, and his *A Place In the Sun* ranks very high on my all-time favorite films list. A new, inexperienced girl named Millie Perkins had snagged the coveted title role (over Susan Strasberg, who had created the role on the stage). I was being considered for the young Jewish boy, Peter, who is infatuated with Anne Frank. I wasn't really right for it and the role eventually went to Richard Beymer (who would later play opposite Natalie Wood in *West Side Story*). Another Broadway play Fox was putting into production was *Blue Denim*, which Charlie Brackett was going to produce. Carol Lynley, who had played the lead in the play, was brought in from New York to test for the movie. They asked me to assist. Usually when they're testing a specific actor for a role, as they were doing in Lynley's case, the cameraman concentrates on her, with the assisting actor mostly shot with his back to the lens. But the young director doing our test had ambitions and wanted to shoot the scene as if he were actually doing the movie. Consequently, it was a really good screen test, giving me equal time with the actress. Brackett saw the test and realized I could be quite good in the part. He talked with me about it, but finally said, "Ray, this boy is a real innocent, and I'm afraid after your cynical character in *Ten North Frederick*, an audience might not buy it." Instead he signed the marvelously gifted Brandon DeWilde, who was really the right age (seventeen). Yes, at the age of thirty I was still passing as a teenager. And in some ways, I think I still thought of myself as one. The age factor was beginning to be a curse.

Soon, however, the studio announced my next picture. Jerry Wald, the prolific producer of *Peyton Place* and many other films, had picked me to co-star with the popular singing star Pat Boone in a light comedy called *Mardi Gras*. I had already done my wardrobe tests when, suddenly, I was yanked from the film. Another rising young singing star, Tommy Sands, was available, and Wald thought it would be good box office to team the two new favorites, building up the musical portions in the film. Instead, I was assigned a co-starring role in another Charlie Brackett feature, *The Remarkable Mr. Pennypacker*, based on the play that Jimmy Dean and I had auditioned for back in New York. For the movie, Clifton Webb and Dorothy McGuire were cast in the roles played on Broadway by Burgess Meredith and Martha Scott. I was happy by this turn of events, as *Pennypacker* seemed a better project to me. Clifton Webb, of course, was riding a crest of popularity following his appearance in several films as Mr. Belvedere.

The character of Mr. Pennypacker was remarkable because he was a bigamist in the Pennsylvania of the 1890s—with one family in Philadelphia, the other in Harrisburg. He was also a successful businessman, a freethinker, a Darwinist and the father of a total of seventeen children. My role, Horace Pennypacker III, caused chaos when he arrived unannounced in Harrisburg looking for his father. This, of course, lets the cat out of the bag. Mr. Pennypacker admits that the Philadelphia wife has been dead for some years, much to the relief of the Harrisburg wife (McGuire). I *looked* even younger in this one! It was a very pleasant, diverting little comedy.

It was also a joy to work on, particularly because of Webb and Dorothy McGuire. The co-starring cast included Charles Coburn, Jill St. John, David Nelson and Ron Ely (later better known as Tarzan in a television series). I adored Clifton Webb. He was very popular in the Hollywood community, particularly in the social set. He was also a known homosexual, though it was never mentioned, living with his aging mother, Mabelle, whom he cherished.

After we'd been shooting for about a week, Webb informed Jill, David, Ron and myself that he'd gotten us tickets for Noel Coward's opening in *Nude with Violin*, a play he'd written and was touring in with Eva Gabor. Mr. Coward, of course, was a legendary theatrical personality, considered by many to be one of the "greats" of show business (he thought so too). He was one of Clifton's closest friends.

Following the performance, Clifton, who hadn't been able to attend the opening, had arranged for us to go backstage to meet the great Mr. Coward. I was very excited by that prospect. Of course I was from "the theatuh" while my fellow players were only movie actors and I didn't think they knew that much about his illustrious past. When we returned to work the next morning, Clifton was eager to know how his young charges had liked the play. Ron Ely made the mistake of speaking first. Now Ron was a big handsome hunk with limited acting experience, and he blurted, "Oh, it was okay, but that Coward guy was kinda—" (he indicated swishy). I thought Clifton was going to explode! He quickly exited the set. He later told me that he'd gone to Buddy Adler's office to demand that Ron be fired—"I don't want anyone that stupid working in my picture!"—but Adler said it was impossible to replace him as he was already too established in the film and it would be too expensive to reshoot. Mr. Webb steered clear of Mr. Ely from then on.

One evening, the debonair actor invited me to his beautiful Beverly Hills home for dinner. The grand piano was covered with photographs of his famous friends—Vivien Leigh and Laurence Olivier, Fred Astaire, Noel Coward, Gertrude Lawrence, and Cary Grant. He was really very sweet, not at all like the acerbic characters he played in most of his films. He was very affectionate towards me, but other than a goodnight kiss on the cheek, more like a father and son, he was never aggressive in any way.

Another evening, however, in less elegant surroundings, we were invited to a small dinner party given by actor Richard Deacon (who had a small role in the film and, later, would be a regular on the popular *Dick Van Dyke Show*). Deacon had particularly planned the evening for Clifton, thinking he might take a shine to one of the actors he'd invited. The actor he had in mind turned out to be none other than Val (remember the "marine" who had helped me raise the flag over Iwo Jima?) Val showed up wearing very short, ripped-off jeans, frayed at the bottoms, with his enormous cock practically poking out from below. Clifton was appalled, thinking him quite crude, and refused to have anything to do with him the rest of the evening. So much for blind dates.

* * * * *

One night a group of Fox contract players were invited to a big benefit at the Beverly Hilton Hotel, following the premiere of *Kings Go Forth*, a new Frank Sinatra-Tony Curtis-Natalie Wood release. Mr. Sinatra would entertain at the soiree. At a nearby table I noticed Joan Collins. Every once in a while she'd glance at our table. Sinatra was almost finished with his show when Collins suddenly got up and stormed out of the room. She didn't have quite the flair Bette Davis had had at the Ambassador Hotel, but she was still young and "Alexis" was still in her future.

I was still working on *Mr. Pennypacker*, and the next day I was leaving the studio commissary and I noticed Miss Collins and Joanne Woodward, talking nearby. Collins saw me and said "Hi!" I joined them and she introduced me to Miss Woodward, who excused herself, saying she had to get back to her set. Joan said,

Above left: A publicity still from The Remarkable Mr. Pennypacker, *Jill St. John played my half-sister*
Above right: The noted writer Christopher Isherwood visiting me on the set of The Remarkable Mr. Pennypacker
Below: 20th Century Fox chief Buddy Adler hand-picked us for "major stardom", left to right, me, Dolores Michaels, Jill St. John, Barry Coe and Lee Remick

"I saw you at the Sinatra show last night.""Yes," I answered."What happened? I saw you exit, but you never came back." She made a face, answering, "Oh, it was something personal. I was angry with Frank."Then she pouted and said,"I'm never going to another premiere! The fans all thought I was Natalie Wood!" We continued polite chitchat, then she said,"They're shooting my big bathtub scene this afternoon, why don't you come by?"That was an invitation I couldn't refuse, so I said I'd be there. She was working on *Rally 'Round the Flag, Boys*, with Paul Newman and Joanne Woodward. It was her best role to date, she said.

Late in the afternoon I wandered over to the soundstage. Sure enough, there was the beauteous Miss Collins reclining in a bubble bath. After several takes, director Leo McCarey was satisfied and she climbed out of the tub, draping herself with a large white towel. Very sexy. I was enamored immediately. She invited me to her dressing room for a drink. We had a second while she dressed and redid her makeup. We were having such a merry time she suggested we continue at a nearby bar. The martinis soon loosened me up and I moved to the leather couch beside her. Soon we were holding hands, laughing and having a smashing time. Suddenly she said she had to go, kissed me on the cheek and was out the door."By the way," she hollered,"can you come to a small dinner party next week?"

I arrived at her apartment a bit late, which was unlike me, as I'm usually early to most functions, then have to sit in my car until the appointed hour. Debbie Reynolds and Eddie Fisher were just leaving as I pulled up. They looked like they were arguing about something. The small party consisted of Joan, Gary Crosby (Bing's son), the handsome Barry Coe (he'd tested for my role in *The Last Wagon*), and a couple of girls, unknown to me. After dinner, the young ladies excused themselves and left. The drinks were flowing. Joan was being quite provocative, and everyone started getting lovey-dovey. *Jesus*, I thought, is this going to turn into a "four-way?" I fantasized about that possibility for a moment—would I? could I? —Well maybe with Joan and Barry, but not with Gary. My fantasy ended abruptly as she booted us out shortly thereafter.

By now I'd become thoroughly infatuated with the stunning Miss Collins. I escorted her to a party at Johnny Mathis' house—where he and Eartha Kitt sang—and our names were linked in a couple of gossip columns. One day the Fox publicity department asked me to stop by their office. "Now what's this about you and Joan Collins?" I was asked. "I think I'm in love," I replied. The jaded publicity guy laughed, shaking his head. "Ray, you don't fall in love with Joan Collins, you *fuck* Joan Collins!" At an opportune moment, I brought this delicate matter up to Joan. "Oh, God," she sighed. "They like to think I'm sleeping with everybody! I wouldn't have time to be as active as their dirty little minds like to think." Unfortunately, that was the end of my "love affair" with Joan Collins.

I continued seeing Diane Baker, mostly escorting her to studio functions. She was playing the older sister in *The Diary of Anne Frank*, which was a very prestigious film debut for her. I also had dinner with Millie Perkins a couple of times. Those occasions also made the gossip columns. George Stevens Jr., the son of the movie's director, called me on the carpet for seeing Millie. Since she was playing the virginal Anne Frank, he said the studio didn't want her name bandied about in gossip columns. While that was probably true, I think George Jr. was also a bit upset because he had a crush on Millie and had dated her himself.

Another Fox contractee I saw a few times was the very young, very adorable Tuesday Weld. At the time, Tuesday was playing a featured role in *Rally 'Round the Flag, Boys.* Even though she was barely fifteen years old, she was sensationally sexy, a Lolita for sure. She lived with her mother, Jo, in the Hollywood hills, but had her own quarters in the house. Jo Weld was quite a character herself. One evening, while waiting for Tuesday to finish dressing, we proceeded to get almost smashed on martinis. I'm surprised she let me drive off with her young daughter. Tuesday, of course, developed into a marvelous film actress (*Play It As It Lays* and *Pretty Poison*, for two) and should have become an important star. But she had a knack for turning down the wrong scripts (*Bonnie and Clyde* being one).

Meantime, the Fox publicity department was starting to move into full action. A press release stated that the studio had allotted $2,500,000 to publicize the studio contract players that Buddy Adler had personally handpicked for "major stardom." One day I was told to report to his office for publicity photos. It was the first time I'd met him. I was there with Lee Remick, Jill St. John, Barry Coe and Dolores Michaels, and we posed for photographs with the distinguished looking

Mr. Adler. I was very nervous and as I was leaving, instead of exiting through his office door, I went into his closet! I'm sure that made a good impression.

Next, they had me doing a few fan magazine layouts. One was titled *Let's Play Sixies*, featuring three "fun loving" couples in a Malibu beach spread. I was paired with Dorothy Provine, a striking blonde under contract at Warner Bros.; Dick Sargent, also at Fox, was with Shirley Knight (a new girl at Warners); and the third couple was Michael Landon and his (then) wife, Dodie. Another had the provocative title *Confessions of a Hollywood Bachelor: The Women in Ray Stricklyn's Life*. The "lucky" ladies included Bette Davis, Joan Collins, Diane Varsi, Susan Kohner, Diane Baker, Dorothy Provine, Kipp Hamilton and Phyllis Gates Hudson. If you believed what you read, I was quite the lothario. The article raised a few knowing eyebrows, believe me. Another silly spread was a color layout in *Photoplay*, a Halloween party I was supposedly having (in July) at my Milner Road home. This one showed young Hollywood bobbing for apples, pinning the tail on a donkey and sundry other juvenile antics. It was also arranged for me to be a model, along with several other promising male and female talents, at a Costumers Ball held at the Ambassador Hotel. Joan Crawford was the special guest of honor, but she'd only agreed to come if the designers presented her with an award naming her the "best dressed actress in films." They obliged and I happily posed for photos with, perhaps, *the movie star* of all time.

An important publicity break was an article in the prestigious *Newsweek* magazine, featuring a two-page spread of Buddy Adler's handpicked "stars of tomorrow." There we were, arm in arm, walking toward the camera, all smiling at the thought of our bright futures, l. to r.: Don Murray, France Nuyen, Bradford Dillman, Diane Varsi, Ray Stricklyn, May Britt, Barry Coe, Lee Remick, Stuart Whitman, Jill St. John, Gary Crosby and Dolores Michaels.

Little did I realize that my studio contract days were about to be abruptly ended.

* * * * *

One evening I was dining at a new restaurant in Hollywood, Panza's Lazy Susan, located at the corner of LaBrea Avenue and Fountain. The small eatery, featuring Italian cuisine, had become a popular hangout for young Hollywood.

Joan Crawford's just been named "Best Dressed Actress in Films." She wouldn't have attended otherwise.

The clientele was a mixed crowd; straights and gays. The parents of Steve Drexel, the Henry Willson client who lived in the North Fairfax Avenue apartment complex, owned Panza's. Henry had gotten Steve a few jobs, but nothing major, so he was working as host in the restaurant. John Smith, Willson's pet client (next to Rock) was doing quite well, however, co-starring in his own Western television series.

This particular evening I noticed Nick Adams sitting at one of the tables. He was with a blonde girl, rather plain, almost mousy in appearance. He waved, motioning for me to come over. This was the first time I met Shirley Knight. She was fresh from Kansas and she'd come to Hollywood to pursue an acting career. I didn't think she stood much of a chance, wanting to tell her to go back home. I was surprised when she said she was testing for a Warner Bros. contract. Not only did she get the contract, she became an absolutely brilliant actress, receiving two Oscar nominations (*The Dark at the Top of the Stairs* and *Sweet Bird of Youth*), and, today, as a character actress, has won several Emmy awards for her television performances. We would become good friends in those early days.

While dining, I noticed Henry Willson enter. He was a heavy investor in Panza's Lazy Susan, so the restaurant became like a second office to him—except here he could cruise the handsome young men at the bar, many of whom had come in expressly hoping to meet him. The divorce between Rock and Phyllis was getting messy, with threats being made to expose his homosexuality. I had been approached about being a possible character witness for Phyllis, if necessary, which I would have done, but we were all hoping it could be avoided. When I'd finished eating, I went to the bar area to have an after-dinner drink. I sat at the far end; opposite from where Mr. Willson was holding court. However, on his way to the restroom, he spotted me. As he passed he snidely said, "I wouldn't testify for that bitch Phyllis, if I were you. If you do, it won't be good for your career." Was that a threat? Fortunately, the case was settled out of court and I put Willson's remark behind me, assuming it was the alcohol talking.

* * * * *

Not long after the unpleasant incident with Henry Willson, Alec phoned to tell me the distressing news that 20th Century Fox wasn't picking up my option. I was stunned. Everything seemed to be going so well. I'd attracted strong reviews in *Ten North Frederick* and *Photoplay* magazine had named me one of "the most promising new actors of the year." An excuse was given that they didn't have enough films on their upcoming production slate that I would be suitable for. Another valid reason, the studio was in dire financial straits, hence the eventual sale of the back lot, and they were cutting down on their contract lists. In just a few years, the contract system would be almost non-existent at most of the studios.

Despite the studio telling Alec that there were no films in the immediate future that I'd be right for, I didn't buy that for a minute. I knew there was *one* property they'd recently acquired that I was perfect for. That was *Compulsion*. It had recently closed on Broadway, after a modestly successful run, with Roddy McDowall and Dean Stockwell starred (both having been former child stars at the studio).

The loss of my contract sent my spirits plunging, the depressions returned, my insecurities boiled to the surface. I decided it was time to return to Houston for a visit. Since mother had written that *Ten North Frederick* was about to open at the Metropolitan Theatre, I decided to go then, thinking it might boost my deflated ego. The Fox publicity department arranged some Houston press to coincide with the film's opening, which was helpful, and they put my name on the marquee alongside Gary Cooper—"Houston's own Ray Stricklyn." The *Houston Press'* entertainment editor, Paul Hochuli, had written dozens of articles about me over the years, keeping my Houston friends up on my career activities. This time he

Arriving at the Houston airport for the opening of Ten North Frederick, *greeting me are sister Mary Ann, her husband Clayton and my nieces Kathy and Karen*

outdid himself. When I picked up a copy, shortly after my arrival home, I was the *headline* on the front page with a large photo and story. It must've been a slow news day. Whatever, I was impressed and so were my Houston friends. So, on the surface, my life appeared to be very rosy. In truth, I was in a very nervous mental state.

The mood seesaw continued for several days, then I had a call from the West Coast. It was Alec. "Ray, I've got very promising news. Richard Zanuck's office called wanting to know your availability about possibly doing *Compulsion*." I almost dropped the phone. Richard Zanuck was the young son of former Fox tycoon Darryl F. Zanuck, and he was going to produce the picture. This transpired so soon after my contract had been withdrawn that Zanuck was unaware that I was no longer under exclusive contract. Of course I was elated by this hopeful news. *Compulsion* dealt with the infamous Leopold and Loeb murder case in Chicago, a tragic story of two young men who murder an even younger classmate "just for the thrill of it," thinking they are so superior and brilliant that they'll commit the perfect crime.

I returned to Hollywood with high hopes. The story goes that Richard Zanuck had made an offer for Dean Stockwell to repeat his Broadway role, but his agents had turned it down, demanding more money than had been offered. Negotiations had bogged down, and, presumably, this is when Zanuck said, "We'll use Ray Stricklyn instead," and a call to Alec was made. Of course it's an old ploy to use one actor against another when negotiating money. Unfortunately for me, this strategy worked. Once Stockwell's representative really thought the studio might use me, they reached a financial compromise, and he was signed for the role. I was bitterly disappointed. Roddy McDowall was also disappointed, as his role went to Bradford Dillman. Orson Welles was set for the Clarence Darrow part, and Diane Varsi was in for the brief romantic interlude. Diane told me her relationship with Stockwell was quite violent, which some said contributed to her quitting her career shortly thereafter. She just walked away. A few years later she attempted a comeback, appearing in a couple of films, but her life was cut short and she died at too young an age.

I had liked being under contract, it was like having an extended family, plus the security of a weekly paycheck was most comforting. With the loss of

Compulsion I sank back into my dramatic mood changes. I also began to take it out on poor Alec, blaming him for my career setback, that he should have fought harder. Of course, it was my own insecurity taking over, but I didn't realize it then. Alec quickly arranged for me to guest-star on the very popular *Wagon Train* series, then I did the equally popular *Perry Mason*. I would later do both shows again. Working, of course, was the answer to my depressions. And I returned to my studies with Dr. Bitzer, which was always a positive step.

At the beginning of each Hollywood year, the town becomes frenzied with award fever. All the studios, plus the actors, directors, producers, writers, editors, composers, etc., start the onslaught of publicity campaigns in the trade papers, hoping first to snag a Hollywood Foreign Press Golden Globe nomination, which will then lead to the big one, an Oscar nomination. The year 1959 was no different. One morning Alec called. "Have you seen the morning paper yet?" "No, I'm still in bed." He suggested I get up and read it. To my surprise I had been nominated for a Golden Globe as "Most Promising New Actor of the Year" (a category they no longer have). Of course, I was thrilled. For a couple of days, before it's forgotten, the publicity causes a stir within the industry. My fellow nominees were Bradford Dillman, John Gavin, Efrem Zimbalist Jr., Ricky Nelson and David Ladd (young son of Alan). I didn't win, nor can I recall now who did. Friends kept saying I should try to get an Oscar nomination for *Ten North Frederick,* so I took out a few quote ads, but I didn't have the budget for a sustained campaign. Maria Cooper, Gary's daughter, later said I should have asked her dad for assistance. "I'm sure he would have helped you," she generously said. But, as the years ahead would prove, I found it difficult to ask anyone for help.

Over the months I'd always kept in touch with Susan Kohner, seeing her at different parties or premieres. She was then dating George Hamilton almost exclusively. One evening she was with her father, the noted agent, Paul Kohner. He congratulated me on my Golden Globe nomination, then casually said, "Now's the time you should have the big push. Let me know if I can ever help you."

I thought about what he'd said. He *was* a powerful, respected agent. I spoke with Susan, asking if her father was really interested in representing me? She said he was. I was very torn about breaking off my relations with Alec. The Alexanders had been extremely good *for* me and *to* me. They'd given me a career. But actors are selfish people, at least where their careers are concerned, and I was no different. I was falling into the trap that every agent and client goes through. The smaller agent builds you, gets you started, then the big boys swallow you whole. It may not be fair, but, as I was to find out repeatedly in the years ahead, there's nothing fair in show business. And so, I signed with Paul Kohner and very happy to do so. Of course this caused a riff with the Alexanders and Paul had to share my first two years' commissions with Alec.

Susan's career was starting to go into high gear, particularly when *Imitation of Life*, with Lana Turner, was released during the year (1959). She would later receive a best supporting actress Oscar nomination. But now she had landed her biggest break to date, or so the publicity said, and she was filming her first starring vehicle, *The Big Fisherman*, a three-hour religious epic based on a novel by Lloyd C. Douglas. It promised to be a lavish production, being filmed in Technicolor and a new widescreen process, 70mm Panavision. Producer Rowland V. Lee was hoping it would rival the box-office bonanzas of Cecil B. DeMille's biblical films. Certainly the film had a big budget with Frank Borzage directing. He'd won the first Academy Award for his direction of *Seventh Heaven*, with Janet Gaynor, in 1928 (the year I was born). Susan's co-stars in the epic were Howard Keel as Simon Peter, John Saxon as her lover and Martha Hyer as the villainess. Robert Evans was playing the other top role, Prince Deran. It was a flashy role, similar to the mad Caligula in *The Robe*. Evans was quite handsome and sophisticated, with his jet-black hair and always sun-tanned skin. He'd been under contract at Fox, but was now freelancing. He also wasn't a very experienced actor. Of course, many years later, he would become a powerful Paramount executive, producing such brilliant films as *The Godfather* and *Chinatown*.

After shooting had begun on *The Big Fisherman*, producer Lee decided Evans wasn't working out and wanted to replace him, always an expensive proposition when you have to go back and reshoot scenes. That's when Paul Kohner went into action. He was close to the production because of Susan, and he immediately suggested me to Lee and, since budget was apparently no object, the producer decided to test me. It was an elaborate makeup, first darkening my hair, then adding a moustache and beard, as well as deep bronzed makeup. The test was a success and Lee began contract negotiations with Kohner. As usual, there was an argument over money, though the first time, as far as I knew, where I was the subject. Paul was determined to up my asking price. Lee was just as adamant about saying no. Of course, I just wanted to act. But that was the game producers and agents had been playing for years.

All weekend I worried, so afraid I might lose the role. Sunday morning I went to Dr. Bitzer's church—if positive thinking was going to work, please God, let it be now. Before the service, I was standing out on the patio, having one last cigarette. A little gray-haired lady, with whom I had a nodding acquaintance, spoke to me as she came up the stairs. This particular morning, for the first time, she stopped to chat. Asking how I was, I blurted out, "Oh, I'm so anxious. I'm up for a wonderful role in a new movie, but there's a hang-up over money, and I don't think the producer's going to meet the demand." Her ears perked up. "What movie?" she asked. "*The Big Fisherman,*" I said. She smiled, saying, "Oh, yes, I read the book. Don't worry, I *know* it's going to work out."

Well, God or a Higher Power or whatever you want to call it *does* work in mysterious ways. That particular moment, that Sunday, I was definitely in the right place at the right time. The little old lady turned out to be producer Rowland V. Lee's sister! What are the odds? It was like winning the lotto. Monday morning, Paul Kohner called to say the deal had been set—at his price.

The picture had a long shooting schedule, something like four months. The exteriors were filmed in the desert just outside of Palm Springs, while the interiors were shot later at Universal. It was a Buena Vista release, however, for the Disney Company.

As the evil Prince Deran, who sinks his father in quicksand so he can become king, I had spectacularly rich costumes, heavily embroidered with jewels—rubies, pearls and sapphires. In one scene, as the rival for Susan's affections, I had the very handsome John Saxon stripped, then practically flogged to death by my soldiers. It was great fun to film, with me reclining on a bejeweled, hand-carried throne, while hundreds of extras cheered me on. The scene was also dangerously close to camp. At the end of the film, because of my evilness, God strikes me dead and I go tumbling off a steep cliff!

The picture was released in 1959 in a special road show engagement, rarely done, except by David O. Selznick on his epics like *Gone with the Wind* and *Duel In the Sun*. The night of the Hollywood premiere, I took Kipp Hamilton, a stunning redhead, who also had been under contract at Fox but a little before me. Afterwards, Paul Kohner had a small supper party at one of the fancy Sunset Strip restaurants. Susan was with George Hamilton, and we were joined by two of Paul's clients, the legendary Maurice Chevalier and new heartthrob, Horst Buchholz. They were currently working with Leslie Caron on *Fanny*. *The Big Fisherman* received a very mixed critical response. It was spectacular to look at, some said, but it was also frequently plodding and too long. The film, however, did receive three Academy Award nominations—for cinematography, art and set decoration and costumes.

* * * * *

In my quest to find my "manhood," I had begun seeing a great deal of Dorothy Provine. Her career was building at Warner Bros., where she was starring with Roger Moore (pre-James Bond, of course) in *The Alaskans* television series. One day I was visiting her in her dressing room and Moore popped in. He had a great British wit and was always pulling some prank. This particular day he was in the midst of telling some tall tale and, suddenly, he pulled me down on his lap. We were all laughing, but as I removed myself from this awkward position, my insecurities came to the fore: *why did he do that?* I was so paranoid that I thought he might be trying to tell her I was gay. Probably not the case at all, but my imagination was running wild.

Several times in recent weeks, since being with Dorothy, I had made serious attempts at sexual intercourse. Of course I had to have several drinks in me to have the courage to go that far. She was so attractive, with silky, soft pink skin, that it was easy to feel the desire to go further. I did want to satisfy her. I always attributed my inability to get an erection to "too much booze," but you can only use that excuse for so long. It wasn't really the alcohol, I knew, but a deeper, psychological disturbance. It was very frustrating. Eventually, we stopped seeing each other.

Kipp Hamilton, who had been my date for *The Big Fisherman* premiere, was next on my frustration list. I had first met Kipp, whose brother Joe was married to Carol Burnett, when I did a screen test with her for a new Burt Lancaster film, *The Unforgiven,* which John Huston was to direct. He, of course, was one of Paul Kohner's major clients. Richard Burton was in negotiations to co-star as one of Lancaster's brothers, with a younger brother yet to be cast. Kohner suggested me to Huston, we met, and I was verbally set for the role.

The female lead was a young Indian girl, and Lancaster and Huston had decided they'd cast a comparative newcomer in the role. Four actresses were to be tested—Susan Kohner, Ina Balin, Gloria Talbott and Suzanne Lloyd. They were also doing tests for a smaller female role. The casting director asked if I'd assist in testing with the ladies—for pay, of course. I wanted to keep Huston happy, so I agreed, as he was directing the scenes. It was a favor I never should have done. The scene chosen for the test was one between the Lancaster character and the Indian girl. Of course, I looked much too young to be playing his role, let alone not being right for it, but since the tests were really for the actresses, I went along with it. It was a very long and grueling day, particularly for me, as I was in every test, plus the one Kipp was to do. She was eventually signed for her role, but the four "Indian" actresses were suddenly out. Unexpectedly, Audrey Hepburn, who was a very big star, was announced for the part (and miscast, I might add).

One day Kipp was at a wardrobe fitting. Lancaster and Huston were also there. Apparently the wardrobe man asked who was playing the younger brother. According to Kipp, Huston said, "Ray Stricklyn." But Lancaster, who was also producing the film, piped in with, "It hasn't been decided yet." Kipp relayed this information to me. I quickly called Paul, asking what was going on. He told me that Lancaster and Huston weren't getting along—one reason being a conflict over the Richard Burton casting. Huston wanted him, but Burton (or his agent) was insisting on equal billing with Lancaster and Hepburn. Lancaster wouldn't agree to this (of course this was before *Cleopatra*) and Burton was out of the picture. Then, when Lancaster started hedging about casting me, the director blew his top, threatening to leave the picture. Of course, contractually, he was bound to the film. Now, realistically, Huston wasn't really that concerned over a Ray Stricklyn, but he was riled about his loss of control. Audie Murphy was the eventual replacement for Burton (*quite* a difference!), while a very blond volleyball player named Doug McClure, who flashed as many teeth as Mr. Lancaster, played the younger brother. He would later have a successful career in television.

Prior to my meeting her, Kipp had played a small role in a Frank Sinatra film, *Never So Few*, and the two had a few dates. Going from Sinatra to me must have been a severe jolt for the beautiful redhead. I may be wrong, but I believe Kipp was a virgin at the time, and virgins didn't last very long in Mr. Sinatra's company. So, in a way, I was a perfect follow-up. Certainly I wasn't constantly trying to get her into bed, so she was very relaxed and we had many an enjoyable evening. And our affection for one another seemed to be growing. One late night, however, we'd both had too much to drink and she suggested I stay over. The next morning, there we were, still on the living-room floor, curled in each other's arms. The situation must have unnerved me considerably, because when I started my Ford to leave, I lost control, and the car went careening from her driveway into the one across the street, crashing into the neighbor's garage door. A smashing morning, you might say. *Herald-Examiner* columnist Harrison Carroll printed that Kipp and I had almost eloped, but got cold feet at the last moment. It was an interesting gossip tidbit, but, alas, not a factual one. Between the crash and the elopement, our relationship ended.

Too bad, too. Both Kipp and Dorothy were wonderful, beautiful young ladies. Any normal, red-blooded male would have killed to be in my shoes. I'm sure, in retrospect, that my relationship with them rates no more than a footnote in *their* lives, but in mine they took on a special importance. In my sincere efforts to be "straight" I had only succeeded in making myself more miserable, not being able to satisfy the women or myself. The whole mixed-up situation wasn't fair to either side. It was following these abortive attempts at a heterosexual lifestyle that I came to realize that you can't be something different from what you *are*.

* * * * *

I was still harboring regrets that I hadn't been cast in *Compulsion*. Certainly Dean Stockwell had priority rights to the role, having created it on Broadway, but I still had a gnawing desire to play it.

One morning I went very early to Santa Monica beach, waiting for the sun to rise. This was a frequent pattern during the hot summer months, spending the whole day on the beach, getting as dark a tan as possible. This particular morning, it was still chilly, so I wrapped myself in a large towel and propped myself against the pier wall. I was reading my morning copies of *Daily Variety* and *The Hollywood Reporter*, a daily ritual, when a gust of wind caused a tiny piece of paper to land on my leg. I attempted to flick it off, but it still clung to my skin. I don't know if I really believe in omens, but *that* morning I did. The piece of paper was the torn off corner of a paperback book page—with one word written on it—*compulsion.*

Shortly thereafter, it was announced in the *Los Angeles Times* that the West Coast premiere of Meyer Levin's *Compulsion* would be staged at a new playhouse on Highland Avenue, the Omnibus Center Theatre. *This is it*, I told myself, this is what the tiny piece of paper had been trying to tell me. I immediately called Paul Kohner and asked him to see if *my* role had been cast. He contacted Dwight Hanna, the play's producer, and found out that the part hadn't been filled yet, though the other starring role would be played by a New York actor named Donald Buka. Buka had done lots of theatre work, as well as a few features. He had created the role of the son in Lillian Hellman's *Watch on the Rhine* on Broadway, then repeated his role in the 1943 film version with Paul Lukas and Bette Davis. *Compulsion's* director, Edward Ludlum, immediately agreed that I would be perfect for the Leopold role. After Kohner had negotiated top billing, I signed my contract.

I hadn't done a play since *Saint Joan* in Florida, so I was very eager to return to the stage. Certainly this would be the most demanding role I'd yet attempted. Robert Brubaker was set to play the Clarence Darrow role, with a young, offbeat actress named Sondra Kerr signed for my brief romantic interest. Two actors in supporting roles would find television success in the years ahead: Ted Knight (*The Mary Tyler Moore Show*) and Bernie Kopell (*Love Boat*).

The rehearsals were long and exhausting. A couple of times I thought I wasn't going to be able to cut it and I told Ludlum I wanted to quit. Fortunately, he talked me out of it, and the character slowly began to fall into shape. As in real life, there was a strong undercurrent of homosexuality regarding Leopold and Loeb, an element that had made the original trial so sensational.

127

Our opening was drawing near . . .

The day before the first preview, I had a call from Paul Kohner. Universal had made an offer for me to play a supporting role in producer Ross Hunter's *Pillow Talk*, which was already in production with Rock Hudson and Doris Day starring. The problem was they had to know *immediately*, as they were shooting the scene I'd be involved in the very next night, which, of course, was the play's opening. Actor Dwayne Hickman (of *Dobie Gillis* fame) had first been cast in the role, but he'd suddenly become ill and the studio couldn't postpone until he was well because they had hundreds of extras on call for the nightclub scene and it was too late to cancel them. It was a small role, only two scenes, but an amusing one of an inebriated young man who, while dancing, goes on the make for the virginal Doris. I wanted to do it, but it would have caused total chaos at the theatre to cancel the performance (plus my understudy wasn't yet up in the role). I also thought it would be most unprofessional. Besides, the play was far more important to me. But in Hollywood, then, as it is today, theatre was considered a poor stepchild, only to be tolerated. *Movies come first.* Another reason I was curious to do the film was because it would have been the first time I'd seen Rock since the nasty divorce. I wondered what his reaction would be? Who replaced Dwayne Hickman then me in the role? Nick Adams.

Meanwhile, back at *Compulsion* rehearsals, we were having our own problems. Two days before our scheduled opening, director Ludlum, who could be difficult, decided he didn't want Sondra Kerr to continue in the ingenue role. A friend of his, Patricia Huston, was suddenly available, so he fired Sondra. Since her scenes were with me, that meant added rehearsals. Pat wasn't able to master her lines by opening night, so she went on carrying her script. But she was a brilliant technician and gave a superb reading, with the audience rewarding her with hefty applause. I, personally, had thought Sondra was wonderful in the role. Pat was a stronger personality, but Sondra had a vulnerability that I thought better for the character. Certainly both were capable actresses, just totally different in type and approach. Sondra soon married actor Robert Blake (pre-*Baretta* television fame). From all reports it was a stormy marriage, while it lasted.

Compulsion was ecstatically reviewed by most of the critics. A few carped about Meyer Levin's sprawling script, but the adjectives about my performance

From above: My first "star" billing, the marquee for Los Angeles stage production of Compulsion; *With my co-star Donald Buka in a scene from* Compulsion *based on the infamous Leopold-Loeb murder trial;Another pensive moment from* Compulsion

were something for the scrapbook. I'd never had that kind of response before, so I was on cloud nine: "*DAZZLING*," wrote the *Los Angeles Times* ... "*SUPERLA-TIVE*," said the *Herald-Examiner* ... "*BRILLIANT*" from *The Hollywood Reporter* ... "*MEMORABLE*" said *Film Daily*. Even my hometown paper, *The Houston Press*, covered the opening. Critic Thomas Thompson wrote: "*RAY STRICKLYN ACTS WITH A BRIGHTNESS THAT RIVALS THE SPOTLIGHTS ON GRAUMAN'S CHINESE THEATRE*." Not bad, huh? Thompson, incidentally, wouldn't remain a critic too much longer. But he would become a brilliant, best-selling author with his novels, *Blood and Money* and *Serpentine*.

For the first time as an actor, I felt I'd really accomplished something; that I might really be a good actor. Though I'd attracted some attention with my movie work and on television, *this* was different. This was personal gratification. I loved the stage. Paul Kohner was excited about my notices, commenting that they were "the kind of reviews that make important actors." But, as I was to learn over and over, reviews in Los Angeles are wonderful for a scrapbook and good for the ego, but they don't generate the power you'd expect. Hollywood still looks to the New York critics for approval, as though they're afraid to trust their own local judgments.

After about four months of performances Donald Buka left the cast, being replaced by Michael Hall (who had played the small role of the son in William Wyler's classic film, *The Best Years of Our Lives*). Michael didn't have the stage experience Buka had, but he was younger and, in some ways, better suited for the role. With Donald gone, I was now given solo star billing. Every night when I'd arrive at the theatre, I still got a chill seeing my name in electric lights on the marquee.

With a cast of thirty-one people—that's a lot—I didn't get to know the cast that well. One cast member was a character actress named Naomi Lawrence, who played Loeb's mother. It wasn't until opening night that I found out she was the sister of playwright Jerome Lawrence (who with his partner, Robert E. Lee, had written such smash hits as *Inherit the Wind* and *Auntie Mame*). He came backstage and introduced himself. This meeting led to a long friendship. Another opening night visitor had been Mary Pickford (she was a friend of Donald Buka's), making one of her rare public appearances. She was really a part of film history.

During the entire run of the play, I only missed one performance. The only performance I've ever missed, as a matter of fact. I was shooting a television show during the day—I believe it was at Warner Bros., a series called *Bourbon Street Beat*, with a young Mary Tyler Moore playing my wife. We were running behind schedule and it didn't look like we'd finish in time for me to make the evening performance. My understudy was Craig Slocum, a very good friend from my New York days, and, secretly, I'd promised Craig (or Rusty as he was called) that I'd let him play at least one performance. It was nearing the end of the run, so this night seemed the ideal time for him to get his chance. At the last moment, as it turned out, I could have made it to the theatre in time, but Rusty was primed to go on; I just couldn't disappoint him. Of course Dwight Hanna, our producer, thought I was still working, so I couldn't show up at the theatre to watch the performance. Rusty, like many of us, had a *need* to act. Sadly, a few years later, and after several previous tries, he succeeded in his suicide attempt.

Compulsion ran for six months, which, for a Hollywood stage production, was considered quite remarkable at the time. I was so proud of the play that I insisted mother fly out for the final performance, though I was a little concerned about the homosexual element in the show, wondering how she'd react to that. In the show's last curtain call, I received my first standing ovation. It was a night to remember.

I'd decided to have a big closing night party for the cast and crew, so Milner Road was ablaze with lights, music and noisy activity till the wee hours of the morning. Half the audience seemed to have showed up too, with nearly a hundred people streaming in and out of the house. Poor mother didn't know what had hit her. Pat Huston got into a screaming battle with someone at the front door, using every four-letter word she knew, which was considerable. Mother had never heard language like that in her life. The police finally came when neighbors complained of the noise. With so many people milling about the house, many that I didn't know, it was amazing that none of Edward's expensive paintings were stolen. The next morning, the house a shambles, I stumbled downstairs for a cup of coffee. It suddenly dawned on me that mother hadn't said anything about my performance. I finally asked her what she thought. Her reply: "You were cute." I'm glad she wasn't a critic.

* * * * *

While mother was visiting, she'd been sleeping in a small room off the far end of the living room. Unable to break her lifelong habit of cleaning, she'd lifted the throw rug to sweep. To her surprise, as well as Jim Terry's and mine, there was a trap door beneath the rug. Where could this lead to, we wondered? We hesitated about a second before lifting the door. There was a ladder leading to the room below. It was a fairly nice size, all concrete with no windows. With the aid of a flashlight we spotted an extra large table with boxes and papers piled on top, as well as several file cabinets. There was also a large printing press. *Aha,* I thought, *Edward prints all his money down here!* The cabinets seemed stuffed with old letters and contracts. The printing press, I decided had possibly been used by Edward to print copies of his books of poems and play scripts. I remembered him giving me a beautifully bound copy of a verse play he'd written. Of course, it was never produced—and for good reason—Edward's demands would have scared off any potential producer. The set, for one, would require deleting the first seven or eight rows of theatre seats. Second, *only* Greta Garbo could play the lead! Now chances of that happening—well forget it. It turned out the mysterious room had actually been built during World War II as a bomb shelter.

Jim and I had been living in the house for almost two years now. While Edward may have been an eccentric, he was also very generous. We really had few bills, except for our personal phones, though we eventually offered to pay the water and electric charges. Jim, by this time, had given up any thoughts of being an actor and was actively trying to be a movie producer, always on the verge of making a "big deal." Seldom did they work out. One time his mother, Iva, came to stay with us for a while. She didn't like being in the house, saying it spooked her, so she'd never answer the door if we weren't home. We were out one afternoon and Edward made one of his rare visits. He rang the doorbell. No answer. He pounded on the door. No response. Finally, Mrs. Terry looked through the peephole. "Go away," she screamed, "no one's at home!" Edward shouted back that he was the owner of the house, but since she'd never met him, she refused to let him in. Cursing, Edward finally left.

Though Jim and I frequently had small dinner parties—he did the cooking, specializing in a chicken dish smothered in pineapple—I decided to have a big blowout for Geraldine Page after she'd opened at the Huntington Hartford Theatre in *Separate Tables*, a play she was currently touring in with English actor Eric Portman. Of course she was absolutely magnificent in the Terence Rattigan script, playing two distinctly different characters. All Hollywood was turning out, it seems, to see this amazing actress "in person." We settled on her first night off for the party. I'd already invited about a dozen actor friends, who were eager to be in her presence, when Edward James said he'd even enter the Milner Road house to meet her. He also said Igor Stravinsky, Aldous Huxley and Christopher Isherwood wanted to attend. Suddenly, my party was taking on an entirely new aura. All evening she was surrounded by adoring fans. She laughed about it the next day, but said she would have much preferred being alone with Stravinsky, Huxley and Isherwood—she was as in awe of them as they had been anxious to meet her.

* * * * *

Shortly after *Compulsion* closed, Edward Ludlum called asking if I was ready to do another play. The Laguna Beach Playhouse was doing a summer production of *Kataki*, a two-character play written by Shimon Wincelberg (who also happened to be a Paul Kohner client), which had recently closed on Broadway. The play had received very good reviews, but wasn't considered a commercial property and only had a brief run. Sessue Hayakawa, the esteemed Japanese actor (remember *The Bridge on the River Kwai?*), and Ben Piazza starred. The play was really a tour-de-force for the young soldier—one long monologue, really, as the Japanese officer only spoke in his native language throughout the script. I read the play and loved it. The only problem being that I'd have to learn it in a week! I'm sure the role was longer than Hamlet. But it was an ideal part for me and I couldn't resist the challenge. Too, I was still on a high from the *Compulsion* success, so I was eager to get back on a stage.

With the great assistance of Dick Munro, a new friend, I diligently began learning the massive role. Dick was a film editor at Ziv Studios (they'd produced Craig Hill's *Whirlybirds* series) and had recently been divorced from Lorraine Bendix, the daughter of film and television star William Bendix. He had started hanging around the Omnibus Center Theatre during the *Compulsion* run, working backstage, and doing various odd jobs for producer Dwight Hanna. Dick was quite thin, dark-haired and had pronounced dark circles under his eyes. He was always very helpful to me during the play's run, catering to my every need. I must admit I liked being waited on. He was also my biggest fan, so I was flattered by his attention. He just sort of took over a section of my life—being secretary, cook, driver, friend. If he'd been an actor it might have been an *All About Eve* situation, but he was no Eve, and didn't seem to want anything in return. He was just one of those people who *did* for others. If he had a crush on me, it never became an issue. Anyway, with his help, and tons of black coffee, I managed to memorize the lengthy *Kataki* role. Dale Ishimoto, a wonderful Japanese actor with a strong presence, played the Sessue Hayakawa part.

The two-week engagement was a summer theatre hit. Again, I lucked out review wise. T*he Los Angeles Herald-Examiner* critic was particularly enthusiastic: *"AS THE BOYISH MID-WESTERNER, RAY STRICKLYN—IN WHAT IS CERTAINLY ONE OF THE LONGEST AND MOST CHALLENGING ROLES EVER WRITTEN—PROVES AGAIN THAT HE IS ONE OF HOLLYWOOD'S MOST ADEPT AND PERSUASIVE PERFORMERS. STRICKLYN RECENTLY WON CRITICAL BRAVOS*

The role was longer than Hamlet—with Dale Ishimoto in the stage production of Shimon Wincelberg's Kataki

IN 'COMPULSION.' HERE HE ONCE AGAIN DEMONSTRATES THAT HE IS AN
ENORMOUSLY TALENTED ACTOR OF GENUINE STAR CALIBER." Playwright
Wincelberg was jubilant; saying it was better than the Broadway production. I
doubted that, only wishing I'd really had time to work on the role properly. Fans
from my movie work were frequently waiting at the stage door. I also met three
people who came backstage that would figure in my life many years later. Two
were friends of Shimon's—Esther and Richard Shapiro. The world of television
would certainly hear from them in the future when they created and produced a
little epic called *Dynasty.* I would hear from them too, but it would be twenty-
eight years later. Another backstage visitor was a young man named Lee Melville.
He says I was rather curt. I don't remember the incident, but we too, would
meet again.

* * * * *

When I first started in movies, my father had said to me, "Well, you certainly
won't be doing any Westerns." He was an avid reader of Western paperbacks—the
only times I ever saw him pick up a book. When he made this comment, I must
admit I thought he was probably right. Back in Houston I'd tried horseback riding once and it was a near disaster. The poor animal ran amuck, racing down a
busy street, with my feet dangling out of the stirrups. I was holding on to the
horse's mane for dear life, trying to stay on. Finally, he came to an abrupt halt, tossing me to the concrete below. Fortunately, other than a few bruises and a skinned
arm, I wasn't hurt. I limped back to the stable, leading the horse behind me.

Of course, Hollywood being Hollywood, I ended up doing quite a few
Westerns. After *The Last Wagon*, in which I luckily only had a brief moment on a
horse, I did my share of cowboys on the various television series. I've already
mentioned my Indian stint, as Nochise-son-of-Cochise, on Fox's *Broken Arrow.*
But there were also two *Wagon Train* episodes (one with the wonderful Everett
Sloane) for Universal; two *Bonanzas* at Paramount; Clint Walker's *Cheyenne* at
Warners, ditto *Lawman* with John Russell and Peter Brown. Also at Warners, I
guest-starred on Ty Hardin's series, *Bronco*, in a segment entitled "The Soft
Answer," in which I played Billy the Kid. However, on that one, I hadn't done my
research—nor, apparently, had the director or the script girl, for throughout the

teleplay I was firing away, using my right trigger finger. Ole Billy, however, was left-handed. We received quite a bit of mail about that error. My father didn't let me forget it either.

He couldn't have been more surprised than I was when 20th Century Fox asked me to return to the studio—to star no less—in the title role as *Young Jesse James.* Of course I was thrilled by this turn of events, particularly after having my contract dropped only a year before. It was like "going home" again. As Jesse, I was in almost every scene in the picture. Fortunately, I'd taken a few horseback-riding lessons in the meantime, though I still wasn't going to give John Wayne any competition. There was a *lot* of riding in this one, and while I occasionally bounced, the film's editor eventually made me look like a real pro. I particularly liked the director, William Claxton, as he concentrated more on my acting than my riding skills.

Young Jesse James, of course, was yet another version of the celebrated Missouri outlaw, with Jesse and his brother Frank (played by Robert Dix) finding it hard to adjust to postwar problems. They join the raiders of Quantrell and meet

Cole Younger (Willard Parker) and Belle Starr (Merry Anders) along the way. As one critic wrote: "*THE MAIN ADVANTAGE OF THIS VERSION IS ITS SUGGESTION THAT JESSE WAS POSSIBLY A MEANER AND MORE COMPLICATED FELLOW THAN THAT ESSAYED BY TYRONE POWER IN FOX'S GLAMOROUS 1939 TREATMENT.*" And *The Hollywood Reporter* commented: "*STRICKLYN HAS THE ABILITY TO HANDLE THIS KIND OF MULTIPLE-PHASE PERSONALITY, AND HE DOES MUCH TO SUGGEST ITS NUANCES.*"

As Billy the Kid in "The Soft Answer" episode for the Bronco *television series with Ty Hardin*

* * * * *

While my career seemed to be progressing at a steady pace, the situation at home in Houston was regressing rapidly. Mary Ann called to tell me that our father was in bad shape, mentally and physically. She indicated that his mind might be going. Also, he'd become violent at times, lashing out at mother; even hitting her. One morning she'd found him standing over her bed with a butcher knife in his hand. Understandably, they were fearful for her safety. After prolonged discussions amongst themselves and the family doctor, it was decided that it was best to "put him away" in a home. This was devastating news, of course. My immediate response was one of rage, forgetting that he was suffering a mental disorder. Since I was the designated man in the family, in order to commit him I had to be there to sign the necessary papers. I flew home.

When I arrived at 6709 Avenue O, he seemed to be in a fairly docile state. But his mood changes were rapid and one day he started screaming at mother. My anger was slowly building and I finally lashed out: *"How dare you!"* I screamed back at him, ending with a resounding, *"I hate your guts!"* It was a very ugly moment. But it silenced him.

On the appointed day that he was to be "taken away," my brother-in-law, Clayton and I had to trick him into leaving the house. I finally told him we were going to visit my old friend John Stevens and wouldn't he like to go along for the ride? This appealed to him and he agreed to get in the car. Clayton had already put his suitcase in the trunk. It was a l-o-n-g ride. Not in miles, but emotionally. Fortunately the hospital-home looked like a normal white-framed house, and the attendants weren't wearing hospital garb, so we fooled him. I excused myself, telling him I'd go find John. Instead,

My first solo starring vehicle, the title role in Young Jesse James, *with Jacklyn O'Donnell as my wife*

Clayton and I disappeared into the admitting office. While I'm signing the necessary papers, we heard scuffling down the hall, then a scream. It was obviously my father. The second scream was more piercing. Suddenly, the chaos stopped and there was an eerie silence. My hand was shaking so badly I could hardly sign the papers. In a few moments, a nurse entered the office. She said, and I'll never forget it, "Mr. Stricklyn, we've given your father a sedative. But I'm afraid he's much more disturbed that we'd realized." "Oh?" I nervously questioned. "Yes," she said, "he kept screaming that his son was Jesse James!"

Suddenly my hatred turned to compassion. "I *am* Jesse James!" I retorted, hastily exiting before they could lock me up too.

That was the last time I saw my father—alive.

As Young Jesse James

TAKE FIVE

Tennessee Williams called the 1960s his snake pit years.

Before long, I, too, would be joining him in my own downward spiral. Certainly there was no reason to expect that as 1960 began. I'd just completed *Young Jesse James*, my first solo starring vehicle, the future looked bright, and I was in a very positive frame of mind.

Now a new opportunity came knocking. Almost immediately after wrapping the Jesse James picture, Fox paged me again for another movie. The studio had had a big success with a science fiction film called *Journey to the Center of the Earth*, which had starred James Mason, Pat Boone, Arlene Dahl, and my friend Diane Baker. From a box-office point of view it made sense to try and clone that success with another movie in a similar vein. Arthur Conan Doyle's classic tale, *The Lost World*, had first been filmed as a silent, now producer-director Irwin Allen planned to remake it as a big-budgeted Technicolored CinemaScope entertainment. Once again I'd be playing Jill St. John's brother (as I had done in *The Remarkable Mr. Pennypacker*), joining a stellar cast that included the great Claude Rains, Michael Rennie, Fernando Lamas, David Hedison and the delightful character actor, Richard Haydn. Not only would I do *The Lost World*, but I'd also been cast for William Claxton's next movie, *Desire In the Dust*, which Raymond Burr, Joan Bennett and Martha Hyer were headlining.

Utilizing the massive set the studio had built for *Journey to the Center of the Earth*, we began shooting. The whole film would be photographed on Fox's back lot and sound stages. While the 1925 silent version had been a trailblazer of its kind, Irwin Allen's new film would certainly offer visual improvements over the original, with splendid special effects, such as actual lizards photographed to be huge and fearsome.

The story was that of an expedition led by a famous scientist (Claude Rains) to a remote area of the Amazon, where he believes life has not changed since prehistoric times. The fierce monsters and wild terrain exceeded even his expectations. Among the group are a nobleman-sportsman (Rennie), his girlfriend

(St. John), who falls in love with the covering reporter (Hedison), a dour zoologist (Haydn) and Jill's younger brother, David (yours truly). As the script progresses, several of the party lose their lives before the expedition returns to tell its exotic story.

Sounds okay on paper, but the Allen script was pretty juvenile, and I think most of the cast knew it was little more than a piece of commercial fluff. One evening I had the pleasure of driving Claude Rains home. Like many others, I considered him to be one of the great film actors. Bette Davis told me he was her favorite leading man. During the drive, I said, "Mr. Rains, tell me, *why* are you doing this movie?" He laughed, then said, "My dear boy, for the same reason you are. The money."

After we'd been shooting about five weeks, the Screen Actors Guild was threatening a major actors strike. All the studios had been warned that a complete shutdown would occur if the strike took place. We still had a couple of weeks to go before finishing *The Lost World.* Jill St. John was particularly distressed by this possible delay. When we'd done *Mr. Pennypacker* the year before, Jill was considered a very promising starlet on the lot. Now she was engaged to marry the very rich Lance Reventlow, son of the multi-million dollar heiress, Barbara Hutton, and they'd planned their wedding as soon as the picture was completed. If the strike happened that would botch up their plans. Jill, half-serious, half-kiddingly, said, "Well, Lance can finance the completion of the picture. He has more money than Fox, anyway." The strike *did* become a reality and every studio became a ghost town for about six weeks.

But during the hiatus, Jill and Lance *were* married. They tossed a lavish party at the luxurious new home his mother had bought them. It had a swimming pool that started in the house, then cascaded into a larger pool outside, turning into a waterfall. Quite spectacular. Most of the cast attended the party, as well as Cary Grant, who had briefly been Lance's stepfather during his marriage to Miss Hutton.

The day the strike ended, the *Los Angeles Times* ran a front-page photo of Jill, David Hedison, and myself, going back to work. However, there was a noticeable difference in the way Jill St. John Reventlow was treated after the marriage. She was no longer regarded as a promising starlet—she was now given the red carpet treatment. Yes, money talks. Especially in Hollywood. Money, however, didn't seem to help her main costume in the film. She was clad in a pair of notoriously tight pink toreador pants. So tight, in fact, that every female crevice was pronounced, causing many a snicker from the crew. Also, not one speck of dirt ever soiled those pink pants or dirtied her shirt, nor was there a single smudge on her perfectly made-up face. The rest of the cast, however, going through the steamy jungle, were a mess, sweating and dirty. But not the lovely Jill.

One day I had a late set call. When I arrived, I noticed that none of the actors were working. I thought the crew must have been lighting the set, which often delays filming. But no, the crew wasn't working either—they were all sitting around smoking, playing cards, reading the paper. Finally I asked Claude Rains what was going on, why wasn't anyone working? He smiled, "My dear lad, we actors are on strike again."

It seems that that morning the studio production manager, in an effort to cut mounting overhead expenses, had ordered the removal of our coffee urn from the soundstage. Every set always had gallons of free coffee for the cast and crew. But *not* the set of *The Lost World*. Michael Rennie was outraged at the silliness of such a move and, with the aid of his fellow cast members, had gone on strike, refusing to work. The production manager was making all kind of threats, Rains told me, barely able to keep a straight face.

Marilyn Monroe was working on a nearby soundstage, shooting *Let's Make Love* with Yves Montand and Tony Randall. She was friendly with Rennie and had called him to say hello. He told her about our coffee ban, saying the actors were on strike. "You want your coffee back?" she asked. "*I'll* get your coffee back! I'll go on strike too until they return your coffee." And she did. Believe me, our coffee urn was back in no time, shooting continued, and we finally finished the film. Now how much money do you think the studio would have saved by such an action? Probably enough to pay Marilyn's hairdresser for the day!

I met Miss Monroe only once. I was lunching in the commissary with Rennie, Rains and David Hedison. She and Yves Montand, her famous French co-star, were just leaving and stopped by our table to speak with Rennie. She looked absolutely radiant. The fact that she was having an affair with Montand may have contributed to her glow. Their romance was the talk-of-the-town, particularly since he was long-married to the great French film star, Simone Signoret. I'll never forget the first time I saw her in person, at the 1958 premiere of *Gigi*. I was making my entrance up the proverbial red carpet just as her limo pulled up. It was total chaos as she stepped from the car—everyone just went crazy—the photographers, the fans. She was wearing a bright red lace gown, so tight she could barely walk. But what a vision!

While I was still shooting *The Lost World*, I had an interview for a new Western about to start at Allied Artists. I drove over to the Allied lot on my lunch hour, still in my makeup and costume, to meet director Joseph Pevney. The meeting was for *The Plunderers*, with Jeff Chandler, John Saxon and Dolores Hart set to star. I was there to see about the co-starring role of Jeb, the script's villain. A really good, flashy part. By the time I'd returned to Fox, Paul Kohner called saying the role was mine and I'd start shooting as soon as I wrapped the Irwin Allen movie. However, it conflicted with the *Desire In the Dust* film I was scheduled to do next. But Jeb was a much more interesting character, and a leading role, so Fox released me from my commitment.

Meantime, my friend Dick Munro had rented a house off the Sunset Strip and he wanted me to share it with him. In a rash decision, I said yes. As I've mentioned earlier, I liked being catered to and Dick was a master at that. Of course Jim Terry was upset, as was Edward James. He was about to leave for Mexico again and stopped by the Milner Road house, saying he had to get something out of the *locked* bedroom (*aha, now I'd find out if Tilly Losch had rotted away in there!*). Alas, when he opened the door, it was just a room with tons of magazines and papers scattered about. He proceeded to take certain items out to his car. But I noticed that he had a peculiar habit of wrapping everything in white tissue paper before moving it. I saw him drop a tiny piece of paper, just the corner of a torn-off magazine. I picked it up—it had a telephone number written on it—and handed it to him. He quickly wrapped *that* in tissue paper. Weird.

Jim managed to stay in the house for another year before Edward finally sold it. If I'd been smart, I would have bought it. Jim wanted me to buy it with him, but I didn't fancy the idea. That was a major mistake. In today's market, the house would be worth at least a couple of million.

* * * * *

Of course I'd never been too bright with money. Now sharing the house with Munro, I decided it was time to *act* like a movie star, so with my first check from *The Plunderers* I went out and bought a new, silver gray Corvette sports car. It was a beauty. It was also expensive. John Saxon, who was making more money than I was, wanted to know how I could afford such an expensive car. I couldn't, but I did.

Before shooting started on *The Plunderers,* director Pevney asked me if I'd mind lightening my hair. He thought my being blond would be a good contrast to Saxon's dark good looks. Once this was accomplished—far more successfully than when I'd had it cheaply done for *Stalag 17*—the cameraman said I reminded him of Alan Ladd

The Plunderers was an offbeat drama, telling a timely tale in an Old West setting. It was the story of four unpleasant young drifters (played by Saxon, Dee Pollock, Roger Torrey and myself), who take over and terrorize a quiet, peace-loving town. Jeff Chandler was the one-armed sheriff who finally brings us down, climaxing in a gun battle with my character, the psychopathic leader of the gang.

The day we were shooting my death scene—Chandler had just riddled me with a barrage of bullets—I received a long-distance phone call. It was Mary Ann. She was calling to tell me that our father had just died that morning, May 19, 1960. He was seventy-three. The official cause, said the coroner's report, "sclerosis of the liver." I would have added broken soul to his findings. I told Mary Ann I would do my best to take time off from the picture to be there for the funeral. After I hung up the receiver, I stood there, numb. There were no tears. Just numb. Then, from a distance, I heard the assistant director holler, "Ray, we need to shoot your death scene one more time!" Ironic, I thought. But I played the scene with more realism this time.

The funeral atmosphere was quiet, subdued. More a feeling of relief, it seemed. It was a sad occasion, yes, but I saw no tears shed. Perhaps from Mary Ann, she was always more understanding and closer to dad than I had been. The biggest sigh came from mother. At last she was free of a burden she'd been under for over forty years. Was it my imagination? Already she seemed to be years younger.

I returned to Los Angeles the next day.

I never cried at my father's funeral. I didn't yet feel a sense of loss. Within days I'd put the enormity of this event out of my mind. Or so I thought. But as Robert Anderson wrote in his beautiful play, *I Never Sang for My Father*—"death ends a life, but it does not end a relationship." How true. My tears would come later.

* * * * *

The Plunderers received mixed reviews. It was not quite an 'A' picture, yet it was better than the average 'B' movie. The cast was favorably reviewed, but it was in the foreign market where the film had a considerably stronger reception. Alan Hunter, a member of the Hollywood Foreign Press, wrote this notice for the *Evening Star* in New Zealand: "*IT IS TO STRICKLYN, AS LEADER OF THE GANG, THAT GO THE FILM'S TOP ACTING HONORS IN A STRONG, SKILLFUL INTER-PRETATION. IT'S A ROLE THAT COULD PUT HIM IN THE RUNNING FOR THE*

BEST SUPPORTING ACTOR CATEGO-RY IN THE COMING OSCAR RACE." Certainly I was flattered by his praise, all actors like to read the good notices, but I most definitely didn't expect an Oscar nomination.

So, I was pleasantly surprised when the Hollywood Foreign Press announced their Golden Globe nominations for 1960. Indeed, I had received a best supporting actor nod. Thank God for New Zealand, I thought. My fellow nominees that year included: Peter Ustinov and Woody Strode, both for their

A strong role in The Plunderers *earned me a "Best Supporting Actor" Golden Globe nomination*

Spartacus performances; Sal Mineo for *Exodus*; and Lee Kinsolving for his touching performance opposite Shirley Knight in *Dark at the Top of the Stairs*. And the Golden Globe winner? Sal Mineo. The coveted Oscar, however, went deservedly to Mr. Ustinov.

* * * * *

When I moved in with Dick Munro I had an adorable miniature schnauzer named Pepper. She was in heat. One day an actress friend, Janet Stewart (would you believe she went down with the Andrea Doria?), whom I met through Craig Hill, called and asked if I would like to breed Pepper. She said a friend of hers had an expensive pedigreed male and was looking for the right female. I could have pick of the litter, if I wanted. She said her friend's name was Tony. I agreed, and on the appointed day, we headed toward the address Janet had given me. For some reason, I assumed I was going to a kennel. Instead I was driving up in the winding hills of Beverly Hills, where each house seemed more lavish and expensive that the other. Finally I arrived at the given address. Could this possibly be the right place? To make sure, I rang the outer doorbell. Sure enough, it was the right house. The massive iron gate swung open and Pepper and I entered. A servant directed us to the pool area, where I saw a woman talking on the phone. The masculine Tony I had expected turned out to be a feminine Toni. She offered me a drink while the dogs immediately began sniffing one another. A good start, I figured. Toni mentioned that her husband should be home from the studio soon and she wanted him to meet Pepper. Studio? My ears perked up. Toni, it turns out, was Mrs. Eddie Mannix. For years, Eddie Mannix had been a top executive at MGM, right under Louis B. Mayer in the studio's heyday, and now was holding the same position under the reign of Dore Schary. We had a second drink. Toni Mannix was an attractive woman in her mid-fifties, I guessed. There was also a hard edge to her—maybe Claire Trevor would have played her in a movie. She had been a showgirl, briefly had wrangled an MGM contract, then landed the biggest catch of all—at least to her showgirl pals—the wealthy and powerful Mr. Mannix. Meanwhile, Pepper and her new male acquaintance were scampering all over the yard. Pepper may have been in heat, but she wasn't standing still long enough for the male to mount her. Great, I thought, I have a lesbian dog! About this time, Mannix arrived home. Although he was very small in stature, he was definitely a take-charge guy. He told me to hold Pepper still while he placed the male in the proper position. There we were, the actor and the executive, down on our hands and knees forcing a rape to occur. Surely, I thought, this intimacy should make Eddie Mannix my new best friend. I had a fantasy of him offering me an MGM contract. I'd heard of actors fucking for a job, but this was the first time I thought a dog could do it for me.

Well, to make a long story shorter, the fuck didn't take. Pepper did not become a mother, nor did I get an MGM contract. However, I did become friendly with Mrs. Mannix. She didn't get fucked either, not by me, or I presumed by her husband. You see, she'd recently been in the headlines when her lover, *Superman* George Reeves, was found dead. It was quite a scandal. Was it murder? It was finally ruled a suicide, though his mother tried to pin the blame on Toni, claiming she'd shot him in a moment of jealous rage. There were many rumors—one insisting that, indeed, she had done the dastardly deed, but that Mannix's power and money had gotten her off. This theory was never proven, however. There was also another woman involved, who seemed a more likely candidate, but that, too, was never resolved. So, suicide it was. Toni was also an alcoholic. For several years I escorted her to various studio screenings. But her behavior could be quite abusive if she'd been drinking and her tirades eventually turned her few remaining friends against her. I began to notice, at screenings, that the various stars and producers would steer clear of her if they saw her coming. I finally decided it wasn't too cool to be seen with her, but it was a little after the fact. For a brief period, at Toni's request, Dick Munro lived in the Superman death house, which she owned.

* * * * *

Pat Huston, who had been in *Compulsion* with me, suggested I join an acting group she was attending. She said the guru was a marvelous director/teacher named Sherman Marks. I hadn't been in an acting class since my early days at the Irvine Studio. Of course the Marks group was much more advanced, strictly for professional actors working in the film and television industry. These were actors dedicated to their craft. I particularly enjoyed doing scenes with Shirley Knight, Richard Bull and his wife, Barbara Collentine, Bill Cort, Colette Jackson, David Frankham and an actor named Tom Troupe. The classes were held every Saturday morning on the second floor of an old building off Santa Monica Boulevard in Hollywood, starting at 10 A.M., but often lasting until the late afternoon. Sherman *was* a talker. It was a productive atmosphere to be in, working with actors particularly devoted to the theatre. Here we had the freedom and time to explore a character, something you rarely had time to do on the average film or television show. On film, you were lucky if you had more than a couple of rehearsals, and those were usually for the camera and lighting crews. Then, wham, you've shot it and it's in a can for posterity.

British playwright Harold Pinter had recently created a furor with his controversial, offbeat plays. He and John Osborne were the new wave of writers in the English theatre, and Pinter had scored a great critical success with his play, *The Caretaker*, which starred Donald Pleasence, Robert Shaw and Alan Bates. They were now repeating their acclaimed performances on Broadway. I managed to get hold of a script, flipped over it, then gave it to Tom Troupe and Dick Bull to read. They too were enthusiastic, and we decided to work on a scene for class. Three great roles, we all agreed. Dick would enact the Pleasence role, a homeless bum; Tom would tackle the Shaw character, an introvert, while I would attempt the role of the sadistic younger brother. The first scene we did went very well, so we decided to keep working on the script, going from one scene to the next. Sherman Marks began to be intrigued by the complex work also and, often, to the chagrin of other class members, would spend the entire Saturday class working with just us. It was an exciting, creative period.

As much as I enjoyed working on *The Caretaker*, personally, my mood swings began to alter considerably. I'd be up one minute, and then a wave of depression would hit me the next second. The spells were usually brief, so I didn't attach too much importance to them. Everyone, I told myself, goes through such mood shifts. However, my thinking was sometimes irrational, and I'd make rash decisions without any real thought behind them. I suddenly felt that Dick Munro was too controlling, that he was smothering me with his attention, and I decided I would move. I needed to be by myself, I said. I'd scouted a very attractive little house in the hills, just past the Hollywood Bowl, off Cahuenga Boulevard. It was located at the end of a cul-de-sac, very private, with a charming little garden. Perfect for meditation, I told myself.

It was the worst decision of my life. Being alone, which I thought I needed, would have a price, however; a dear one. I was very lonely and I was also feeling very sorry for myself.

One evening I accepted an invitation from Leon Moore, the handsome black actor who had appeared with me eight years before in *The Climate of Eden*. He was in town, working as a production assistant and friend of opera star, William Warfield, who was appearing in concert. Leon invited me to the performance and supper afterwards. It was a pleasant evening, with all three of us drinking too much.

I was feeling no pain as I hopped into my Corvette and headed home. Then I made a *big* mistake. As I passed the old USO building on Hollywood Boulevard, I noticed a young blond marine standing idly on the corner. I was waiting for the light signal to change, and it seemed that he was staring at me, rather intently. As the signal turned green, he smiled, and I drove off. He was quite attractive in his starched uniform, wasn't he? My mind started spinning and, suddenly, I had this tremendous urge to pick him up. It had been quite some time since I'd had any sexual activity, and the alcohol made me bolder than I'd usually be. I quickly sped around the block, pulling up at the corner where he was standing. "Want a lift?" I asked. "Why not," he answered, quickly climbing into the car. As we were driving up Highland Avenue, he said, "Aren't you in the movies?" My first instinct was to say no, but my vanity took over and I nodded in the affirmative. "I knew I'd seen you before," he replied.

It was after 1 A.M. when we pulled into my driveway. Already the booze was beginning to wear off. Suddenly, I felt very tired and any desire I'd felt was waning fast. *Why have you done this!* I kept repeating to myself. He asked for a drink, so I made him one, then he wanted another. I poured myself a Pepsi-Cola as he kept pumping me about various actors. He was particularly hung up on Elvis Presley. Did I know him, he asked? "No," I said, though I had met him once when he was making his first movie (*Love Me Tender*) at Fox. He then said he'd followed the singer at various concerts, "almost" meeting him once. He continued his endless chitchat, while I was desperately trying to think how I could get rid of him. After downing his second drink, he excused himself and went to the bathroom. He was gone for quite a long time, so I decided I'd better check on him. As I went down the hall, I noticed that he was in my bedroom, checking out the clothes in my closet. "Man, you've got a lot of great duds," he said. I did, too. I hadn't been on *Teen* magazine's list of "best dressed young actors" for nothing. Neatly piled in stacks were at least fifty expensive sweaters, as well as sport coats and a variety of tailored suits and dozens of slacks.

He then sat on the edge of the bed, unbuttoning his uniform's jacket and taking off his shoes. "Let's make out, man," he said, pulling me down beside him. I quickly disentangled myself and, apologizing, said it was just too late and I was too tired. To my surprise, this change of plans didn't seem to phase him and he followed me back to the living room, stopping first in the kitchen to make himself another drink. He seemed preoccupied, though, and suddenly picked up the phone and dialed a long-distance number. He was talking with some girl, explaining that he was with a "movie star" and that she should really come to the West Coast as they could have a "great time." The call seemed endless, but in my state every extra second seemed like an hour. Finally off the phone, he then started looking through my massive record collection, but became upset when he couldn't find a single Elvis Presley recording. "I'm not a fan," I found myself saying, as he carelessly tossed aside dozens of Frank Sinatra, Johnny Mathis, Carmen McRae and Nat "King" Cole albums.

By now it was approaching 4 A.M. I was a total wreck. Finally, I insisted that he had to go. Thank God, he too had had enough and agreed. As we started to get into my Corvette, he insisted that he drive. "I've always wanted one of these, man." *Anything*, I said to myself, to get rid of him. He sped back to the Hollywood area, going a few blocks out of the way, enjoying himself behind the wheel of an expensive sports car. Finally, we reached the USO corner and he got out. "See 'ya around, man." he said, giving me a military salute. I didn't salute back. Instead, I gunned the motor and took off. *Never again!* I swore. *Never again!*

Exactly a week later, on a Saturday evening, I came home around midnight. I put the car in the garage, but as I opened the front door I sensed immediately that someone had been in the house. After nervously checking each room, to make sure no one was still there, I noticed my opened bedroom closet door. *All* my clothes were gone. Not one single item was left, except for a stray sock. My heart sank. In rechecking the bathroom, I now noticed that the window was wide open—obviously where the bastard had entered. I figured that when he'd excused himself the week before to go to the bathroom, he'd been formulating his plan, unlocking the bathroom window for an easy entry. I felt like I'd been raped. I felt unclean.

I couldn't stand to be in the house alone, so I went to the phone to call a friend—but my telephone book was missing. This concerned me, particularly, because I had the private numbers and addresses of many well-known people in the book and I feared he might try to hustle one of them. I left the house and drove over to David Frankham's apartment. David was a fine English actor, and we'd been working on a scene from *Five Finger Exercise* for Sherman's class. I confessed to David what had happened and he suggested I stay the night there. While I was trying to calm down, his phone rang. It was for me. *Who knew I was there!* Immediately, my paranoia assumed it was *him*. Congratulations," the voice said. "Who is this?" I asked." "It's Gene. Gene Persson." I heaved a sigh of relief. "I've been trying to reach you, then Shirley suggested you might be rehearsing with David (Gene was married to Shirley Knight). Anyway, I wanted to be the first to tell you that you and Shirley have been nominated for Golden Globe awards (she for *Dark at the Top of the Stairs*). Warner Bros. publicity just phoned Shirley, saying the nomination would be officially announced on Monday."

And that is how I learned I'd been nominated for *The Plunderers*. Normally, I would have been elated by such good news, but the robbery and my guilt left little room for celebration. I just felt emotionally and physically drained, unworthy of the success I was having.

I refused to stay in my house alone, so Paul Nesbitt offered to stay with me. Paul was a recent arrival in Los Angeles. He was an extremely handsome young blond Adonis and, of course, Henry Willson had lost no time in signing him when he appeared on Broadway (as Adonis, no less) in Noel Coward's *Look After Lulu* with Tammy Grimes. True to form, Willson had changed his name to Chance Nesbitt. Their relationship didn't last too long, though, as Paul wouldn't tolerate the agent's constant harassment. Anyway, thank God, Paul agreed to houseguest with me. The very next weekend, following the robbery, it was late and we were watching television in my back bedroom. Suddenly there was a knock on the front door. It startled me, and I slipped into the darkened living room and saw two men standing outside. One was the marine. The other, much larger in size, had flattened himself against the wall, trying to hide himself. The knocking continued. Paul finally went to the locked door and asked who it was. "Oh, I'm a friend of Ray's, is he home?" "No," Paul lied. "Can I come in and wait for him?" the marine asked. "No," Paul said, "I'm already in bed." "Oh, well, I borrowed a sweater of his and I wanted to return it." Paul suggested he leave it on the porch. Eventually, the two menacing figures vanished. My paranoia was working overtime—*Why had he come back?* I had little left to steal, unless he'd returned to take the stereo and records. Or had he come back to beat the shit out of me? *Or worse!*

I reported the theft to the police, neglecting, of course, to tell them that it had been an "inside" job. I was too ashamed to tell them the truth, though they may have suspected as much. I was also afraid it might leak to the newspapers. In the old days, a studio publicist would have covered up an actor's indiscretion, but I didn't have that luxury. About a year later I spotted the sonuvabitch on Hollywood Boulevard—wearing *my* wardrobe! I started to hail a cop, but thought better of it. I just wanted to forget the whole nightmare. Forgetting it wasn't easy, however. Not for one as guilt-ridden as I.

The next weeks were a blur. I attended the Golden Globe banquet, dating Colette Jackson, an actress from Sherman's workshop. We posed for photos with Jack Lemmon and Felicia Farr, with Janet Leigh and Tony Curtis. But even as a best supporting actor nominee, I didn't feel like I really belonged there. I was a fraud. My Christian upbringing was stronger than I realized. *I must be punished.* My slow descent into my own private hell had begun.

Of course, I now loathed the little house I was in and badly wanted to move. I still had fear that *he* might return. Finally, after pleading with the owners, they let me break my lease. Once again, Dick Munro came to my rescue. He, too, had moved—this time to a house in the hills of Laurel Canyon. The house wasn't as large as our previous one, so I slept on a convertible bed in the living room. It was a satisfactory arrangement, though everything in my life seemed to be "on hold." Although I needed money, I had little desire to seek work, even turning down a couple of television jobs at Ziv Studios. I became angry with a Kohner assistant for submitting me for "such crap." In my fear and insecurity, I became arrogant. Thank goodness I had my weekly unemployment check.

* * * * *

In May of 1961, I was offered an opportunity to attempt the difficult role of Treplev in Chekhov's classic, *The Sea Gull.* It was an Equity production being done at the Hollywood Center Theatre under Benno Schneider's direction. I remembered when Bob Casper had done the role in a New York Equity Library production and what a frustrating time he'd had with the character. Casper, incidentally, had moved to Los Angeles in 1958, and while I'd occasionally see him, I kept it at a minimum. He did a couple of featured roles in the films *Studs Lonigan*, with a young Jack Nicholson also in the cast, and a Fox picture, *The Right Approach* with Frankie Vaughan, Martha Hyer, Juliet Prowse and Gary Crosby. Fortunately, for him, he had a new friend—a brilliant young dancer— ironically, from Houston also.

The Sea Gull production turned out to be no more than adequate, to my way of thinking, and I was no more than adequate in it. The best thing about it was working with a young actress named Jennifer West, who was playing Nina. While she didn't quite make it as Nina, as I didn't make it as Treplev, you could tell she was very talented. Not long after we did the play, she moved to New York and scored a striking success Off Broadway in LeRoi Jones' shocker, *Dutchman.* Her reviews were so outstanding that director Elia Kazan asked her to play the matinees in the new Arthur Miller play he was staging, *After the Fall. T*he roles in both plays were terribly long and exhausting. She'd do a matinee of the Miller play, then dash to do an evening performance of *Dutchman.* It was a grueling schedule. I saw her do both and she was very exciting to watch. There was talk that she might be the *new* Geraldine Page. Those two plays led to Jerome Lawrence and Robert E. Lee signing her to star as Eva Peron in their new drama, *The Diamond Orchid.* Her future seemed assured. But the play flopped, closing almost immediately, and Jennifer disappeared from the theatre scene completely. A loss.

Mentioning playwright Jerry Lawrence reminds me of an evening (one of many) I spent at his Malibu beach house. He'd invited me for dinner, but this particular evening turned out to be a special one. When I arrived, he said he hoped I wouldn't mind, but he'd also invited a neighbor to join us. The "neighbor" turned out to be the legendary Charles Laughton! After a few drinks, this extraordinary actor proceeded to recite Shakespeare out on Jerry's patio. With the stars overhead and the pounding of the surf for background, he did soliloquies from *King Lear* and Bottom's speech from *A Midsummer Night's Dream*. It was a magical moment. He'd recently done *Lear* in London, lamenting that he "never quite got it right." Certainly sounded right to me.

* * * * *

With little work on the horizon, my one sanity was the weekly workshop meetings at Sherman Marks. Over the months, Dick Bull, Tom Troupe and I continued working on *The Caretaker*. Eventually, we'd worked on the whole play, and it just seemed too good to drop the project. The snag was that the play was still running in New York and production rights weren't yet available. Fired by our enthusiasm, we decided to stage the play anyway, using a small theatre connected with the workshop. It wouldn't be open to the paying public, we'd just invite friends, and, of course, it wouldn't be reviewed by the press. We opened it one weekend and the response was extraordinary. Word-of-mouth began to spread and, soon, every weekend was jammed with actors, directors, and writers, trying to get in to see it.

One day I received a call from my old Texas acquaintance, Mildred Cook. We'd renewed our friendship in New York, but now she, too, had moved to Los Angeles—being brought west by none other than Lucille Ball. Miss Ball had recently formed her own theatre company at Desilu, signing up several promising young talents. Mildred was her protege. She also changed her name to Carole, in honor of the wonderful film comedienne Carole Lombard.

Miss Cook was calling for a single ticket to see *The Caretaker*. She was eager to see me in it, she said. She came, she saw and she fell in love with Tom Troupe. Almost that fast too. First, of course, she fell for his talent, then for the man. Tom was, and is, a wonderful actor, and his scene work was always looked forward to in Sherman's classes. He was Italian, dark, intense, very serious, and very methodical. I'd known him slightly before joining the workshop (he'd appeared in *The Big Fisherman*, but we had no scenes together) and I'd occasionally see him at Dr. Bitzer's church. Prior to coming to Los Angeles, he'd played the young Peter in the Broadway production of *The Diary of Anne Frank*. *The Caretaker* ran for several months, each weekend, and was a tremendous experience for all involved.

Although I'd occasionally have an interview for a television show, my good fortune was no longer with me. Only two years before I was being asked *for*. I didn't have to read for roles, I was just automatically set once Kohner had agreed on the price and billing. But the tides had turned. I was also thirty-five years old. While I could still *pass* for a teenager on the stage, a screen close-up would show the lie. Understandably, the casting people had moved on to the latest batch of juvenile actors. My youthful appearance was no longer an asset. Meantime, my financial situation kept getting worse. Then Dick Munro lost his well-paying editor's job at Ziv. Now we were both struggling. My one sanity was the weekly scene work at Sherman's, but even that suffered when you're constantly worried about the lack of money.

* * * * *

Thomas Wolfe wrote that you can't go home again. Hopefully, I was about to disprove his theory. Nina Vance called from Houston to make an irresistible offer, asking if I would like to return to the Alley for a very important project. The theatre had been given the first post-Broadway production rights to Eugene O'Neill's *Long Day's Journey Into Night*, which was considered quite an artistic coup for Nina and the Alley. The New York critics had hailed the work as O'Neill's greatest masterpiece when Jose Quintero directed it, offering Fredric March, Florence Eldridge, Jason Robards and Bradford Dillman four tour-de-force roles. Nina was asking me to play Edmund, the young O'Neill in the very autobiographical work. I accepted immediately.

* * * * *

Since my father's death, Mary Ann and Clayton had sold the old house on Avenue O, buying a new place for mother across the street from them. I would stay there during my Houston stay. Mother seemed like a different woman, more content than I'd ever seen her. And it felt good being home with her, alone. After my recent turmoil in Los Angeles, I felt "safe" for the first time in months.

The Alley was still situated in the old fan factory, but the theatre was now a full-fledged professional company. It was hard to believe that the last time I'd worked there had been in 1949, when I did *Season with Ginger* (or, as it was called on Broadway, *Time Out for Ginger*). A lot had happened to Raymond Stricklin since then.

Our rehearsals were long and difficult, but we were working on a long and difficult play. Nina was in good form with O'Neill. She wasn't a Jose Quintero, true, but she was a good professional director. She'd cast Virginia Payne and a red-haired Irishman named Moultrie Patten to play Mary and James Tyrone. Payne was well known to radio fans, having played *Ma Perkins* for many years on the popular serial. Len Wayland, who I hadn't seen since our disastrous tour in *Stalag 17*, was cast as James Tyrone, Jr.

Our opening night performance was particularly noteworthy, and nerves making, because *The New York Times* had sent critic Howard Taubman to cover the play in its first production outside of New York. Fortunately, he was quite impressed, writing: *"IT IS HARD TO BELIEVE THAT ANY ALLEY PRODUCTION HAS BEEN SUPERIOR TO THAT OF LONG DAY'S JOURNEY INTO NIGHT."* As for my performance, Taubman said, *"RAY STRICKLYN MEASURES UP TO THE CHALLENGE OF HIS DEMANDING ROLE, PLAYING WITH SENSITIVITY AND INTENSITY."* Houston's senior critic, Hubert Roussel, writing in *The Houston Post*, really welcomed me home: *'RAY STRICKLYN, TRAINED IN THE HOUSTON THEATRE AND LATELY ACTIVE IN FILMS, HAS COME HOME TO PLAY EDMUND WITH BRILLIANCE. THIS HANDSOME AND ELOQUENT YOUNG ACTOR IS CLEARLY BOUND FOR THE HEIGHTS."* My one dissenting note came from Ann Holmes in *The Houston Chronicle:* "WE WELCOME RAY STRICKLYN HOME, BUT, UNFORTUNATELY, HE GAVE US A YOUNG O'NEILL OF LITTLE TEMPERAMENT OR PERSONALITY." That smarted. You survive the negative reviews, but you don't forget them. The play was a smash at the box office and we extended the run to twelve weeks. A highlight of the opening night performance was meeting astronaut Alan Shepard, the first man in space. *That* was history and I was thrilled when he invited me to visit NASA, personally giving me a tour of the Space Control Center.

From the depths of O'Neill to the light-hearted froth of Mary Chase's *Bernardine* was next on my agenda. Nina asked me to stay on and play the leading role of Wormy in the comedy. Finally, after all the years of *almost* doing it, I had succeeded. It was a fun part, particularly after the tragedy of Edmund, even though I was too mature to be playing it. A point Hubert Roussel made in his review. On the other hand, Ann Holmes, who hadn't liked my Edmund, loved my Wormy. Go figure. You win some, you lose some.

While playing *Long Day's Journey,* my friend John Stevens introduced me to a young man named Marvin. He was fresh out of college and working in an art gallery. He was young, bright, and great fun to be with. It was the first time since Craig that I had allowed myself to be close with anyone. I knew the relationship would end when I returned to Los Angeles and, for a brief moment, I considered staying in Houston because of him. But, deep down, I knew I still had unfinished business in Hollywood, even if it was a career that seemed to be going nowhere. The movies may have given up on me, but I hadn't given up on my dream. There was still a bit of fight left in this aging juvenile. *Long Day's Journey Into Night* and *Bernardine* recharged my spirits and I returned to California with renewed vigor and hope.

Unfortunately, it was short lived. Before I knew it, I'd allowed myself to be sucked down once again in the mire of depression and a feeling of unworthiness. Once you have known success, it is very difficult to adjust to the loss of it.

While I was in Houston, Dick Munro was also having a rough time of it, having to give up his Laurel Canyon house. So, I moved once again. Having saved a little money from my months in Houston, I took a cheery apartment on the edge of Beverly Hills. The apartment was really more expensive than I could afford, but I was trying to be positive. Surely my luck would change. I had almost no furniture in the apartment, but I splurged on a necessity—a new bed. But, for some crazy reason, I picked a *round* bed (probably because my life was going in circles). With no jobs forthcoming, I often had difficulty meeting the monthly rent. My landlady, who lived upstairs, happened to be a practitioner with the Christian

Science church. I told her I didn't have the rent money one month. She suggested she give me a "treatment" —a positive prayer to a Higher Power. I willingly accepted. I needed help. Her meditation worked. The very next day I got a guest lead on the *Perry Mason* television series. The landlady got her rent and I had temporary peace of mind.

One afternoon there was a rap on my door. I opened it and was taken aback to find Craig Hill standing there. I hadn't seen him in a very long time. He said he'd run into a mutual acquaintance who had given him my address and, he continued, he just had an "urge" to see me. Perhaps it was the seven-year itch, but I was pleased to see him. He was still living with Bill, he said, but he happened to be out of town at the moment. Over a cup of coffee we had polite chitchat, eventually leading to his apologizing for the way he had treated me. I tried to be casual, accepting his apology as though it had been "just one of those things." He said he had an appointment and had to leave, but could he see me the next day? I said yes. I knew then that it wouldn't be just a visit. I fantasized that maybe he'd leave Bill and we could pick up where we left off. The next day, however, proved to be a comedy of errors. As much as I thought I wanted him, the passion was no longer there. We laughed at our clumsy efforts. And that was it. Finally, after all those years, I was free of Craig Hill. And that was the last time I saw him. Eventually, he and Bill did split. Craig moved to Spain, many years ago now, and for a while became a popular film star in Spanish-speaking adventure films. Later, I heard he'd married a very wealthy woman who lived there. Bill Lundmark died several years ago, at too young an age.

During this period I made two very close women friends. One was Jacquelyn Hyde, who had moved from New York to try her luck in Hollywood. She was a good friend of my former *Compulsion* understudy, Craig Slocum, and he suggested she look me up. She had very dark hair (which became red in future years), with luminous Bette Davis eyes, and a unique voice—sounding at times like Billie Burke in *The Wizard of Oz*, then the next moment she was Tallulah Bankhead in her lowest register. Her movie career started very promisingly with a featured role in Woody Allen's first film, *Take the Money and Run*. That was followed by a lengthy stint as one of the marathon dancers in Jane Fonda's breakthrough film, *They Shoot Horses, Don't They?* We became very close and shared many an intimate moment—not sexually—but she was a good listener and we felt free to discuss any subject. But over the years her luck would run out and she became a self-destructive personality. Perhaps that's the reason we got along so well—we had that trait in common.

The second new friend was character actress Gertrude Flynn. I'd seen her play Amanda in *The Glass Menagerie* in a Los Angeles production, and had been terribly moved by her performance. I went backstage and introduced myself and we became dear friends from that moment on. In her youthful days she'd had a successful ingenue career in a number of Theatre Guild plays in New York. She also had the distinction of being Jessica Tandy's understudy in the original production of *A Streetcar Named Desire*.

Through Gertrude, I met Sarah Hardy, who was introduced as her daughter, but she wasn't really. Gertrude's own daughter had died at a very early age and Sarah became the substitute. I would spend many an evening with them—all of us drinking way too much. We weren't alcoholics, of course, just social drinkers.

In 1964, I received a call from Carole Cook and Tom Troupe, informing me that they were going to be married, and asking me to be an usher in the ceremony. Tom was divorced from "crazy Sally," as Carole called her, and had a young son named Christopher. Tom had kept active in television and theatre work, and Carole had continued her close association with Lucille Ball, frequently appearing on her *I Love Lucy* series. When her contract with Desilu ended, she signed with Warner Bros. and played opposite Don Knotts in a comedy called *The Incredible Mr. Limpet,* as well as a co-starring role in *Palm Springs Weekend,* which showcased a group of Warners' young stars—Troy Donahue, Connie Stevens, Robert Conrad, Ty Hardin and Stefanie Powers.

It was a wedding to remember. It was planned just like a stage production, with Hal Martin, a friend of Carole's, acting as director and stage manager. The rehearsals became so hectic, the poor church pianist practically had a nervous breakdown and quit the "production," with a professional musician brought in to replace her. As I recall, there were six male ushers in the procession, as well as Tom's young son as ring bearer. Lucille Ball was the maid-of-honor.

When it was time for the ceremony to start, I, along with another usher, entered to light the candles on each aisle pew. I felt like I was auditioning, as it seemed each aisle seat was occupied by a prominent casting director. The ushers, who included our friend Bob Osborne, all lined up at the front of the stage—I mean, the altar. The overture started—okay, the wedding march—and young Christopher came slowly up the aisle, carrying the wedding band on a pillow. Unfortunately, the church's floors had been highly waxed and polished, and poor Christopher slipped, sprawling to the floor, with the pillow and the ring flying in the air. Miss Ball was behind him when this mishap occurred, and she immediately dropped to all fours, crawling down the aisle searching for the lost ring. It was hysterical. The "audience" was screaming with laughter, as though they were watching a sketch from Lucy's television show. Finally, she retrieved the diamond, handed it to the embarrassed Christopher, and took her place beside me at the altar. Then Carole made her entrance, wearing a beautiful off-white wedding gown with a train that seemed at least a block long. While she was slowly making her way up the aisle, Hal Martin started a whispering campaign among the ushers, each repeating to the next what he had said. Finally, it got to me: "Tell Lucy she's not in her light!" Well, I wasn't about to do that. If anyone knew where to find her light, it was Lucille Ball.

About a year after the wedding, Carole had a major career boost. She was signed by director Gower Champion to star in the Australian production of *Hello, Dolly!* The musical was still a huge hit on Broadway, so it was considered quite a coup to be the first actress to inherit the coveted role that Carol Channing had created. She was a smashing success in the role and it ran for over a year.

* * * * *

Phyllis Gates, now that she'd divorced Rock, had sold the Warbler Place house and was living in a Beverly Hills apartment. She'd also enrolled at UCLA, taking several courses, one in interior design. Since she had exquisite taste, it was a good profession for her to pursue (she didn't, however). She was still bitter over the divorce and was threatening to write a book exposing her ex-husband. I told her I thought that a very unfair thing to do and, for a while, put a damper on our friendship. Fortunately, not for too long. She knew I was having a rough time financially, but I found it very difficult to ask anyone for assistance, so I never tried to borrow money. Soon I had to sell my Corvette. I am sure I could have saved myself a lot of heartache, as well as a Corvette, *if* I had been willing to admit I was broke.

One day she stopped by my apartment. She said she'd met someone that she thought I should meet. His name was Richard St. John, she said, and he was looking for someone to help him drive back east—and he was willing to pay the driver. Besides, said Phyllis, it would give me an opportunity to visit New York again. That appealed to me, so I told her to have him call me. When he drove up in front of my apartment, I noticed that he was driving a new white Cadillac convertible. He was in his fifties, with white hair, and a becoming tan. He was dressed very casually, but the clothes had an expensive look, and he was an attractive man. We chatted for a while, he seemed most pleasant, and I agreed to make the trip with him. A reason I wanted to go to New York was to see the Off Broadway hit, *Boys In the Band,* as I'd heard there would soon be an L.A. company and I wanted to be a part of it. St. John's plan, he said, was to stop off in New York City for a few days, then go on to Swampscott, Massachusetts to join his wife at their home there. After a couple of weeks, they'd be making the drive back to Los Angeles. I made plans to stay with my friend Craig Slocum, hopefully catch a play or two, then fly back home (he was paying, of course). Mr. St. John was also an actor, but he was getting a rather late start in this most difficult of professions.

Although I was surprised when he said he was married, I wasn't surprised when he propositioned me. I'd been around too long not to spot someone who was becoming smitten. Older men, however, had never been a turn on for me. Still, he was very nice, he was attractive and he was generous with his money. We arrived in New York, he checked in at the Plaza and offered to get me a room there. I declined, saying Craig (or Rusty) was expecting me. That evening he invited me for dinner at Sardi's, the famous theatrical restaurant. The next day he called, saying he'd gotten tickets for Barbra Streisand in *Funny Girl.* Of course, she was extraordinary and you knew a major star had been born. Then we went to see Carol Channing in *Hello, Dolly!* which was wonderful entertainment, with delightful supporting performances from Charles Nelson Reilly, Eileen Brennan and Mary Jo Catlett (all three would become my friends in the years ahead). He was leaving for Swampscott the next day, but he bought me a ticket for *Boys In the Band* before he left. He asked if I'd be staying in the city for the next two weeks and I said no, I couldn't afford to stay but a few more days. When I left him that evening, he gave me $500—payment for helping him drive, he said. Certainly more than I'd expected. He asked if he and his wife, Claire, could call me when they returned to Los Angeles? Sure. Why not?

The very next day he called from Swampscott. He'd come up with a "brilliant idea," he said. Why didn't I stay in New York for the two weeks, then drive back to Los Angeles with him and his wife? I was having a good time in the city, plus I'd arranged a meeting with Richard Barr, the producer of *Boys In the Band*, so I accepted his offer. I had known Barr before, during my early New York days, and before he became an important producer—particularly noteworthy for bringing the works of Edward Albee to the stage. *Who's Afraid of Virginia Woolf?*, with Uta Hagen and Arthur Hill, was one of the great American plays, certainly one of the most exciting theatrical experiences I'd ever had.

Dick St. John's wife was the former Claire Hastings. She was from a very wealthy newspaper family, owning the Swampscott paper for one. She was also much older, a woman now in her early seventies. They'd met when she was on a cruise and Dick had been the group's tour guide. They struck up a friendship and, eventually, to everyone's shock in staid Swampscott, they were married. Everyone was sure he married her for her money. The whole situation reminded me of the plot of *The Heiress*. Claire had married when she was young, against her stern father's wishes, and for a while had been disinherited. But the young husband died and she was welcomed back in the family. To herself, she vowed that she'd never marry again—unless it was to a much younger man—because she refused to go through the pain of losing another husband. She figured the odds were with her if she found a younger mate. They had been married about five years when I entered the picture. It seemed a very happy arrangement. He catered to her every need, was a perfect gentleman and, most importantly, seemed to genuinely care for her. The trip back to Los Angeles was fine, with Dick and I alternating with the driving. Claire seemed to like me, mostly, at that point, because I was a safe driver. Soon I would become one of their "family."

If I'd been a working actor, or secure financially, the next years would never have happened. Phyllis had introduced me to Craig Hill. Now she had introduced me to Richard St. John. Both had a profound effect. One out of honest affection, the other out of desperation.

TAKE SIX

The St. Johns were returning to Los Angeles to oversee completion on a luxurious new home they were building in the Mt. Olympus section. The large construction had a spectacular view of the city. The house was not at all similar to Claire's estate in Swampscott, which was a simpler, shingle-framed home with massive grounds. They checked into a hotel until they were able to take occupancy. Since Dick was determined to have an acting career, she had, reluctantly, agreed to spend half the year in Los Angeles, which she really didn't like. The new home was a most generous gift to him.

I knew I was being mentally seduced, with Dick constantly showering me with expensive gifts. And, since I'd been broke for so long, I accepted his generosity. Of course I was being reeled in for the kill. I was aware of this and was dreading the night when I had to succumb to his advances, but that didn't stop me from accepting his offer to buy me a new car. Since I'd lost my Corvette I had been without wheels, a necessity in Los Angeles. We settled on a slightly used aqua colored Corvette, very similar to the one I'd had. In accepting this major gift, I knew I had passed the point of no return. At first, I thought I could handle the situation, that I was a mature man, and knew what I was getting myself into. Money can be very seductive. At thirty-six years of age I thought I was a bit mature to be a "kept boy," but I looked ten years younger, and thought I could play the game. But as the weeks turned into months, I knew I was living a lie. I was weak, getting very used to the luxurious living, the fancy restaurants, the new clothes, the parties, and the cash. I told myself I couldn't afford to give this up. I still wasn't working; I had little money except what he gave me, so I was almost completely dependent upon him. Of course, he liked it that way. He knew he had a hold on me. I told myself to go out and get a regular job, but that was too easy. Surely, I thought, my luck would change and I would start working as an actor again. Participating in a lie, however, was beginning to take a toll on my self-respect. Too, I had regard for Claire. I liked her and felt very guilty about my relationship with her husband, though I'm sure she was well aware of the situation. One time she said to me, "I just don't want Dick to be hurt." It was a veiled request, but I read her underlying meaning. I felt myself drowning again, but I was too weak to seek outside help.

As with me, Dick thought he could buy his way into being an actor. I suppose it's been done, and he did do a few television jobs, mostly through their social contacts. He and Claire would entertain lavishly, wining and dining people in the industry. Harriet Parsons, the lesbian daughter of columnist Louella Parsons, was a frequent guest. I liked Harriet, however, and she had been a very successful producer for a while at RKO—putting out several good pictures—including *The Enchanted Cottage* with Dorothy McGuire and Robert Young; *I Remember Mama* with Irene Dunne and *Susan Slept Here* with Dick Powell and Debbie Reynolds. Another "conquest" was the powerful columnist Hedda Hopper, whose syndicated column in *The Los Angeles Times* was widely read. But there was *one* thing money couldn't buy, and that was talent. While Dick was up to the limited demands of a small part on television, he was way out of his league in tackling a lengthy, serious role. For a brief period he joined Sherman Marks' workshop, but that didn't last long, for which I was grateful.

And, of course, he loved meeting celebrities. One evening Hedda Hopper brought the distinguished actor Raymond Massey and his wife to dinner. And, later, Claire and Dick, while they were back in Swampscott, would rent the house to Vivien Leigh when she was in Los Angeles filming *Ship of Fools*. Unfortunately, I didn't get a chance to meet one of my favorite actresses. Claire, however, was appalled when she returned to the house to find the elegantly tiled floors very damaged. It seemed the famous Spanish dancer, Jose Greco, who was also appearing in *Ship of Fools*, would entertain Miss Leigh with his flamenco group. There were heel marks embedded deeply in the tile.

I made the mistake of saying I knew Liberace, as well as the silent film star Mae Murray and actress Isabel Jewell. Dick insisted I throw a party for them. I resisted having the party at his house, however, preferring to hold it in my modest apartment. He paid for everything, of course. Then, a few days later, through his friendship with Hedda Hopper, it would appear in her column, linking his name with the celebrities.

I had met Liberace through his personal assistant, Bob, and had been to several parties at the flamboyant star's home. He was always the perfect host, of course, and his lavish, overdone house was a marvel to see. A lot of money had obviously been spent, but it was very garish, with everything in gold. When I had been ditched by Craig Hill and was so distraught, Liberace kindly offered me his house in Palm Springs for a change of scenery. I spent several days there, alone, and it was a very thoughtful gesture.

Mae Murray, however, was another story. In the late 1920s she'd been one of MGM's most valuable and popular stars (sort of a Lana Turner of her day), with her biggest film hit being *The Merry Widow* opposite John Gilbert. She really wasn't considered a good actress, but she had personality and, in films, that is sometimes more important. Her career died, as did many others, when talking pictures arrived. I'd met her when a friend of mine, Bill Gass, who had briefly been my manager, was trying to assist her in reviving her long dormant career. She'd made an attempt with a nightclub act in Las Vegas (naturally dancing to the strains of "The Merry Widow," which was always identified with her). But the novelty act hadn't been too successful. Now Bill Gass had the outrageous idea of starring her in a revival of Tennessee Williams' *The Glass Menagerie*—with me playing the role of the son, Tom. It was a role I'd always wanted to do, so I happily met with them at a beach restaurant in Venice. During dinner I made the mistake of saying how great it was she was making a "comeback." The very word sent her into a frenzy of denial—"I've never been away!" she haughtily answered. I'm sure she wouldn't have had a clue about the role of Amanda Wingfield. Perhaps she might have captured Amanda's dreamy, at times childlike quality, but the complexities of the role I'm sure would have totally escaped her. After dinner we went to the nearby Santa Monica amusement park. As luck would have it, over the loudspeaker came "The Merry Widow" melody. That's all she needed. She suddenly started waltzing around the park, her black taffeta dress and big picture hat twirling in the evening breeze. Of course she attracted a considerable amount of attention. Her powdered white face and bee-stung red lips were definitely from another era.

Yet, even in 1964, there were those who recognized her as she waltzed through the park. She seemed to revel in the attention. It was really quite sad. Of course *The Glass Menagerie* never happened. After my little party, where she met the St. Johns, she would frequently call me—often needing money. As usual, Dick was generous and would come to her rescue. She was later found wandering the streets of St. Louis (I think it was), having gotten off a bus, thinking she was in New York.

Another old-time actress Bill Gass introduced me to was the petite blonde, Isabel Jewell. Isabel's career, of course, was later than Miss Murray's—her heyday being in the mid-30s and early 40s. She was a good actress, however, having appeared in at least three classic films—*A Tale of Two Cities* and *Lost Horizon*, both with Ronald Colman, and she played the small role of Amy Slattery in *Gone with the Wind*. She'd also had a good part with Bette Davis in *Marked Woman*. Bill, always trying to assist an actress in need, had produced a local production of Tennessee's *The Milk Train Doesn't Stop Here Anymore* for her, which is when we first met. Occasionally, in the 1960s, she'd get a small role (like the *Bernardine* film), but the pickings were pretty lean. Like me, she was a chain smoker, and she'd frequently have dinner at my place. Although she now no longer drank, somehow, during the evening, she'd seem more loaded than the rest of us, with her speech getting more slurred and unintelligible as the night wore on. She rarely left the couch, even to go to the bathroom, but somehow, she was taking pills. She was really very dear, even offering to loan me money, which I knew she didn't really have either. One morning I found an envelope with cash under my door. I thanked her profusely, but I never kept the money. The next time I'd see her, I'd slip the bills into her purse. Isabel always said she wanted to be cremated. But when she died, her body wasn't discovered for several days and had started to decompose. Bill Gass, however, in one of his irrational moments, insisted that she had to have a public funeral. "Her public," he reasoned, should be able to stare at her in her casket. It was macabre. But it got more so. The funeral home, thinking she was going to be cremated, had done nothing to stop the body from decomposing more. They refused to makeup the face for the service. Frantic, Bill asked me to call one of the studios to see if a makeup man would do the deed. Against my better judgment, I called one. In horror, I was turned down. Bill finally found a young girl, who was working in the makeup department at the May Company, to do the gruesome task. Poor Sharon, who'd never seen a dead person in her life, was a nervous wreck. She said she'd almost fainted when one of Isabel's fingers fell off. But, considering the odds, Isabel looked pretty damned good—the face, anyway.

* * * * *

After months and months and months of inactivity, I suddenly had a spurt of good fortune. I became a favorite of the casting director for a Sunday morning television series called *This Is the Life*. The filmed scripts had religious messages and were heavy on dialogue. The program wasn't a prestigious one, certainly, but it was work, and I was indeed grateful. Since the budgets were limited, they had to have actors that were fast and ones who could handle lots of dialogue. I could do that. Former child actress Gigi Perreau played my wife on one episode, and soap opera star to be, Susan Seaforth, on another. I did at least ten of the half-hour scripts.

Then I was asked to play the supporting role of Helen Keller's brother in *The Miracle Worker* at a summer theatre in Phoenix, directed by Jack Sydow. It was a very good production with Eileen Brennan giving a marvelous performance as Annie Sullivan. We hit it off immediately, and, once again, after having too much to drink, we attempted the bed scene. Let's just say we were much better on stage. Eileen, of course, would go on to a very fine career, including an Oscar nomination for her hilarious performance in *Private Benjamin* with Goldie Hawn. It was seriously hampered, however, when she was hit by a car and almost killed, but, she persevered, and every once in a while I see her in a television performance, I'm happy to say.

In an attempt to break Dick's hold on me, I decided my near-Beverly Hills apartment was too expensive, and I found a small place in the back of a house on North Curson Avenue in Hollywood. I moved my round bed and set up very modest housekeeping in the three-room-with-bath apartment. I even took in a roommate; a singer named Don Minter. Dick wasn't happy about that, but I was trying to show some independence. When Don moved in, I put the round bed in the living room and gave him the bedroom. The bed took up most of the space.

All in all, 1965 was shaping up as a fairly decent year. Nina Vance called again, inviting me back to the Alley to do an English play, *The Knack*. The ten weeks in

Houston were good, though the play was considered "too racy" by some, causing a bit of a stir. Of course the St. Johns showed up, en route to Swampscott.

Shortly after I returned to Los Angeles, I was asked to repeat my role of Edmund in *Long Day's Journey Into Night* at a new summer theatre in Orange County. I almost said no when I found out they'd already set Jody McCrea to play the older brother, Jamie, enacted so astutely by Jason Robards on Broadway and in the film version. Jody had been featured in several Frankie Avalon-Annette Funicello beach movies, had little stage experience, if any, and I snobbishly thought the role way beyond him. First of all, he was a big, hulky guy, radiating health, totally opposite of the dissipated character in O'Neill's script. But the management explained they were in a contractual bind. They'd originally set Jody for a light comedy, but for some reason that had been canceled, and in order to honor his contract they put him in the O'Neill play. I finally said I'd accept if they cast my friend Gertrude Flynn in the Mary Tyrone role. They agreed. I also got them to use Jacquelyn Hyde in the small role of the Irish maid.

Jody and I were put up in a large apartment, with three bedrooms, so I asked Jackie Hyde to stay with us. It was most disheartening to find Jody, in the mornings, reading *Batman* comic books instead of learning his long and difficult role. In fairness, he did tell me later that he'd been studying the comic books because he was reading for the new *Batman* television series. One evening Jackie and I had been for a stroll along the waterfront, where all the wealthy yachts were moored (John Wayne's included). When we returned to the apartment, we entered, surprising Jody, who was sprawled on the couch, completely nude, watching an old movie Western that starred his parents, Joel McCrea and Frances Dee. He grabbed a towel and covered his crotch area, though he didn't seem too phased that we'd caught him in an intimate moment. I had one of my summer colds, so I quickly excused myself and retired to my room. Jackie wasn't so quick, however, and he decided to make a move on the actress, grabbing her and planting a big kiss on her lips. She managed to escape his advances and locked herself in her room. The next day, a rather sheepish Jody apologized—sort of— offering Jackie a lame "I felt an obligation to try." Not too flattering to the actress, I'm afraid. In retrospect, I think Jackie was sorry she had resisted—after all, he was a good-looking hunk.

However, he wasn't too swift in theatre protocol. On opening night, his parents, who were still a very handsome couple, came to the play, but he told them not to come back for the third act because it was "too depressing" and, also, he was offstage for about forty minutes. So, unbelievably, he left the theatre and joined them at a nearby restaurant. Granted, he got back to the theatre in time for his next entrance, but, in the meantime, the stage manager was losing his mind!

Of course, his parents may not have come back anyway. It wasn't a good production. Though Gertrude, Jackie and I managed to come off reasonably well, it's just not a play you attempt to do in summer stock, where shows are put together rather hastily. Film actress Joan Caulfield followed us in *Affairs of State*, a comedy much more suited to stock. Later in the summer season, I was asked to return to play the young college professor in Edward Albee's *Who's Afraid of Virginia Woolf?* I should have known better, after the near fiasco with O'Neill, but I couldn't resist the chance to be in this marvelous play. But, again, it's not a script you tackle in summer stock. Just learning the barrage of lines, particularly for the Martha and George characters, is daunting in itself. In fact, Henry Beckman, our George, was never able to master his lines. A hypnotist was even called in, hoping that would help, but it was to no avail. Beckman, usually a fine actor, had his lines pasted all over the stage—on the back of the couch, on tables, on backs of chairs, or in various books, which he'd pick up pretending to be looking for something. He was—his lines. It was a mess. But, I must say, he was a pro and did it very well. But it was very difficult for the rest of the cast, as we never knew when he'd finished a line, or indeed, if he was going to get one out. Consequently, it left us sputtering and in limbo, not knowing when to speak or not, making us look like we didn't know our lines. And who got the best reviews? Right. Henry Beckman.

I'd suddenly had this flurry of work, but they were small paying jobs. Still, it was good to be busy at what I loved most. Dick St. John, of course, was still very much in the background. My being out of town eased the situation a bit, but he usually found a way to show up at one of the theatres I might be playing in.

The one high profile job I had during this period was a guest shot on a new 20th Century Fox series, *The Long Hot Summer,* which was based on the hit movie that had starred Paul Newman, Joanne Woodward, Orson Welles, Lee

Remick, Anthony Franciosa, and Angela Lansbury. I was cast in the role Richard Anderson had done in the film, the weak fiancé of the Woodward character, played on the series by Nancy Malone. Nancy and I recalled our stint on *Lamp Unto My Feet* years before in New York. She laughingly said she'd still pick me over Steve McQueen and Robert Loggia. I hoped this exposure would lead to more of the better television shows, but it didn't.

Then, out of the blue, I got another movie. It had been five years since *The Plunderers*. The new film was *Arizona Raiders* for Columbia. I was cast as Audie Murphy's younger brother (which I'd missed out on being when Burt Lancaster booted me out of *The Unforgiven*) in the Western, being directed by William Witney. Also in the featured cast were Buster Crabbe, my old Flash Gordon idol, Ben Cooper, Michael Dante and Gloria Talbott. I only had about four scenes, but they were good ones, before I died in Audie's arms. The *Daily Variety* film critic liked the movie a lot. Considering its budget, he said the film had an "almost epic" look, and he singled me out with: *"RAY STRICKLYN IS A SOLID CLICK, SCORING BIG IN HIS FEW SCENES."*

We filmed *Arizona Raiders* in the Phoenix desert, but I almost didn't finish the movie. The day before I was to shoot my death scene, I suddenly had tremendous pains in my side and stomach. The production manager called a doctor, who diagnosed it as acute appendicitis. I should be operated on immediately, he said, or they could burst. Since I only had one more scene to do, I opted not to have the operation until I finished the picture *(the show must go on!)*. The producer was grateful, but also nervous in case something tragic happened. As the scene was written, I was supposed to ride into the frame, be shot, then fall into Audie's arms. The doctor said it was too dangerous for me to ride a horse, so they had a double ride into the scene, be shot, then cut to me in Audie's loving arms. I died beautifully.

The ever-constant Dick St. John, knowing of my attack, flew to Phoenix to bring me back to Los Angeles, then rushed me to his doctor. It was a very comforting thing for him to do, and I was indeed grateful for his assistance and care. But being grateful was one thing, being intimately involved was another. More jaded friends of mine said I had a "good thing" going—a rich, married man, who was away a good deal of the time. "Just shut your eyes and bear it" was their suggestion. I tried that. But I hated myself more and more each day, each week, each month. I felt like a whore. But I was too weak and I kept the relationship dangling. I knew, however, that I didn't *like* anything about my private life. Dick was offering his affection and assistance and I was just *taking*. I was now seeing myself as the villain, not him. Something had to give . . .

TAKE SEVEN

When I'd returned to Houston in 1965 to do *The Knack* at the Alley, I'd left my dog, Pepper, with friends in the San Fernando Valley. They had a large yard, so I thought that would be a great luxury for the animal. The house, however, was on a busy thoroughfare. As too often happens, the gate was left opened and dear Pepper ran into the street, being killed instantly. There's little worse than losing a beloved pet and I swore I'd never allow myself to go through that anguish again. *No more pets.*

A year later, however, I was weakening in that resolve. Phyllis called and said it was time I had another pet. She knew I was partial to schnauzers and she said a friend's dog had just had a new litter. Why didn't we go look at them? I knew I'd likely be hooked even before we reached David Galligan's apartment. As fate would have it, I would end up with more than a dog.

Phyllis explained that David was working as a furniture refinisher at CBH Antiques on Melrose Avenue, one of the fancier and more expensive shops along Decorator Row. As Phyllis was so interested in interior design, she was a frequent visitor at the shop. She and David had become friends and he was teaching her how to refinish. His apartment was down an alley in West Hollywood, lined with similar small abodes (Tuesday Weld lived across from him when she first arrived in Los Angeles). From the exterior the apartment was quite average, but the moment you stepped through the door it was another story, decorated in excellent taste with beautifully stained hardwood floors. Obviously a lot of attention and time had gone into making the place attractive.

David looked to be about seventeen or eighteen, although he was really twenty-four. He had a thin, boyish body, with brown hair highlighted with sun streaks. In other words, he was quite attractive. Phyllis had also told me that working at CBH Antiques was only a temporary job, as he was really just starting out as an actor. He seemed a perfect juvenile type—in fact, he reminded me a little of my earlier self. He had also done a good bit of modeling, including a fashion magazine layout with Tuesday Weld.

After complimenting him on his apartment, we immediately went to the back porch area to look at the puppies. There were only two left. I finally picked the little female. With that decision made, we settled down with a drink. He had a terrific sense of humor, I thought, and, even more, seemed very hip about movies and theatre. His knowledge on that score appealed to me right away. Usually younger types have never heard of a Katharine Cornell or a Helen Hayes, but Galligan knew them all, even to giving their credits. He could even quote the box-office receipts on the latest Broadway plays!

Phyllis suggested we have dinner, so we went to a nearby Mexican restaurant. As each margarita glass was emptied, a new one was ordered. I learned that he was from San Francisco, had won an award as the youngest person, at twelve, to ever swim the span of the Golden Gate bridge, was of Italian descent, and that his real last name was Mozzetti. He changed it to Galligan, his mother's maiden name, because most casting people assumed he'd be a dark, swarthy Italian-type, when, of course, he was just the opposite. He'd appeared in a few plays in San Francisco, notably two offbeat musicals, *Street Scene* and *Sandhog*. I could also tell he was very definite in his likes and dislikes, having an opinion on just about everything. He obviously wasn't some Hollywood twinkie—you know, cute but without a brain in their head.

There was an obvious attraction, I knew that. *Godammit, Phyllis, this is the third person you've introduced me to!* First, Craig Hill, then Richard St. John (who was still very much in the picture), and now this opinionated youth! During the course of the evening, I also discovered that Mr. Galligan had a live-in lover, Alan, who was a dog groomer. And so the plot thickened. Eventually, we all said our goodnights. But, instinctively, I knew this encounter was just a prelude.

I didn't know, however, that I would see him quite so soon. As I was to find out many times in the future, when David Galligan made up his mind about something he worked fast. He went home that very first night and told his roommate that he was moving. There was no question in his mind. Understandably, Alan was stunned. The very next day, he packed his belongings and moved out, taking temporary refuge in a loft above CBH Antiques. All he had was a cot and his clothing.

David Galligan

And so we started a relationship, one that I assumed was a temporary one. How wrong I was! Even though I had a roommate, easygoing Don Minter, David began staying at 1010 North Curson Avenue. Don, who was a very attractive and promising singer, understood at first, but it was quite apparent that the three-room apartment was way too small for three people. It wasn't fair to Don, of course, so he moved out. Fortunately we remained friends. And, so, the "pushy" Mr. Galligan moved in. He was the man who came to dinner—and stayed. I didn't know what had hit me. Secretly, however, I rather liked the idea.

Everything had happened so fast there had been no time to tell David about Dick St. John and his importance in my life—at least financially. Besides, that relationship wasn't one I was proud of, so I tried to keep that side of my life as secret as possible. Fortunately, at this particular moment, he was back in Swampscott. Not for long, however.

It became a three-way merry-go-round, though there was little for me to be merry about. I told Dick that I had to have my own life; that he had his, and I needed to have someone permanent in mine. But he wouldn't let me go. And, frankly, I was reluctant to have him completely out of mine. He was practically my sole support, except for my weekly unemployment check. It was an awful situation, one of many indecisions and frustrations. Understandably, David couldn't stand him. I'm sure Dick felt the same way, but he was quite cagey and would occasionally include David in dinner invitations at some chic restaurant.

Meanwhile, I was caught in the middle, loathing myself more with each passing day. David and I were fighting, while Dick was more attentive than ever, continuing to ply me with gifts—which I continued to accept. To make a bad situation worse, we were all drinking too much, trying to escape the mess we were in.

My mind was in a state of chaos. I needed to get away—from both David and Dick. A real estate acquaintance, Carl, said he had a vacant house, the tenant had died, and I could stay there until it was sold. And so, I moved to the house in Laurel Canyon. David was miserable, I was worse than miserable. Dick, however, was delighted. I invited my mother out, thinking she'd be a somewhat stabling influence, and she was. Of course Dick really did a number on her—dinners with him and Claire, taking us to Las Vegas and Lake Tahoe. He even bought me a new car, a little red Fiat.

While I put on a decent facade, inside I was completely crumbling, heading for a nervous breakdown I was sure. I couldn't take this double life any more. It had to end. I missed David terribly, and I knew that I *needed* him in my life. I didn't know how I'd survive, but I knew I *had* to make a clean break from St. John. Once mother had returned to Houston, I moved back home, back to the little apartment on Curson.

Of course, Dick was crazed by my decision. His obsession was most destructive, for all of us. He was really beginning to lose it, sneaking around the apartment late at night, peering in windows, even breaking in once. I finally told him I couldn't see him at all—under any conditions. But he continued his destructive behavior. Eventually, I threatened to go to Claire. That stopped him, temporarily. But he would still park his car in front of the house, sitting there for hours at a time. It was most disturbing and unnerving.

One night, our friends Gertrude Flynn and Sarah Hardy, invited David and me for dinner. They lived at the top of Laurel Canyon on Wonderland Avenue. If you parked on the street in front of their house, you had to walk up an endless flight of stairs. *If*, however, you took a treacherous back road it would eventually lead you to the rear of their house, with no stairs to climb. The back road was a very narrow, bumpy dirt road, only wide enough for one car to go through at a time. There was a tremendously steep cliff to one side and, if you misjudged, you could easily go crashing hundreds of feet below. How we maneuvered it after many a drunken evening is a small miracle.

This particular evening, however, we noticed Dick following us in his Cadillac convertible, a stunt he had done several times in the past. But he'd never tailed us into Laurel Canyon before. Nor did he know the back road to Gertrude's.

As we turned onto the dirt road, I was sure he would stop following us. But he didn't. Instead, in his madness, he started driving way too fast, bumping into the rear of my car. He kept rear-ending me. It was so dangerous. Finally, we got to the end of the road, to Gertrude's house and dashed inside, locking the door. He sat outside for a while, obviously in a very distraught state. I watched out the window as he attempted time after time, to turn the large Cadillac around in the tiny parking area. It would have been easy for him to plunge over the side of the cliff. At last, he succeeded, as the dust from his spinning wheels scattered behind him.

Finally, the nightmare with Richard St. John was over. For nearly five years I'd allowed the situation to run its course—out of my own neurotic need and desperation. But my self-loathing had nearly destroyed me in the process. I didn't know *how* I was going to exist, but I was relieved the whole ugly experience was behind me.

A few years later, I heard Dick had died. Yes, before Claire. She had married a younger man so she wouldn't have to go through the pain of burying another husband. But the fates didn't see it that way. I started to send her my condolences, but I decided against it. That part of my life had been buried too. Except for the ashes of remembrance.

* * * * *

There were, perhaps, two positive experiences during this whole period that stand out. One was our revival of *The Caretaker*. Sherman Marks had moved his workshop to the safer and more luxurious area of Beverly Hills, leasing the charming Beverly Hills Playhouse on Robertson Boulevard. It was a marvelous little theatre, located at the end of a long alley. *This* time we had the legitimate rights to do the play, and both the press and the public beautifully received it. *The Hollywood Reporter* critic wrote: "A FASCINATING THEATRE PIECE, A TREAT FOR ACTOR AND AUDIENCE ALIKE UNDER THE SKILLFUL DIRECTION OF SHERMAN MARKS AND BY VIRTUE OF THE PERFORMANCES BY RICHARD BULL, TOM TROUPE AND RAY STRICKLYN. MARKS ORCHESTRATES THE 3-ACTS AND THE 3-CHARACTERS TO MAXIMUM EFFECT."

Daily Variety was similar: "THIS PERFORMANCE SHOULD SEND THE AUDIENCE WAXING POETIC IN A STRONG AND EXCITING PRODUCTION. RAY STRICKLYN, TOM TROUPE AND RICHARD BULL SHOW THEIR DEFT TALENTS FOR CHARACTERIZING PINTER'S PEOPLE. TROUPE IS MAGNIFICENT, BULL PERFECT, STRICKLYN FINELY ETCHED. THE PRODUCTION WAS A MARVEL OF THEATRICALITY."

The Glendale News-Press echoed the praise: "AS ACTED BY TROUPE, STRICKLYN AND BULL, EACH ROLE IS A MEMORABLE PORTRAIT. WE WERE

ENTHRALLED BY A NEARLY PERFECT PERFORMANCE." We had opened in October 1967 and ran for many months. In many respects, I think it perhaps the finest overall production I was ever a part of. Everything just *worked*. And Sherman's direction had been the best I'd encountered since my cherished Circle-In-the-Square days with Jose Quintero.

I also appeared in the workshop's next production too, playing the title role in Joe Orton's black comedy, *Entertaining Mr. Sloane,* with Dick Bull and his wife, Barbara Collentine, fighting over who would seduce Mr. Sloane first. Bob Richards directed this one. I also tried my hand at producing. Jerry Lawrence entrusted me with the rights to a new long one-act play he'd written, *Live Spelled Backwards,* a fascinating script about the effect of drugs on a group of lost souls in Tangier. Two of the characters were loosely based on a Tennessee Williams' type and a Barbara Hutton/Doris Duke persona, "The Richest Woman in the World" (played by Jacquelyn Hyde in my production). Gertrude Flynn was also in it, playing "The Woman Who Knew Everything—Badly." Under Bob Richards' guidance, it was very well received. This was the beginning of my long and fortunate experiences at the Beverly Hills Playhouse.

Another "up" moment during my down period, was when Marvin Paige, a prolific casting director who had used me several times over the years (the *Combat* series, for one, with Vic Morrow), set me to star with Tommy Kirk in a low-budget movie about stock car racing. We filmed *Track of Thunder* (a 1967 United Artists release) entirely in Nashville. Tommy Kirk had been a popular Walt Disney child star, but now he was grown up, and we were cast as friendly rivals, fighting for supremacy on the track as well as in the romance department. We were both a bit mature for our roles, but we managed to "pass," looking in our early twenties. The object of our romantic attention was a beautiful young brunette named Brenda Benet. She was a knockout in the looks department, reminding me a little of Natalie Wood. As a simple farm mother of Kirk, Marvin had cast Faith Domergue, who had been an exotic Jane Russell-clone in the early 1950s when Howard Hughes signed her to an RKO contract. To me, she seemed a bit out of place on a Nashville farm. When the film was released, playing mostly in drive-ins, *Daily Variety* was kind: "THOUGH TOO MATURE FOR HIS ROLE, RAY STRICKLYN BRINGS A CHARISMATIC CHARM TO HIS ROLE AS THE RICH

BOY." The beautiful Brenda Benet should have had a future in films, but her life was cut tragically short. She married television star, Bill Bixby (*My Favorite Martian* and *Courtship of Eddie's Father*), but it wasn't a happy union and they divorced. Shortly after, their baby died. Brenda never fully recovered from this tragedy and, sadly, ended her own life. Tommy Kirk, who I later found out was gay, also had an increasingly difficult time of it. He disappeared from view completely.

* * * * *

David and I weren't having an easy time of it, either, although he was at least working. He'd taken a job at Donald Gould's—one of the shops located in Farmers Market. The shop carried expensive household appliances and was the most elegant of the many boutiques in the famous mall. Eventually he became store manager. A new woman had been hired who introduced herself as Virginia Greenfield. She was in her fifties, plainly dressed, and wore little makeup. Beneath her nondescript appearance, David could see she had an attractive face and figure. "You *can't* be a Virginia," he teased. "With those legs you must be a Marlene." So, from that moment on, that's what our group called her. They became fast friends and, in time, she would become equally close to me, becoming a part of our little family. She also blossomed from the plain Virginia into a stunning woman, with a new hairstyle, a smart wardrobe, and the proper makeup. Galligan had "remade" her completely. In the forties, Marlene had had a promising career as a band singer, working under the name of Virginia Fait. She'd appeared with a couple of name orchestras—Jack Teagarden, for one—and she said Frank Sinatra used to come into the club and listen to her numbers. But she retired when she married, and had two daughters, Nancy and Maxine. Their father, she said, had been a gambler and had died at an early age. Maxine, at the time, was living in San Francisco, and Nancy, a real knockout in the looks department, was between husbands.

With David's job at the shop and my unemployment check, we were managing to eke by, but it was rough. He did a few television shows, like *Batman* and *The Lieutenant,* with Gary Lockwood. He was also in the two-hour pilot for the *Medical Center* series (with two greats, Edward G. Robinson and Kim Stanley, as guest-stars) and he did a small part in the film, *The Navy vs. the Nightcrawlers,* with Mamie Van Doren. He also helped actor Paul Kent form the Melrose Theatre, which became a most respected Equity-waiver playhouse, appearing in their productions of *The Goddess* and a one-act oddity named *No Why* with Gertrude Flynn. On the other hand, I had no acting offers. I was also agentless. As a result, I was drinking a lot, we both were.

My friend, Jim Terry, who had finally despaired of his constant rejection trying to get low-budget movies produced, had moved to Whittier and lived with his mother. He, too, was having a difficult time financially. Over the years, at Christmastime, low on funds, he made fudge as a gift for his friends and business associates. Everyone commented on how good it was. His recipe was special and he decided to try his hand in the candy business. *This* time he was successful. Before long he had his own small factory in Whittier, with hundreds of orders for his unique fudge. He called it Phanny's Phudge, and was catering to a number of outstanding outlets. Jim knew I was in trouble and asked me if I wanted to help him at the factory. So I drove to Whittier and back every day for almost a year, wrapping Phanny's Phudge in the colorful boxes. Eventually he even trusted me enough to let me cook a few batches. While I was grateful, it didn't stop the waves of depression I was wallowing in. Finally, using the long drive as an excuse, I quit.

Around this time David had a falling out with Donald Gould and quit his job at Farmers Market. Now we were both unemployed. Fortunately, Margaret Amick, who also worked for Gould, said her daughter, Pat, was looking for help at a printing and mailing company in Burbank. She particularly needed a good typist. And so we both went to work for Walter Miles. Like everyone else, it seemed, Walter was also a frustrated actor. There were just the four of us working and we worked hard. We handled all the mailing for NBC studios, for one, which was a massive job in itself. My typing, however, wasn't on a conventional typewriter—I had to pound out address plates, by the thousands, on a big old noisy machine. It was backbreaking work—you really had to hit the keys hard—and the noise was deafening. Doing that for eight hours a day was my "punishment" I irrationally told myself. I was hiding out in a small print shop in Burbank. But one day, to my dread, Walter asked me to deliver a bundle of mail to NBC. Suddenly, I was in the corridors, going to executive offices, dropping off mail. The very same corridors where I'd once had interviews, where I'd been hired to star in a television show. I found it thoroughly humiliating. I was also in terrible mental shape.

But I was about to have a temporary reprieve. Ross Brown, a casting director who had used me frequently in the past, called to say that PBS was getting ready to do an "all-star" version of *The Andersonville Trial,* with no less than George C. Scott directing. Ross said they were using only 'name' actors, even in the smallest roles—cameos he called them—and Scott had okayed me for the role of a soldier who swears in the testifiers in the courtroom drama. I was so down on myself that I couldn't believe George C. Scott even knew who I was, but Ross said when he brought my name up, Scott said, "Yes, of course, I wondered what had happened to him?" The fact that they considered me a "name" surprised me and gave a small shot to the damaged ego. But I wondered how many other "names" were pounding out address plates on a noisy machine in Burbank?

We rehearsed the show just like a play, which it had been, of course. Scott, who had been going through his own private hell with alcoholism, was on the wagon after being in a rehabilitation center. He had a friend with him—a caretaker really—to make sure he didn't take a drink. Some of the "names" appearing in *The Andersonville Trial* included William Shatner, Richard Basehart, Cameron Mitchell and Jack Cassidy in the leading roles, with fine actors like Martin Sheen, Buddy Ebsen, Albert Salmi and John Anderson doing cameos. I hadn't done anything in so long, plus being in the company of all those working actors, I was extremely nervous. In fact, I don't think I've ever been as unsure of myself, before or since. Even though I had only one basic speech—the swearing in oath—I kept blowing my lines. I'd never done that before in my life. It was humiliating, particularly in front of all those actors as well as dozens of extras. I wanted to leave the studio I was shaking so badly. I was sure I would be fired and part of me was hoping it would happen. Scott, however, was very sympathetic. He took me aside and put his arm around my shoulder as we walked down the corridor, trying to rebuild my confidence. I think he sensed, from his own downfall, that I was suffering and that my shakes weren't just from nerves. He knew an alcoholic when he saw one. Of course I refused to even consider the possibility. I wasn't an alcoholic, I was just a social drinker. When the show aired it received magnificent reviews, and eventually won the Emmy for best dramatic production of the year. Jack Cassidy, who was normally associated with musical comedies, was a revelation in his dramatic role.

From George C. Scott I went back to the printing factory. My reprieve had been brief. Also it had been a traumatic experience, with only Scott's kindness getting me through the taping. My already shaky confidence was now pretty well demolished. More than once I'd told myself I would rather die than not be able to act. My neurotic need was that strong. I had slowly been killing myself these past years. I think those awful years began with my father's death, compounded by my shame over the marine incident, then hating myself even more for my "prostitution" years with Dick St. John. And, of course, the drinking stopped me from looking at my situation with a clear and honest view. David was the only constant in my life, but even that relationship was in jeopardy in the state I was in. Emotionally and physically I was drained. And my sex drive was completely nil, and had been for some time.

Fortunately, I would receive a positive Christmas present in 1970. Once again Nina Vance would come to the rescue. The Alley Theatre's new multi-million-dollar complex had finally been completed. It was a castle, a formidable fortress, all off-white concrete with towers and bridges. It was a new landmark in downtown Houston. Nina asked if I'd like to come home and open the new theatre? What an honor, I thought. Of course, I accepted. And the play? It wouldn't be an easy one. In fact, it would be one of the longest and most difficult scripts ever written—Eugene O'Neill's five-hour trilogy, *Mourning Becomes Electra*. Because of its length it was rarely performed, and the three leading characters—the mother, Christine, the daughter, Lavinia and the son, Orin, were terribly complex roles. If I couldn't remember *one* line for *The Andersonville Trial*, how could I master an arduous role in a five-hour trilogy! Fortunately, the play wouldn't be done until December, so I had a few months to learn the lines. And learn them I did, having the script completely memorized before rehearsals began. Not always an ideal way to work, but on a project of this size, it was a big help. I would become particularly friendly with the ingenue in the play, a dark-haired actress from New York named Robyn Goodman.

With judicious editing, which the play badly needed, Nina cut about an hour off the running time. Still, four hours is a long sit. But it opened the new theatre with a big splash and we had a successful run. I was in my element again and feeling better than I had in months. As always, *work* as an actor was my salvation. David flew in from Los Angeles to see the show with good friends of ours, Jan LaMaak and newlyweds, Sandy and Jimmy Sangster. Jimmy was the British director of a number of horror movies for Hammer Films, and had written the screenplay for Bette Davis' *The Nanny.*

Nina had also contracted me for the next play at the Alley, *The Night Thoreau Spent In Jail,* written by Jerry Lawrence and his partner, Bob Lee. The title role was a wonderful one and I wanted to play it. Without my knowledge, Jerry had written Nina some weeks before, suggesting me for the role, but she'd already cast another actor who was coming from his season at the Tyrone Guthrie Theatre in Minneapolis. Nina offered me, instead, the role of his older brother. It was a good supporting role, and it beat sorting mail for Walter Miles.

The first day of rehearsal we just sat around a large table reading the script. It wasn't successful. The actor playing the Thoreau role mumbled his way through the lengthy part. Michael Moriarty was a tall, thin, attractive blond who looked to be in his mid-twenties, though I think he was a little older. Nina was worried. She took me aside after the reading, saying, "I think I've made a big mistake, Ray. You should be playing the role." I silently agreed. "I'll give him a few days," she said. Nina wasn't actually directing the play, a young woman named Beth Sanford had that task, but Nina was obviously very involved.

The first few days of rehearsal Moriarty continued with his mumbling. Our opening scene together was a welcoming home moment and he grabbed me in a big embrace, spinning me around. His grasp, however, was so tight that I couldn't get my breath when he released me. I was in a good deal of pain. He had crushed my pocket cigarette lighter into my chest. The stage manager rushed me to their doctor and he said I had a contusion. From then on I wouldn't let the actor near me during rehearsal. "We'll do the welcoming home scene after I've healed," I said. However, when I wasn't involved in a scene, I began sitting in the theatre watching the rehearsals. I couldn't believe what I was seeing. Moriarty was no longer mumbling, instead he was blossoming, with each scene growing in emotional power. My God, I thought, he's going to be absolutely brilliant. He positively glowed. I immediately got off my ass and started participating in our scenes together. Our relationship was growing, both on stage and off. I was now his biggest fan. Here was one actor, I knew, that had the potential to be a great actor.

After rehearsals we'd go to the bar across the street from the theatre, sitting for hours, discussing the pitfalls of an acting career. He seemed particularly interested in my once promising movie career, then my fall into oblivion. He said he was afraid that might happen to him and he didn't want to repeat my mistakes. He'd just finished a movie, about to be released, called *Bang the Drum Slowly.* It was a low-budget baseball story, he said, but he had no idea whether it was any good or not. He had the lead with another young unknown actor named Robert DeNiro (it was better than *good,* with powerful performances from both players).

The opening night of *Thoreau* went beautifully and, as expected, he gave a positively glowing performance. You could sense the audience rapport; he had them in the palm of his hand. It was magical. The reviews would confirm my

With Michael Moriarty in Lawrence & Lee's The Night Thoreau Spent In Jail. *He created theatrical magic*

184

opinion—this was a *star* on the rise. But not just a star—he was a truly gifted actor. There is a difference.

The second night I arrived at the theatre, anticipating another magical evening. The play opened with our welcoming home scene. He spun me around, hugged me, we exchanged a few lines of dialogue. Then, suddenly, he sat on the edge of the stage, his head bowed in his hands. What was he doing? Was this a new piece of staging? Maybe he was one of those Actors Studio types who can't repeat the same thing twice? He just sat there, not responding to my dialogue. Amazingly, because of his charisma, the scene was holding. The audience was completely with him. Then, suddenly, he raised an arm—"Ladies and gentlemen, I'm sorry but I can't possibly continue and give you the kind of performance you deserve or that I'm capable of." With that, he got up, then exited from the stage. I sat there, alone on stage, as stunned as the audience. The stage lights were lowered, the house lights came up, and the audience was dismissed.

I ran backstage, wending my way through the chaos in the halls. Nina and Beth and the stage manager, Bettye Fitzpatrick, were in a huddle. I tried his dressing room door, but it was locked. "Michael, it's Ray," I whispered. He opened the door, letting me in, then locked it again. "I think I'm having a nervous breakdown," he said, explaining to me what had transpired. His wife, Francoise (she'd been a ballerina with the Joffrey Ballet), who had been visiting during the Christmas holidays, had asked him for a divorce. He was cracking under the strain, he said.

As I left his dressing room, Nina immediately called me into her office, asking what they should do? "It was terribly unprofessional," she angrily said, "I think we're going to fire him." I pleaded his case. Yes, I argued, what he did was wrong, but his talent was so great he deserved a second chance. A rehearsal was called immediately. To everyone's surprise, his understudy, Joel Stedman, knew the lines of the long and difficult role. Consequently, they *did* fire Michael. He was stunned by this unexpected news, thinking he was irreplaceable. The next day I met him in front of the Rice Hotel to say goodbye. Just before hopping into his taxi to go to the airport, he suddenly grabbed me and gave me a strong embrace. "Thanks, Ray, for all your support." Then he added a bizarre line: "If I can ever do anything for you, let me know. I'll even kill you if that's what you want." And he was gone. I mulled that statement over for a long time. He had sensed my years of unhappiness, my heavy drinking, and my slow self-destruction. He was offering to end my misery, if necessary.

Joel Stedman did a good job as Thoreau, particularly considering he'd had little rehearsal. He wasn't Michael Moriarty, however. That incident spoiled the rest of my Houston stay.

Shortly after this debacle, Michael and Francoise (they'd temporarily reconciled) were in Los Angeles and attended a lavish birthday party Sandy and Jimmy Sangster had for me at their plush estate. At the party, Michael gave me a script, asking me to read it. He'd been offered the leading role in a new Broadway play, *Find Your Way Home*, written by the British playwright John Hopkins (who would marry Shirley Knight). It was a real shocker, dealing with a homosexual hustler and his victim. He said he was petrified of accepting the challenge. After reading it, I knew it was a sensational role. I told him he *had* to do it. And he did

He also became Broadway's newest rage. It made him a stage star and won him the coveted Tony Award as best actor of the season. On top of that, he picked up an Emmy Award for his performance as the Gentleman Caller in a television special of Tennessee Williams' *The Glass Menagerie,* toplining Katharine Hepburn, no less. Several additional Emmy awards would be in his future. I was so proud of him—I lived vicariously through his success. For several months we exchanged letters, but, after a time, this stopped and we were no longer in touch. Of course I continued following his career. His later years, however, seemed to be disturbing. In 1997 a tabloid paper carried a distressing article headlined: "I'M AN ALCOHOLIC AND PROUD OF IT!" I hope that was just fourth estate sensationalism.

After *Thoreau* I stayed on at the Alley for one more play, doing a small role in *Our Town*. I had been in Houston for about five months, on salary, so that had been a real blessing. Nina would bring me back, later in the year to play Lord Byron in Tennessee Williams' *Camino Real*, which she was directing. This was one of Tennessee's trickiest and most difficult plays, full of symbolism and obtuse characters. Lord Byron wasn't a large role—just one long and beautiful monologue. If done right, however, it was a show-stopping scene. I was looking forward to attempting it. I had seen the original Broadway production staged by Elia Kazan with Eli Wallach starring. The play had only moderate success at the time.

Our *Camino Real* turned out to be a very unhappy experience for me. For the first time Nina and I disagreed on interpretation completely. As I saw it, the role should be played in total stillness, in just a spotlight, with a very simple delivery. As a result it becomes quite powerful. Nina, however, had me gesturing all over the place and moving about. Also, the character should be in a simple, drab costume, but she had me dressed in silver tights with a flowing white silk shirt and a huge, shiny, silver cape. She said it represented the romantic poet. I thought it looked like a comic character out of some dated operetta. Between the costume and the staging, I was completely inhibited. I hated it. Consequently, I lost my voice during a performance, barely audible as I finished the scene. One night, there was news that Tennessee Williams, himself, would be in the audience. I dreaded the evening. Would he remember me? Did I *want* him to remember me since I thought I was so bad in the play? But I needn't have worried. When he came backstage two men, who seemed to be supporting him, were escorting him. He didn't stop to speak to any of the actors—he just gave a royal wave with his hand as he was assisted down the corridor. This was the last time I saw Mr. Williams. It was a sad remembrance. Toward the end of my run, I took the liberty of playing Lord Byron *my* way. In this instance, I was right. Simpler was better. As the lights would fade on the scene there was now thunderous applause. It was that kind of moment, if played correctly.

But it had been a bitter experience. A disaster as far as I was concerned. I decided I *couldn't* and *wouldn't* act any longer. I called my old friend, John Stevens, telling him I was quitting acting. He replied, "You can't, Ray, it's your life blood." "More blood than life," I retorted.

I wondered if Michael Moriarty was serious about killing me?

* * * * *

Because of our love for the theatre, David and I frequently went to see the different plays in Los Angeles, from the biggest theatres to the smallest. It was in one of these smaller venues that he first saw an actor named Ed Harris playing the small role of a cop in William Saroyan's *The Time of Your Life*. Even in a minor role, David had a knack for spotting exceptional talent. He also had developed a critical mind, being able to dissect a script, to see the positives and negatives in each individual production. And if he didn't like something he was quite vocal in his critique. His comments could be very witty and equally bitchy. At some social function he was spouting off his opinions. A woman named Carol Stone, overhearing his tirade, introduced herself. "You're such a bitch, how would you like to write for me?" The "me" was a publication called *Fashion Week*. She was the editor. "If you can write like you talk, you should be our film and theatre critic." And so, the former championship swimmer, the former model, the former furniture refinisher, the former salesman, the former mail sorter, the former actor— became a writer. It was the start of a course that would alter his life. Of course this new profession gave me a new job too. I had to type all his copy. That became an almost full-time job (except I wasn't getting paid for it). Before long he had branched out doing interviews, first with fashion celebrities, then expanding to chats with famous film and stage personalities. This led to doing interviews for a number of national magazines.

Of course, switching professions wasn't easy for him, either. He was a good actor and I'm sure he had second thoughts about giving it up. However, I think one job may have made his decision a bit easier. A few months before he'd auditioned and gotten a featured role in a tour of *The Impossible Years,* a Broadway comedy that was going to star television comedian George Gobel. David was playing one of several young men lusting after Gobel's teenage daughter. The actors cast as the young lotharios were all very attractive and, as it turned out, most of them were gay. The tour wasn't going well, however, and, despite George Gobel, it was not the box-office bonanza the producers had assumed it would be. And the reviews didn't help—"SUMMER STOCK ARRIVES EARLY," wrote the *Boston Herald Traveler,* or Elliott Norton's "A DREARY IMPOSSIBLE PLAY." When the show reached Chicago, the *Chicago Daily News* was particularly bitchy: "SUFFICE IT TO SAY, IF I WERE MR. GOBEL, I'D BE MORE WORRIED ABOUT LEAVING MY SON WITH THIS GROUP OF YOUNG SUITORS THAN MY DAUGHTER." Ouch!

David worked for *Fashion Week* for several months. And while the fashion paper wasn't widely read, his pithy and knowledgeable notices began to attract attention within the film and theatre community. They may not like what they read, but it was definitely readable and quotable. This led to his being asked to write a theatre column for the Hollywood trade paper, *Drama-Logue*. In time, he would also be a reviewer of plays and films for the publication, as well as a contributor of lengthy interviews with celebrities. That was a lot of writing. It was also a lot of typing—for you know who.

Lee Melville, the gentleman who said I'd been "curt" with him when he came backstage to congratulate me on my *Kataki* performance, way back in 1959, was made editor of *Drama-Logue* at the same time David came aboard. Melville was a definite plus to the paper, restyling it, enlarging it, giving it a professional gloss it had lacked. *Drama-Logue's* original focus had been on the latest casting notices—what was happening at the various theatres, large and small, as well as at the film studios. With Melville now at the helm, plus the hiring of better writers, the reviews began to take on greater prominence. It was a constantly expanding publication and like a bible to the young (and not so young) struggling actor.

While typing some of Galligan's reviews, I'd frequently scream, "You *can't* say that, that's cruel!" I'd try to rewrite some of his more scathing notices, attempting to soften the blow for the poor actor. Sometimes I'd succeed, but, usually, he stuck to his critical opinion. Getting a negative review is a devastating thing for an actor. I'm sure they've altered many a life and career. In our gut we know they're only the words of one person, but that one bad review is usually the one we remember—even if the others have been glowing. No question about it, within the theatrical community of Los Angeles, David Galligan was either loved or hated, depending on what he'd written about you that week. Agree or disagree with him, he did make an impact. Among our friends, the joke was, "Ray's the nice one."

TAKE EIGHT

Although I didn't realize it at the time, 1973 would be the start of a whole new life. It was only a part-time job, a temporary situation, I told myself, until my phone rang once again with an acting opportunity. Even though I had "quit" acting after *Camino Real,* and though we may be down and out, we actors are a strange breed. We always think tomorrow will be the day our luck changes. It's not a realistic assumption, of course, but it's what keeps us going. That thread of *hope.*

Through David's many dealings with press agents for his sundry articles, he was in contact with most of the public relations firms. One was John Springer Associates. Springer's West Coast outlet was headed by a woman named Donna Quinn. She was very young, mid-twenties, at most. She was also a dynamo, with an ambition to "get ahead." The fact she was very attractive, with flowing ash blonde hair and a sexy figure, didn't hurt her chances either. She and David hit it off immediately. One evening at some publicity function, she indicated that she needed to hire someone for her staff. He suggested me.

As an actor I had slightly known John Springer in New York where he maintained his main office. Besides being a crack publicist, he was also the biggest movie fan in the world. His client list was most impressive—and had been from the very start—Henry Fonda was his first client in the early fifties. And, in 1973, Henry Fonda was *still* a star client. He'd represented Marilyn Monroe for a period, and now he was swamped with demands for the most famous stars in the world, Elizabeth Taylor and Richard Burton. Veteran actresses like Myrna Loy, Sylvia Sidney, Maureen O'Sullivan and Martha Scott continued on his list as well. They were part of film history.

Donna Quinn, however, didn't really know that much about the "older" stars. I did. We were a perfect match. And so, I began my part-time association with John Springer Associates. At first I had very mixed feelings about the job, but, still, it was better than sorting mail and pounding out address plates for Walter Miles. The West Coast office was very small in staff—just Donna, myself, an adorable secretary named Vicki Garretson and Donna's boyfriend, Daniel. He wasn't on the payroll, but he should have been, as he was constantly around, assisting Donna in her upward climb.

My first major assignment was a lulu. It was a publicity junket to Oroville, California, a small northern community, where Richard Burton and Lee Marvin were shooting a new film, *The Klansman*. The producers were bringing in press from all over the world to publicize the start of the picture. An added attraction, and primary reason a lot of press would be covering the event, was because they knew that Elizabeth Taylor would be there with Burton. But as I was flying to my destination, all hell was breaking loose on the ground below. Elizabeth had stormed off the location when she learned that Burton had presumably slept with a young waitress, even giving her a ring. Of course, this indiscretion, like everything else they did, made worldwide headlines. This would be the first of their many separations.

Into this swarming hellhole I came, a novice in dealing with the press on such a massive level. There were easily a hundred photographers and reporters covering the event, now far more interested in the Burton-Taylor saga than in covering the start of a movie. I arrived at the remote location site, found Mr. Burton, and introduced myself. With a drink in hand, he nodded. He'd obviously had more than one beverage, I decided. In fact, he was quite intoxicated. And so, it turned out, was Lee Marvin. Attempts to get them to complete a scene were useless. But, from what I was told, that was the usual condition of the two stars while filming *The Klansman*, which turned out to be one of their lesser efforts.

The big press conference was held in the bar area of the local hotel. The two stars were at separate, large, round tables, with about a dozen reporters sitting at each table. They'd ask their questions, then another group would sit down and the process would start again. I was seated near Burton at a small table. Of course, he had a great gift for the gab, a real charmer, and everyone was laughing and having a raucous time. He was telling one of his wild stories, making sweeping gestures, and he attempted to stand to stress his punch line. Instead, he fell backwards into a bunch of plants. But, just as he fell, two men standing on each side of him lifted him immediately and he continued his story as though nothing unusual had happened. Perhaps it wasn't unusual. The men grabbed him with such finesse I had a hunch they'd played the scene many times before. I steered clear of Lee Marvin, but I wondered if he still had a giant dildo in his dressing room?

And that was my baptism in the world of public relations. Mr. Burton didn't even know I was there. But, as John Springer told me, the important thing is that I *was*. My second attempt at being a press agent involved the temperamental singing star Peggy Lee. She was planning a party, so I was at her Bel Air home, assisting as best I could. Although I had been a big fan of her music, I didn't become a fan working with her. I found her difficult and demanding and, from my point of view, often unreasonable. Every other day it seemed she was ready to sue somebody. She called John Springer after I'd met her for the first time, saying she "guessed I was okay, except that I shaved my eyebrows." That bit of false information didn't endear her to me either.

I had only been with the office a short time when I was asked to do a role in a new movie being shot in Vancouver, Canada. I would only be on location for a week, so Springer, who was very understanding, said I could do it. I would have done it regardless, but it was nice to have his blessing. A friend of mine, Jeffrey Bloom had written and was directing *Dogpound Shuffle*, a charming film centered on two hobos and a dog. English actor Ron Moody (who'd scored as Fagin in the *Oliver!* film) and television favorite, David Soul (*Starsky and Hutch*), were the stars, with Elliott Kastner producing for a Paramount release. I only had two scenes, playing a wealthy man who hires the two hobos (one's a dancer, the other a harmonica player), to entertain at a party he's giving. At Jeffrey's request, I'd let my hair grow very long, to my shoulders, which was the fad of the period (Springer hated it and bluntly suggested I cut it!). I'd first met Jeffrey when he married Pamela McMyler, who was also featured in the film. Pam was an adorable, fiery little redhead, a good actress, who had gotten a Universal contract after her performance in Steven Spielberg's first short film, *Amblin,* which had also started Spielberg's career. Pam and Jeffrey, both in their twenties, were particularly good friends with Jacquelyn Hyde which is how I became close with them. With David and Jackie I had many a delicious meal at their Sherman Oaks home. Jeffrey knew of my great desire to act and this was his first chance to help me. He was always very generous. He even flew David and Jackie to Vancouver during the filming. It was a real "family" affair. Later, producer Kastner and Jeffrey became embroiled in a big battle with Paramount and, eventually, they dropped their option on the film. It finally had a hasty release, but was sold almost immediately to television. Too bad, it was a very good film.

Donna Quinn, in the meantime, had talked John Springer into moving our small office in Century City to a very large suite in the same building on Avenue-of-the-Stars. At that particular moment business was very good, so Springer reluctantly went along with her request. He was usually very tight with money. But we were suddenly handling a number of important films such as Roman Polanski's *Tess*, which would get a best picture Oscar nomination and *A Touch of Class*, earning Glenda Jackson her second best actress win. We also handled Lina Wertmuller's classic Italian film, *Seven Beauties*, which garnered nominations, and Ingmar Bergman's devastating Swedish film, *Scenes from a Marriage*. Plus we were active with our star clients—the Burtons, Janet Leigh, Tony Randall, Shelley Winters, Liv Ullmann, Lynn Redgrave and, of course, Henry Fonda.

Donna, however, suddenly announced that she was leaving the firm. Although she was still seeing Daniel, off and on, she had met an older, very wealthy gentleman and they were going to be married. Although I still considered the job only "part-time," I was now made head of the West Coast office. It was a big responsibility. With business booming, I needed help. John recommended, and hired, a former employee of his, Kim Garfield, who had also worked in MGM's publicity department. Kim had just moved to Hollywood so it was advantageous for all concerned. She had the experience that Donna lacked. We hit it off immediately and became good friends as well as business associates. Kim was in her late thirties, I guessed, with short blonde hair and a voice that made Tallulah Bankhead sound like a soprano. Often a phone caller would say, "Thank you, sir," when conversing with her. She also happened to be a lesbian—and proud of it. We were busier than ever and we needed to hire additional employees. John's son, Gary Springer was hired (he was also an actor, and had appeared with Al Pacino in *Dog Day Afternoon*). And we talked David into joining us, though he continued doing his own personal interviews for publications, and his column and reviews for *Drama-Logue*.

One day, John Springer called to tell us that we'd be handling the debut of a new toy—Rubik's Cube—some Hungarian puzzle that would become the rage (and frustration, if you tried to unscramble it). The toy company had already hired Zsa Zsa Gabor—because she was Hungarian, we presumed—to be spokesperson for the unveiling of the puzzle. We all raised our eyebrows at their choice of celebrity. Ms. Gabor had a notorious reputation for being difficult to work with. Of course the toy company hadn't had any dealings with her—yet. A big press party was planned for the introduction of the toy, to be held at Zsa Zsa's gorgeous Bel Air estate. For this she would be paid a very healthy $25,000.

Ms. Gabor, in her sometimes-unintelligible manner, summoned Kim and me to her mansion. We were supposed to go over the celebrity guest list. I gathered together the office list of "star" names and addresses and we went to the lady's house. She was seated out by her pool chattering on the phone. Her face was lovely, with flawless skin, but she was considerably overweight. Hanging up the phone, she said, "Let's start, dahlink."

Since I didn't have the star names in any particular order, I rambled off the first name on the list. It happened to be Cesar Romero. Mr. Romero was one of the most charming and well-liked gentlemen in Hollywood. He was also very social with a reputation for attending "the opening of an envelope." Immediately Zsa Zsa screwed up her face. "Oh, no, dahlink, I don't vant no 'B' movie stars at my party!" Okay, I said, scratching a line through Mr. Romero's name. "What about Glenn Ford?" I offered. "No, no, dahlink, he comes to my house and drinks all my liquor and never even sends Zsa Zsa thank you flowers." Okay, off went Mr. Ford's name. "Invite Elizabeth Taylor, dahlink." I said Miss Taylor was in Europe. "Ask her anyway, she'll fly in. I was her stepmother once. She'll come." Fat chance, I thought. All right. She wants the *big* names. "How about Gregory Peck?" I asked. Another ugly face. "No, no, he's married to that French bitch!" Henry Fonda? You couldn't get much classier than that. Again, "I know he's important, dahlink, but his wife was only an airline stewardess." My blood was beginning to boil. He wouldn't come anyway, I wanted to shout! On and on we went. I mentioned the name of a prominent columnist: "I know ve should ask him, dahlink, because he'd put my name in the paper, but his wife's a kleptomaniac, you know. She might steal something." Then she thought for a moment—oh! how she craved publicity!—

"I know," she said, "we'll ask the toy company to hire security guards to follow her around." I almost laughed in her face; I couldn't believe what I was hearing. But on and on she rattled. "Ask that cowboy star." *What* cowboy star, I wondered? I wanted to say, "Who? Hopalong Cassidy?" He was the only one I could think of who might be in her age range. "You know, dahlink, he's so cute on that TV show." Who? Clint Walker? Ty Hardin? Michael Landon? It turned out to be James Drury, who had been *The Virginian,* but the show hadn't been on the air for some time and, as far as I knew, Drury was no longer in the business. "I suppose we have to ask Kathryn Grayson," she sighed. "She's a good friend of mine. But she won't come, dahlink, 'cause she's too fat." For whatever reason, two names she wanted were Cornel Wilde and Connie Stevens.

The toy company had provided us with very expensive elaborate invitations, which we promptly mailed to just about every star in Hollywood—except, of course, Henry Fonda, Gregory Peck, Glenn Ford and Cesar Romero—inviting them to Ms. Gabor's for the unveiling of Rubik's Cube. The very day we mailed them, happy that we'd gotten them out so fast, she called, frantic: "Dahlink, don't send an invitation to Cornel Wilde yet. First call him, ask if his wife is still alive. If she's still alive, ask him if she's still a drunk?" I was almost hysterical with laughter. And, wouldn't you know, the very first person to RSVP was Mrs. Cornel Wilde—Jean Wallace—and yes, she did sound a bit tipsy. And she *was* still alive! I no sooner hung up than she called back, screaming, "I can't have the party at my house! All those people will ruin my carpets!" She was adamant. Now the toy company was paying her a handsome fee for lending her "name" and house—but that was no longer going to happen. We had to scurry to find a chic restaurant that could handle the crowd on such short notice. Finally, we managed an arrangement with the Bistro in Beverly Hills. But that would cost an additional $25,000. The toy company was not happy to be sure. But it was too late to turn back.

The evening of the affair was upon us. She called again wanting me to invite some cable television interviewer but I couldn't understand the name she was saying. "Zsa Zsa," I said, "I'm sorry, but you're speaking so fast I can't understand you." "Vat do you mean you don't understand me! I do the *Merv Griffin Show* all the time and everyone understands me! Da whole vorld understands me!" Then she added, "You're stupid, dahlink!" I slammed down the receiver, hanging up on her. *"That's it!"* I hollered to Kim and David, "I won't work with her anymore!" And I didn't. Kim, trying to calm me down, said she thought she could handle her. "I'll call her back," she said. "Dahlink, thank goodness it's you. Dat Ray is so stupid!" Trying to change the subject, Kim said, "Oh, I've got good news. I think George Cukor is going to attend." Cukor, of course, was one of Hollywood's best and most respected directors. But apparently not to Ms. Gabor. "Oh, no, dahlink, ve don't vant no queens at my party!" I also had assumed that she'd be inviting her sister, Eva Gabor, but that question was answered with a haughty, "No, no! Why should I let her cash in on my publicity!" By the time this four-week nightmare was over she had us all in tears. On the last day of dealing with her, she said to Kim: "Dahlink, you're Jewish yes?" "Uh, yes," Kim replied. "Vell, dahlink, you're very nice for a Jewish girl." She did have a way with words.

And the party? I came to help Kim and David check in the guests, but I disappeared the moment I saw Zsa Zsa arriving. Even so, she almost didn't make it to the event. She'd called Kim earlier in the day to say she couldn't come as one of her pet dogs had died. *That* did get my sympathy as she did love her animals. The only compassion I ever saw displayed. Of course she made a late entrance at the Bistro. The room was jam-packed, but mostly with toy executives and their wives and friends. Very few celebrities showed. I did see Cornel Wilde in the crowd, but without his wife. Kathryn Grayson was there. She *was* overweight, but Zsa Zsa had more excess pounds on her own frame. I spotted Connie Stevens in the mob. One celebrity, however, attracted more attention than anyone else—and he hadn't even been on our invite list—O.J. Simpson. He would attract much more attention in the years ahead—*and then some!* To cap this whole bizarre incident? When the toy executive introduced her, Zsa Zsa took the mike saying, "Vye am I here, dahlink?" We all asked ourselves the same question. It's funny in retrospect, but at the time it was a publicist's nightmare. Rubik's Cube became a big commercial success, so, in the long run, that's what was important.

Some years later, when Gabor was arrested for slapping a Beverly Hills cop, I wanted to tell the judge that the best way to punish her was by banning her appearance on any talk show, and by ordering the press not to mention her name once. She thrived on the notoriety, craving the publicity, and she milked the incident for all it was worth, and, of course, the press and talk shows lapped it up. Her whole career was based on being a much-married celebrity, having little to do with her lack of ability as an actress. Fortunately, most of our other clients were much more professional and reasonable, my particular favorites being Henry Fonda and Janet Leigh.

And I was soon to add a new favorite—Bette Davis.

* * * * *

The next two years, 1977 and 1978, would be my banner years as a publicist. Ones I was proud of. It started when Springer phoned with the exciting news that we'd be handling the 1977 American Film Institute tribute to Bette Davis, a most prestigious event, saluting her lifetime achievements. She was the first actress to be so honored. Of course, John knew I had made *The Catered Affair* with the actress in 1956, but he wasn't aware that I'd known her far better after that. He said my having been an actor with her could be good or it could have the reverse effect, depending on her mood. I'd soon find out.

Well, the next six weeks turned out to be a positively marvelous experience, the most exciting time I'd yet had in my days as a publicist. First of all, I knew her career backward and forward so that part was easy I didn't have to do much research. Also, Bette knew how important this tribute was to her career, so she was on very good behavior. Of course, generating press wasn't difficult— the world wanted to interview her—so it became a matter of

A portrait of Bette Davis taken by famed photographer George Hurrell

who to turn down. Importantly for me, she liked having people around her she knew, that she trusted. We got her former makeup man from Warner Bros., her former hairdresser and we got the famous photographer George Hurrell to do a portrait sitting. She was house guesting in the home of a West Hollywood friend, antique dealer Charles Pollock, and every day I'd be there holding interviews and/or photo sessions in his stunning home. Then, after a full day of working, we'd settle down for the evening Scotch and vodka, usually in the kitchen.

George Stevens Jr., who produced all the AFI tributes, had lined up a stellar list of fellow stars to laud her. Jane Fonda would be host, with Henry Fonda, Olivia de Havilland, Robert Wagner, Natalie Wood, and Geraldine Fitzgerald among those who told stories of working with her. Over the years there have been many other AFI affairs, but *this* is the one that was the most exciting, and I don't think it's because I was personally involved. It was because Bette Davis herself *caused* the excitement. There was an electricity in the Beverly Hilton ballroom, just as there had been electricity in so many of her film performances.

The evening after the event, Geraldine Fitzgerald, who had played my mother in *Ten North Frederick*, was opening her nightclub act, singing Irish songs, in the club at Studio One, a very popular gay discotheque in the heart of West Hollywood. The club was always crowded, but word had gotten out that Miss Davis would be there that particular evening. The place was absolutely mobbed, with hundreds of young men (and not so young) lined up to get a glimpse of their idol. Geraldine, of course, was an old friend, dating all the way back to 1939 when they'd done *Dark Victory* together, and she'd promised her she'd be at the club opening. Bette's host, Chuck Pollock, escorted her, and the supper party also included Olivia de Havilland with Bob Osborne, Paul Henreid and his wife and I was with Betty Lynn. When we exited the club, there was an even bigger turn out of fans, cheering as Davis passed. Being a press agent, and an admirer, I wanted to say to some of the boys, "Hey, Olivia de Havilland's here too!" This almost equally great star was ignored in the frenzy surrounding Bette. Ah, fame . . .

During one of our Scotch and vodka evenings, Bette had said to me, "I like you, Ray. You're a survivor like me." I don't think she realized the depth of her statement.

* * * * *

The very next year George Stevens Jr. asked the Springer office to again handle the tribute. A reasonable decision, since the honoree was Henry Fonda. Like Davis, he was a joy to work with, a real pro. Again, I put my best foot forward. Fonda knew the value of promoting a project. He wouldn't do a lot, but he was always willing if the publicity had a purpose. Without a doubt, he was one of the most loved of all film actors.

And what a star turn out he had for his AFI tribute! Of course, Jane and Peter Fonda were prominent, but all of Hollywood, it seemed, wanted to salute him. There was Barbara Stanwyck (his favorite leading lady), Jimmy Stewart, Gregory Peck, Bette Davis, Charlton Heston, Jack Lemmon, Richard Burton, James Garner, Kirk Douglas, Gene Kelly, Fred MacMurray, Lillian Gish, Marsha Mason, Dorothy McGuire, Richard Widmark, Jane Alexander, Ron Howard, Billy Dee Williams, to remember a few. Jimmy Stewart, a lifelong friend, was particularly amusing in his speech. In 1940, they'd both been nominated for the best actor Oscar. Stewart won for *The Philadelphia Story.* The actor recalled it this way: "Hank, I admired your performance so much as Tom Joad in *The Grapes of Wrath* that I voted for you. Of course," Stewart added wryly, "I also voted for Alfred Landon, Wendell Willkie and Thomas E. Dewey."

While the evening was in progress, Bette Davis came frantically searching for me. "I've lost my speech," she said. "We've got to write another one, fast." So we quickly found an empty room at the hotel and sketched out something for her to say. Of course, being the pro she was, she didn't once look at her notes. As I was escorting her back to her table, with Jimmy Stewart, she said, "Come and get me the second this is over! I've got to get out of here!" I dutifully followed her order, and as we were fighting our way through the mob of people, she stopped suddenly, poking a woman's back with her finger. The startled woman turned. It was Cloris Leachman. "I'm Bette Davis," she said, as if the whole world wouldn't know that. Miss Leachman said, "Yes, I know." "Well, I'm doing a television movie and you just might be right to play my daughter," Bette said. Leachman took a breath, then said, "Yes, I think I've already been submitted for it." "Hmmmm," said Davis. Then she added, "I understand you don't allow smoking on your sets." There was a pregnant pause as Leachman regained her composure, "Well, I'm sure we can make an exception in your case." "We'll see," Davis said, grabbing me by the arm as we exited to her waiting limo. When the television movie was made, however, it co-starred the wonderful Gena Rowlands, not the non-smoking Cloris Leachman. You never know how a casting decision will be made, do you?

Over the years with Springer I spent more time with Henry Fonda than any other client. I'm sure I was at his stunning Bel Air home at least once a week. His wife Shirlee indeed had been an airline stewardess, but their lengthy marriage had been a very successful one even though she was considerably younger. She also had exquisite taste—a classy lady. During the course of one interview, Fonda said, "If you really want to act, somehow you will." I was sitting there listening, and his words seeped into my brain.

When his autobiography, *Fonda: My Life*, as told to Howard Teichmann, was published, he was too ill to help publicize it. Shirlee agreed to do a few interviews. One day I particularly remember driving her to a television studio in Hollywood. On the way back I drove down Santa Monica Boulevard between Highland and LaBrea avenues. She noticed all the young men idly standing on the corners. "What are those kids doing?" she asked. "Hustling," I answered. It was a notorious area for gay pickups. This seemed to surprise her. "I guess I don't get out of Beverly Hills enough."

The night Hank won his best actor Oscar for *On Golden Pond*, Kim and I were at the house. It was hard to believe, with his lifetime of work, that he'd only been nominated once before (*The Grapes of Wrath*, 1940). Of course he was too ill to attend the award ceremony, but, in case he won, we knew the press would descend on the house. Indeed, he did win, with Jane Fonda accepting in his behalf. "We'll be right over, Dad," she said, and sure enough, in about forty-five minutes, followed by dozens of reporters and photographers, Jane and her husband, Tom Hayden, arrived carrying the golden statue. Hank was sobbing as she handed him the award. It was a most moving moment. Ernest Thompson, the handsome young playwright who had written the play and the screenplay for *On Golden Pond*, had also won in his category and he showed up with his Oscar in one hand, Diana Ross in the other. It was a very special night.

Although we knew his death was imminent, it was still a great shock when the moment arrived. Of course John Springer flew in from New York. Joanne Carson, one of Johnny's ex-wives, and a friend of Shirlee's, called the office saying Shirlee was too distraught to make any arrangements, but she felt there should be friends at the house to offer comfort and sympathies after the funeral service. Who should I invite, I asked? "He loved actors," Joanne said, "call up everyone he's ever worked with." That was a wide call. Close friends like Jimmy Stewart, Dorothy McGuire, James Garner, Walter Matthau, George Peppard and Martha Scott, those were easy to think of. I knew Olivia de Havilland was in town, and they'd done a movie as well as a Broadway play together, so I called her. She seemed surprised that she was being asked, but graciously said she'd be honored.

Besides the immediate Fonda family, and all the Springer office, I suppose there were fifty or sixty mourners at the house. Shirlee, though in grief, was very gracious. Jane, however, was quite the reverse. She was furious. *Who* were these people intruding on her privacy? She went to another part of the house, refusing to welcome anyone. Jane blamed John Springer. Actually, I had done most of the

inviting. John tried to explain to Shirlee that Joanne Carson had initiated it and I had assumed it was with her approval. It was an unfortunate misunderstanding.

Peter Fonda, however, was a perfect gentleman throughout the whole ordeal. He and David particularly hit it off, and had a long, private conversation. He told David about the period of time when he and his dad had been estranged. One day, he said, he called Fonda senior from his ranch in

With a favorite client, Henry Fonda

Montana, and said, "I just wanted to tell you that I love you, Dad." Fonda hung up on him. Peter immediately phoned back, again expressing his love. Once again, his father slammed down the receiver. This effort was repeated a third time with the same shattering effect. Peter said he immediately got on a plane, flew to Bel Air, rang the doorbell, and when Hank opened the door, he again said, "Dad, I wanted to say I love you." At this point, according to Peter, the two fell into each other's arms, weeping, and it was the beginning of old wounds being healed. As David and I were leaving the house, Peter walked us to my car. He apologized for Jane's behavior, saying she hadn't yet come to terms with Hank's death. Although she had specifically produced *On Golden Pond* for him, hoping it would win him his long overdue Oscar, even that hadn't completely reconciled some of their differences. Now it was too late, Peter explained. It was a revealing conversation.

One last Fonda story. When they first started location shooting on *On Golden Pond*, Katharine Hepburn, as a good luck token, gave Hank a gift, saying, "This was Spence's favorite hat" (referring, of course, to Spencer Tracy). The actor put it on and wore it in the first scene they shot. During the course of filming, the actress asked him if he'd do a painting for her; sort of memento of their working together. Although not widely known, Fonda was a superb artist, and he was very flattered that she wanted a painting of his. As he said, "She is very rare. You don't come across a person of her caliber often." Once they completed filming, and he returned to California, he was unpacking his luggage and there were three items he noticed. Three hats. He knew immediately what to paint for Miss Hepburn. Painted in dry brush, on the left is Tracy's favorite, a beat up, brown, crushable felt. In the middle is his rain hat, and on the right, his tan fishing hat. The painting was one of his very best. He, of course, gave the original to the actress, but a very limited number of lithographs were printed of the painting, and Shirlee gave me one after his death. "Hank wanted you to have this," she said. He'd signed it, "To Ray, with warmest good wishes, Hank." It's one of my most prized possessions.

As for Katharine Hepburn, well, I only had the pleasure of meeting her once, at the home of director George Cukor. When she was on the West Coast she lived in his guesthouse. I was there early one morning sitting in on an interview he was doing. We were seated in the living-room, which had a big picture window, and I happened to look through the window just as a woman appeared, walking briskly down an outside path. As she neared the house, I recognized Miss Hepburn. Her body was wrapped in a large white towel, with a smaller towel fashioned like a turban around her head. Suddenly, she noticed that there were people in the living room, and she quickly scampered behind a clump of nearby bushes. "Oh, that's Kate," Cukor laughed. "She's going for her morning swim. She hates it when I have unexpected visitors. To punish her, I'll insist that she come in and meet you." A little later, he heard her in the kitchen area talking with his secretary. "Kate, get in here! There are some people I want you to meet." Minding her favorite director, she dutifully made an appearance. She was drying her hair with a towel, wearing no makeup, yet she looked magnificent. Such bones! She was most cordial, though not eager to join in any discussion. She also appeared smaller in stature than I imagined. She was such a giant on the screen, I guess I assumed she'd be a giant in person too. But most of the great film ladies, I'd noticed, like Davis and Crawford, were petite—they were just powerhouses on the screen.

Another incident involving George Cukor was at a private party Mary McCarty was giving. Mary was celebrating her new success as a co-star on the *Trapper John* television series. David and I were invited to the small gathering, maybe a dozen people, including Jane Powell and Alexis Smith and her husband, Craig Stevens. Mary, who had a terrific sense of humor, was regaling us with some story when the doorbell rang. She excused herself and I saw her conversing with a man at the door, but she kept shaking her head, as if she were saying "no" to some question. With a very perplexed look on her face she shut the door. Almost immediately, she returned to the double doors—unlatching both sides—pushing them wide open. Then she clapped her hands, "Ladies and gentlemen, your attention, please! I have the great honor to announce the arrival of a true legend in her own time—Miss Mae West!" We all dutifully applauded as the legendary sex goddess made her entrance—literally being held up by two aging muscle men. It was as though her feet never touched the ground, she just sort of glided across the floor, as if she were on roller skates. Then clapping her hands together one more time, Mary announced: "And another legend in *his* own time, Mr. George Cukor!" Again, we applauded as the director entered on the arm of a very handsome, very young Italian lad. *Only in Hollywood!* At one point in the evening, Miss West had to go to the ladies room (yes, even legends have to take a dump), but I noticed that her two muscle men, with arms folded and legs apart, stood guard at the door, making sure no one made a surprise entrance. As Miss West had once said, "Hollywood has had only three geniuses—Charlie Chaplin—and I'm the other two."

* * * * *

While John Springer was in town, I joined him in visiting with Irene Dunne and Gregory Peck in their respective homes. Over the years, John had produced several notable evenings at Town Hall in New York, with a retrospective of a star's career, showing film clips and discussing their lives and various movies. His evening with Bette Davis had been particularly successful, and he was to do others with Paul Newman and Joanne Woodward, Sylvia Sidney and Myrna Loy. Though interested, Peck and Dunne never did the evenings. Next on his schedule was the reclusive Lana Turner. After he left town, I met with my old childhood favorite. She was very nervous about the upcoming event and was particularly wary of the press, but the evening eventually became a great success.

Springer also decided during his brief stay that we no longer needed our fancy Century City offices, so we had to search for a cheaper place. We finally found a suitable suite on Santa Monica Boulevard in West Hollywood. It wasn't as elegant, but it was comfortable and, in many ways, we liked it better. Mainly because it was near our homes and we didn't have to fight the endless Century City traffic.

David insisted it was time we brought some new, fresh talent into the office, and he was responsible for signing up two promising actors, Ed Harris and Brian Kerwin, as new clients. Both were very fine actors that he'd gotten to know from seeing them do excellent work in the smaller theatres around town. Ed, in fact, had given one of the most exciting performances I'd seen when he played Chance Wayne in Tennessee Williams' *Sweet Bird of Youth* opposite a very talented actress named Karen Kondazian. He fairly exploded on the stage (in the nude, too). His histrionics made Paul Newman's film performance look pale indeed.

Another new client was the very young Drew Barrymore, who was about to enchant audiences in Steven Spielberg's blockbuster, *E.T.* She was adorable when she'd come to the office with her mother, Ildeko (sometimes called Jaid). Little Miss Barrymore could also be a spoiled brat. David and I frequently brought our new puppies, two adorable Shih-tzus named Brewster and Baybay, to the office. Of course, Drew was almost a baby herself, but she was old enough to know better. She kept picking Brewster up, then dropping him. David asked her to be careful. One day, however, she pinched the little dog very hard, making it squeal. David promptly got up from his desk and went over and pinched her. *She* squealed, running to her mother, who was talking with Kim. Fortunately, Ildeko sided with David; otherwise I suppose we could have had a child abuse suit.

I only had a few dealings with Elizabeth Taylor. I can't say they were particularly pleasant ones. They were after her divorce from Richard Burton. I had long been a fan, particularly for her beautiful performance in *A Place In the Sun*, when she was her most radiant, and, later, her stunning work in *Who's Afraid of Virginia Woolf?* But now she was drinking heavily, was quite bloated and no longer the great beauty she had always been. I also thought she had the worst taste in clothes—an Audrey Hepburn she wasn't. She'd had some falling out with John Springer and, after many years, was on the verge of leaving the office. I was a stranger to her, so she seemed very wary, pretty much ignoring my presence when I met her for the first time in her hotel suite. We mainly dealt with her through the gracious and beautiful Chen Sam, who always kept her cool and sense of humor, no matter how difficult Ms. Taylor got. Chen Sam told Kim and me that she longed to quit her job as Elizabeth's assistant, but she never did. She would soon become her publicist. At the Variety Club International gala tribute to Miss Taylor, Kim and I were seated at a table with Esther Williams and her husband, Fernando Lamas, June Allyson, Barbara Eden, Tom Troupe and Carole Cook, who was teasing Allyson mercilessly about her kewpie-doll looks. The minute the tribute started, Fernando Lamas noticed that it was being filmed. Scowling, he said, "Hey, this thing is being televised! We should be getting paid for being here." As soon as the camera panned past our table, Esther and Fernando made a hasty exit. At yet another Taylor tribute, I forget which one, we all went upstairs to her suite afterwards. Her hubby at the time, Senator John Warner, entertained us because La Liz locked herself in the bedroom and didn't come out for ages. Our one last encounter with the actress was when Kim and I visited her on the set of a television movie she was filming with Joseph Bottoms (I believe it was called *Return Engagement*). It was during a break and she was at the coffee machine, pouring herself a cup. Because she'd just recently recuperated from her umpteenth operation, Kim asked her how she was feeling. She snapped back, "Christ, how do you expect me to feel!" I've always regretted that I didn't really get to know her, for she's reputed to be one of the "great dames." Unfortunately, at that time in her life I didn't see the positive side.

* * * * *

During all my years at Springer I'd never discussed my former acting career with a client. Well, maybe Bette Davis, but that was different. In the late 1970s we were handling a festival of Swedish films being shown at the Academy, particularly featuring the masterpieces of Ingmar Bergman. Bibi Andersson, who had appeared in a number of his films, was in town for the occasion. She was a striking blonde actress, often a brilliant one. After spending a whole day with her, riding from one interview to the next, we ended up back where she was staying, unwinding with a couple of drinks. She said she was sick of talking about herself—something I'd rarely heard an actor say—and she asked me to tell her something about myself. The alcohol had relaxed me, so I told her that I had been an actor, had some success when I was younger, and that I missed it terribly. I explained that I felt a *need* to try again, but I was fearful of attempting it. She seemed to sense my anguish. Then, like she was a very sympathetic and friendly therapist, she took my hand, saying, "You must do it again, for yourself. Not for the glory, the money or the fame. Do it for *you.* Do a play, see if you still feel the same way. You may find that you no longer have that same urge or you don't have the talent you once thought you'd had. But find out. That's the only way you're going to find inner satisfaction." It was a sobering moment.

* * * * *

Bibi Andersson's advice was carefully stored away, but I wasn't ready to expose myself to more hurt and rejection. I thought of calling Nina Vance, to see what plays the Alley had scheduled, but the unhappy memory of *Camino Real* was still lingering and I didn't make the call. However, it was time for me to visit Houston again. Mother had fallen in the backyard, badly hurting her spine, and she had been confined to her bed for a long period. Since she could no longer take care of herself, Mary Ann and Clayton, out of necessity and compassion, sold her house and brought mother to live with them in their new, larger home. Although she could eventually move around with the aid of a walker, she never fully recovered and her condition continued to deteriorate. I know it was a very stressful time for Mary Ann and Clayton. It also added one more guilt to my burdened shoulders—that I had taken none of the responsibility. Exactly *what* I could have done, living in California, I don't know, but it compounded my feeling of my own selfishness. In October 1979, mother died. She was ninety-years-old. I cried at her funeral, something I hadn't been able to do for my father. I miss her to this day. Dear Aunt Ada hung on for another four years, again with Mary Ann and Clayton taking full responsibility for her in her later years. She was ninety-seven when she left us. Ironically, when I was in Houston for mother's funeral, David called to say I had an *acting* interview! From out of nowhere, a casting director wanted me to do a one-scene role on *The Rockford Files* series, with James Garner. And so I flew back to Los Angeles the day after the funeral and made my brief "return" to television. I felt guilty about that too.

* * * * *

My years with John Springer, for the most part, had been good, positive ones. I'd gotten myself out of debt—only to make new ones, of course—but having a steady paycheck was a luxury I'd rarely had. By now, my relationship with David had become one of deep friendship. Although we went through many a stormy session, our need for one another was strong enough to withstand my withdrawal, completely, from any sexual activity.

We had certainly outgrown our little apartment on North Curson Avenue— where I'd lived for over ten years—and, with the aid of David's mother, Patricia, we decided to buy our first house. While I liked the place we picked, once I was *in* it, getting to it was another matter. It was on a hillside right next to the Hollywood Bowl. During the summer months, particularly, the traffic and parking were a nightmare. The Bowl, of course, attracted thousands of viewers every night, so fighting to get to my garage was a major battle. Although on a warm summer night it was very pleasant to sit on the porch and hear the glorious symphonic music wafting through the hills.

A bigger negative than the traffic, however, was the increasing vandalism in the area. Our garages were set on fire, destroying several cars (fortunately, not mine). And one evening, while walking Mamie, our dear Schnauzer, I was in the alley near the garages and I found a man who had been shot. I wanted to call for help but he said he was only wounded and didn't want the police involved—drugs being the reason. An acquaintance of his showed up and helped him out of the alley.

The real tragedy, however, was coming home from work one evening to find Mamie dead on the bedroom floor. She had been poisoned. I figured she must have eaten something when I had her out for her morning walk, even though I had her on a leash. But our loss was only heightened by the mayhem further up the hillside. The grounds were littered with dead animals. The count had reached twenty! It was a massacre scene. We were positive we knew who the monster was that perpetrated this vicious act. A nearby neighbor, a little further up the hill, had recently landscaped his yard. Apparently a dog was continuously digging up his lawn. He'd left a warning notice on a telephone pole near the garages—with the ominous message—*Keep your dog out of my yard! Or else!* We tried to press charges, but the police said they could do nothing unless we had proof—and that meant actually catching him in the act. It was a cruel end to our dear Mamie's life. We had loved that animal, even more so because she had brought David and me together in the first place.

We'd been in the house for only three years, but it was unbearable to continue living there, so we put it on the market. It sold quicker than we thought and we hastily bought a duplex on North Genesee Avenue, on the edge of West Hollywood. This turned out to be a wise investment, as the other side of the duplex would help with the mortgage payments. David had superb taste in decorating, though his tastes could be on the expensive side. But, having worked at CBH Antiques, he knew good furniture and, when possible, he only wanted the best.

About a year after we'd moved in, our tenants in the other duplex bought their own home, and we talked our friend Marlene, who was still working at Farmers Market, into taking the apartment. She was happy to be near her "recreator." In time, David decided we *had* to have a swimming pool. I thought he was out of his mind, the expense, first of all, but when Mr. Galligan made up his mind about something, it somehow became a reality. Not a bad trait, necessarily, but one that could make the heart beat a little faster. Of course, with his excellent taste, it was a beautifully designed pool and sauna, surrounded by used brick. With all the plants and flowers, which he loved, the backyard was really most attractive. In time, he decided we should turn the garage into a pool house. Eventually, it was transformed into a marvelous little guesthouse, complete with kitchen and bath. David, of course, was a wonderful swimmer. I, however, mostly used the pool for cooling off after sitting too long in the hot sun. We had many a backyard pool party, with the drinks flowing like tap water.

One day we received a call from our dear New York friend, actor Billy McIntyre. He said Maureen Stapleton, who was one of his closest friends, was coming to Los Angeles. She *loved* playing movie star guessing games, he said, so would we entertain her with such an evening? We solicited the aid of Bob Osborne, who was a whiz at concocting fun movie games, and welcomed the actress to our humble abode. Maureen was, and is, one of the finest actresses, so we were honored to have her as our guest. To her surprise, and dismay, I beat her at the games. Devouring all those movie magazines as a child paid off in this instance. Maureen also liked to drink. After she'd relaxed a bit, we asked her to tell us one of the many legendary stories that circulated about her. A favorite being when she was filming *Bye Bye Birdie* at Columbia. This was the musical that had made Ann-Margret a hot new star—a "sex kitten"—as her publicity releases said. Maureen, with her co-stars Janet Leigh and Dick Van Dyke, were at some big studio function, with every male in the room panting as Ann-Margret made a late entrance. Loudly, Maureen shouted at her, "Sit over here, honey, it's safer! I'm the only one in the room who doesn't want to fuck you." It had been a long, but enjoyable evening, and it was nearly 3 A.M. before she decided it was time for us to drive her back to the Chateau-Marmont where she was staying. David and I had to practically carry her into the hotel lobby, laughing all the way. As we turned to leave, we saw her chasing the night clerk behind the counter. He ran for his life!

With the added expense of a new pool and spa, we decided to rent out the guesthouse. Gower Champion's hit, *42nd Street,* was coming to the Shubert Theatre for an open-end-run. Carole Cook, who was one of the show's leading players, suggested we rent it to Lee Roy Reams, also featured in the musical. Lee Roy had a big musical comedy voice and would practice his vocal lessons daily. His melodic tones seemed to fascinate Brewster, our male Shih-tzu, and he became quite enamored with Lee Roy. I think Brewster was playing up to him because he knew he was in a hit show. It paid off too. The dog in the show became ill and, thanks to Lee Roy, Brewster joined the cast. My *dog* could get an acting job, but I couldn't! It was just like the plot of *42nd Street*—you know, the star becomes sick, the understudy goes on, and is an overnight sensation. Brewster's tale wasn't quite so glorious, however. No Ruby Keeler he. He made the mistake of snapping at one of the chorus girls and was *fired*! Like my mother had warned me, I told him *girls can cause trouble*. Brewster would make a couple of other stage appearances in the next few years, but his tail wasn't in it and he retired at an early age. Lee Roy stayed in the apartment for a year.

That had been a happy situation, so we decided it was a good idea to rent to show people, for a limited amount of time. Some became long runs, however. In most cases, happily so. British actress Jane Carr, fresh from her triumph in *Nicholas Nickleby*, would be with us for almost three years, becoming a close friend in the process. Some other very talented people who stayed with us: Kelly Bishop, who won a Tony Award for her *A Chorus Line* performance; Barbara Walsh, so magnificent in *Falsettos;* and Olympia Dukakis' brother, Apollo.

* * * * *

During my years at Springer, I'd only done four small acting jobs, starting with the *Dogpound Shuffle* movie; one scene parts on *The Rockford Files* and *Medical Center*, the latter with Chad Everett, Arthur Hill and guest-actress Stephanie Zimbalist. The fourth effort was as a sheriff in a Mexican film called *La Ilegal*, dealing with aliens attempting to cross the border. It was directed by Arturo Ripstein. That came about because we were handling his first English-speaking film, *Foxtrot*, with Peter O'Toole and Charlotte Rampling. One day he was at the office and, to my surprise, recognized my name. He said one of his favorite films was *The Big Fisherman!* I couldn't account for his taste, but as a result, he asked me to be in his movie. Scott Wilson (who gave such fine performances in *The*

Great Gatsby and *In Cold Blood*) was the only other American actor in the picture. I never saw *La Ilegal*, however, so I don't know how it turned out.

We were very busy at the office, going from one project to another. One of particular interest was a ballet documentary, *Children of Theatre Street*, directed by Robert Dornhelm. Documentaries are not the easiest films to get publicity for, but I had no trouble with that one. The reason being I had Grace Kelly, Princess Grace of Monaco, as the bait. She had narrated the film and had come to the states to help promote it, agreeing to do a few choice interviews. We had a very private cocktail party in her honor at the Bel Air Hotel, and I had the pleasure of escorting her around. She was dressed in a simple gray suit with a scarf at her neck, nothing glamorous. She was still a very beautiful woman, but I had the feeling she really wanted to kick off her shoes, have a martini, and hear the latest Hollywood gossip. I mentioned that I'd played stock at Elitch's Gardens in Denver two seasons after she'd been the resident ingenue there (before her movie stardom), and that solicited a warm remembrance. "Ah," she said, "those were the happy days." The rumors were flying that she was having an affair with the documentary's

With Grace Kelly, Princess of Monaco at the Bel-Air Hotel

young Austrian director, Bob Dornhelm, but that was never confirmed. He'd just smile when questioned about it. It's pure assumption on my part, but I believed the rumor.

Besides Princess Grace, we were also very active with Evelyn Keyes' wonderful autobiography, *Scarlett O'Hara's Younger Sister*. David and I became quite close with Evelyn, frequently having drinks and dinner with her. She was always giving me hell about my smoking. Ditto Tony Randall, who wouldn't allow smoking on *his* sets. Janet Leigh was a particular favorite of mine, perhaps the friendliest and most accessible of all the stars I worked with. Like Davis and Fonda, she was a real pro as far as the press was concerned. I escorted her to several functions when we were representing her book. I particularly remember a tribute to Gene Kelly. We sat at his table and Janet presented him with his award.

Other projects that were exciting to be involved with were the Oscar campaigns for several films and players. We were thrilled when Robert Preston, one of the nicest, got his nomination for *Victor/Victoria.* Also when both Richard Burton and Peter Firth nabbed nominations for *Equus.* I've already mentioned Glenda Jackson's win for *A Touch of Class*, and Roman Polanski's best film nomination for *Tess.* Giancarlo Giannini, the Italian star of *Seven Beauties*, was a real charmer, and a deserving best actor nominee. But we were equally disappointed when Liv Ullmann's brilliant performance in Ingmar Bergman's *Scenes from a Marriage* was disqualified by the Academy because it had first aired on Swedish television. It was, by far, the best female performance of that year. Fortunately, the New York Film Critics thought so too.

Shelley Winters, however, was another story. We handled her autobiography and it became an instant best seller. Of course, Shelley was a marvelous talk-show guest, as she held nothing back, often saying outrageous things. But she could be difficult, frequently backing out of interviews at the last moment. I particularly remember one evening she had been booked for *The Tonight Show with Johnny Carson.* About an hour before she was to be picked up by a studio limo, she called saying she wasn't feeling well and couldn't do the show. She'd pulled this on other occasions, but I pleaded with her, finally screaming that she *had* to go. First of all, Carson would have been livid at a last-minute cancellation. I learned that if you screamed back at Shelley she seemed to relate to that kind of treatment. We made it to the show in time and, of course, she was a fabulous guest.

She later thanked me for "talking her into it." The appearance sold a lot of books too. Class, however, wasn't Shelley's strong suit. On a personal level, one afternoon, David and I had been invited to a brunch at our good friend Marisa Pavan's Pacific Palisades house. Marisa was and is a beautiful woman, married to my old friend Jean Pierre Aumont, who was in Paris. In her earlier days she had been nominated for an Oscar for her role as the daughter of Anna Magnani in *The Rose Tattoo.* It was a small affair—with her mother, Mrs. Pierangeli, French singing star Line Renaud, David and I. Actress Rita Gam was to be another guest, but she called at the last moment and asked Marisa if she could bring Shelley Winters— "Shelley's feeling lonely," Rita said, "and doesn't want to be alone on Labor Day" (it's not as if it were Christmas). Marisa hurriedly set another plate at the outdoor dining table. The two actresses arrived and we sat down at the table. Shelley's hair was still in huge rollers with a kerchief wrapped about her head. During the lunch, she proceeded to take the curlers out of her hair, placing them on the table. We all gulped, but kept on eating. Mrs. Pierangeli, however, refused to ignore

this social no-no, finally blurting out, "I don't know how you have such a beautiful child, it must be Vittorio's genes!" (She was referring to one of Shelley's ex-husbands, Italian actor Vittorio Gassman). The caustic comment didn't seem to phase Miss Winters, however. Good actress? Yes. Class? No. But I liked her, she was really rather sweet underneath the gruff exterior, and could be a pussycat.

We worked with some interesting personalities, all diverse, each an individual: Jessica Tandy and Hume Cronyn. Lynn Redgrave. Richard Thomas.

With Shelley Winters, backstage at The Tonight Show

Director Harold Prince. Harry Belafonte. Lee Strasberg. Sylvia Sidney. Alan Jay Lerner. Hope Lange. Anthony Quayle. Doris Roberts. Even Andy Warhol, Divine, and Tab Hunter. It was particularly satisfying to watch Ed Harris' movie career begin to rise. There's no finer actor working. There was also a woman named Charlotte Chandler.

TAKE NINE

In 1982 I received a phone call from Phill Thomas, who was working in publicity at one of the networks. He told me he had written a new comedy entitled *How Does Your Garden Grow?* He was planning a reading of it and wanted to know if I'd be interested in playing one of the roles. I first said no, but he was persistent, suggesting he drop a script by the office. The play was a homosexual comedy, with serious undertones, dealing with a bisexual young man torn between an older gentleman and his girl friend. Since *Boys In the Band* had been such a success (no, I didn't get to play in it when it made its L.A. bow some years before), I thought it wouldn't hurt to help Phill. After all, it was only a reading. Patty McCormack, who had received an Oscar nomination when she was a child for her despicable Rhoda in *The Bad Seed,* was going to read the girlfriend role. I would be the older gentleman. Bill Gamble, a very attractive young man, would eventually play the leading role. We did the reading, and it got all the laughs Phill had anticipated. Some months later, he called saying he'd raised the money to do an Equity-waiver production at the Cast Theatre in Hollywood. Waiver theatres were springing up all over Southern California as a cry from union members who wanted and needed a place to act. As long as a theatre only had ninety-nine seats or less, Equity okayed the movement. It caught on fast. With Phill twisting my arm, and flattering me, I finally accepted his offer. David, who hadn't liked the script, didn't know if it was such a good idea. But just being in rehearsal again was a joy, and it was *good* to be on stage again. John Springer even flew in from New York to see it. He didn't like the play either, but he was positive about my work and said he didn't mind my doing a play now and again, as long as it didn't interfere with my work at the office. The reviews were mixed, mostly negative for the script, which, they felt, was a series of one-liner jokes. Despite this, we ran for six weeks, and I enjoyed doing it. It whetted my appetite to do more.

Not too long after, I would try again. An actor named Nathaniel Christian was trying to produce the West Coast premiere of Michael Sawyer's *Naomi Court,* which had a moderately successful run Off Broadway. It was a real shocker, dealing with a homoscxual hustler tormenting a middle-aged man who had invited him to his apartment. Actually, the script was almost two separate plays, the first dealing with a woman who may, or may not, be losing her mind—with both taking place in an apartment complex named Naomi Court. The second act dealt with the above confrontation and was the meat of the script. The two male roles were terrific parts, but very violent and physical. Nat would play the hustler and, at Lee Melville's suggestion, I was approached about playing the man. The minute I read the script I knew I wanted to do it. Eventually, the money was raised (barely) and rehearsals were ready to start. But who to direct? Our offbeat choice turned out to be actress Mary Jo Catlett. Although she was now living in Studio City, when I first met her she was living just down the street from us on North Genesee; we had become very friendly with her when our friend Billy McIntyre houseguested with her. In New York, Mary Jo was mainly associated with musical comedy, being a particular delight in Carol Channing's *Hello, Dolly!* Since moving to Los Angeles, however, she had won the hearts of the theatre community with her wonderful performances in *Come Back, Little Sheba* and *Philadelphia, Here I Come,* and captured Los Angeles Drama Critics

Sharing a moment with New York friend actor Billy McIntyre and the great Fox star, Alice Faye

Circle awards for both performances. *Naomi Court* was certainly a dramatic change for her, but she turned out to be an inspired choice as director.

I'd suggested my friend Gertrude Flynn for the woman in the first playlet, but for some reason, Gertrude, whom I loved dearly, wasn't able to grasp the role. We decided she'd have to be replaced. It was a touchy situation, but I think she was relieved at the decision. Since we were about to open, Mary Jo had to step into the role, and played it most movingly. The production received very good reviews. The original New York production had received a strong notice from *The New York Times*—"A STUNNING, HAUNTING NEW PLAY THAT BREAKS YOUR HEART BEFORE INTERMISSION AND THEN PROCEEDS TO SKEWER IT WITH AN ICE PICK IN THE SECOND ACT." Our production would elicit similar praise. Polly Warfield, in her *Drama-Logue* notice wrote: "AN EXCITING, RESONANT THE-ATRICAL EVENT THAT KEEPS ON REVERBERATING IN THE MIND LONG AFTER THE LIGHTS GO DOWN." She continued with: "THIS MAY BE THE BEST WORK MARY JO CATLETT HAS EVER DONE, WHICH IS SAYING MUCH, AND RAY STRICKLYN'S MUTED, SENSITIVE DAVID AND NATHANIEL CHRISTIAN'S HARPER, A FERAL DEMON LOVER, TOGETHER CREATE AN EXQUISITELY CHOREOGRAPHED PAS DE DEUX OF MOUNTING TERROR THAT ENDS IN PHYSICAL, VISUAL FIREWORKS AND SHOCK." The important *Los Angeles Times* review was equally rewarding to read. Critic John Mahoney said: "AN EXTRAOR-DINARY CAST . . . BUT IT IS SO UNCOMPROMISINGLY SHOCKING THAT A FEW PATRONS MAY BE EXPECTED TO WALK OUT AT ALL PERFORMANCES." And indeed, that happened. The tension was just too great. We, of course, figured we'd succeeded in playing the author's intent. But it was brutal. At the end of the play, after the hustler's been tormenting me for an hour, the audience applauded wildly when I finally pushed him out the window, presumably crashing to his death.

This one I really hated to see end; but, like all plays, end it did. I really wanted to continue acting now, but that didn't look too feasible. Still, I received further encouragement when the annual *Drama-Logue* awards for "outstanding achieve-ment" were presented. Mary Jo, Nat, and I all received acting certificates. We were thrilled, me, most of all, I'm sure. I was tempted to write Bibi Andersson in Sweden, telling her I had followed her advice and the results had been very positive. Having had this little success made my days at John Springer easier;

certainly, I was happier. But in other ways, the job felt like a noose. *I should be acting!* As the months went by, however, I only had the memories of a rewarding experience.

* * * * *

Actress Hope Lange, however, would alter my immediate future. Hope had been at Fox when I was there, though I never met her. She had received an Oscar nomination for *Peyton Place* (1957) and had gained television popularity when she starred on *The Ghost and Mrs. Muir* series. Now she was a client at the Springer office. We were chatting one day and she mentioned that she was having director Jose Quintero and his friend, Nick Tsacrios, over for dinner. "Oh my God," I said, "I *love* Jose Quintero!" I then told her about my *Grass Harp* days years before in New York. "I haven't seen him since the mid-Fifties." She responded with, "Please join us for dinner." I did. It was just the four of us, and Jose seemed as happy to see me, as I was to see him. He and Nick had just moved to Los Angeles, and he was starting an acting workshop. He asked me if I was still acting. I said not really, but I had a great desire to try again. By the end of the evening, he had invited me to be an observer in his class. I couldn't wait for the sessions to begin. But first he was staging Tennessee Williams' *Cat on a Hot Tin Roof* for the Mark Taper Forum. He'd cast an unknown young actress named Kirstie Alley as Maggie-the-Cat. That was the start of her climb to television and film stardom.

His classes were a revelation. But they meant so much more to me now. I was older, I'd been through my own personal turmoil, and each precious word he spoke seemed to sink into my very being. I enjoyed watching the various scenes being done in the workshop, but it was his critiques that were so telling. Quite remarkable. Indeed, he was a poet to me.

Most of the actors in the group were highly trained professionals, but there were two or three novices, who clung to every word Jose would say. But I was doing the same thing, too, and, at times, I felt like a novice also. And I was just *watching.* One young man caught my eye immediately. He looked to be in his early twenties (he was twenty-four), was devilishly attractive, with an athlete's physique. He reminded me of the young Warren Beatty, or perhaps in today's market, *Batman's* Robin, Chris O'Donnell. He seemed to be just an observer, too, as I had yet to see him do a scene. I asked Jose who he was. He said he'd met him at the gym and his name was Sean.

Also attending the workshop was Karen Kondazian. She was a well-known actress in local theatrical circles, particularly for her performances in the works of Tennessee Williams, whom she idolized. She had scored in *The Rose Tattoo*, and also in *Sweet Bird of Youth*, the latter being the production in which I saw Ed Harris give such a powerful performance as Chance Wayne. One evening Karen approached me, saying she and Clyde Ventura (he'd directed *Sweet Bird*) were getting ready to do a production of Tennessee's *Vieux Carre* at the Beverly Hills Playhouse (the home of our triumphant production of *The Caretaker* years before). She said there was a role in the play, a Mr. Nightingale, that she thought I might be right for. I said I hadn't read the play, but I'd gladly look at it. I read it and fell in love with the character immediately. It was certainly different from any role I'd ever attempted. Mr. Nightingale was a heartbreaking character, a dying homosexual artist, living in a seedy New Orleans boarding house. The play was really autobiographical of Tennessee's young years as a writer in the French Quarter— the young writer in the play represented Tennessee, the older man a thinly veiled version of the haunted Tennessee. Other leading roles were the landlady (which Karen would play), and the prototypes of Stanley and Blanche (from *Streetcar*). There were also assorted misfits who wandered in and out of the Vieux Carre boarding house. It was a large cast.

I mentioned to Jose that Karen had asked me to read for the role. He suggested I work on a scene, present it in class, and see how it went. Good idea, I thought. I asked Jose about maybe doing a scene with young Sean, but he said Sean was too inexperienced to tackle such a difficult role. He recommended another young actor, who turned out to be *very* good. When the Springer office would close around 6 P.M., we'd rehearse in the office for hours on end. It was a very intimate scene, with the older man seducing the youth. It was very moving, also very sexy. At times it became difficult to remember I was only doing a scene. But I restrained myself.

In class the scene came off beautifully. Karen wanted me to audition for Clyde

Ventura that weekend. "Go for it, Ray," Jose said. "You can be magnificent in the role." That was all I needed: *his* seal of approval.

Although there were other character actors auditioning, Karen and Clyde told me I had the role immediately following my reading. I was elated. They finally selected a sensitive and attractive young blond named Robert Wightman to play the writer. In some ways he reminded me of the Michael Moriarty I'd known when we did *The Night Thoreau Spent In Jail*. At the top of the play, my character, Mr. Nightingale, makes his entrance accompanied by a handsome young hustler that he's picked up. The landlady rebuffs their entry however, and the youth leaves, much to my anger. It was only a brief moment, maybe a dozen lines exchanged between the man and the trick, but it sets up my character. Clyde had auditioned several young men for the role, but then asked me if I would like to choose among them. "It's your pickup," he laughed. I immediately replied, "None of them. I have the perfect choice for the role." And so, Sean, fresh from Orange County, was cast in his first role. It would be a momentous selection.

Milton Katselas, Eric Leonard, and Karen Kondazian were producing *Vieux Carre*. Milton was a prominent New York director, who had become active as a movie and television director. He'd also staged a well-received version of Tennessee's *Camino Real* at the Mark Taper Forum, with Earl Holliman and Karen Black starring. He also headed L.A.'s most successful workshop at the Beverly Hills Playhouse, which he now owned, filled with well-known television and film actors. He also had another theatre, the Skylight, which is where we rehearsed *Vieux Carre*. Eric Leonard, who became my number one supporter, was Milton's right-hand associate.

We rehearsed in the evenings, so, of course, I continued my daily routine at the office, though my thoughts were really focused on Mr. Nightingale and not the public relations world. Fortunately, Kim and David took over most of my workload, one of the perks in having your boss live in another city. Because of the intimacy of our brief scene, Sean and I were becoming friendlier; he was also relying on me to help him since this was his first play. But there was a simplicity in his playing, and he was handling his few lines quite well. I, however, was becoming more infatuated each evening. If I wasn't onstage, I made sure I sat near him in the theatre, watching the rehearsal. But there was nothing overt in my attention, and I was never aggressive in my attitude. I was too mature and too wise to open myself to rejection. But I felt truly *alive* for the first time in years, and I attributed that to the joy I was having in the rehearsals.

Vieux Carre was a very complicated play. Robert Wightman, as the young Tennessee, was a dream to work with. He was going to be superb in the role, that was evident. Michael Nader had been cast in the Stanley Kowalski-type character, and you felt there was an underlying intensity, a streak of violence that might explode at some unsuspecting moment, which was perfect for the role. I liked Michael. He was very open about his prior addiction to drugs and alcohol, which had been a setback to his once-promising career. His good fortune would be returning soon, however. During our run he tested for the running role of Dax on the very popular *Dynasty* series, and eventually was cast in the role, playing opposite Joan Collins.

When *Vieux Carre* was originally done on Broadway with Sylvia Sidney in the landlady role, it had not been a success. The New York critics were still being brutal in reviewing Tennessee's later works, from which he never fully recovered. After being hailed as America's greatest playwright, he was now treated by many

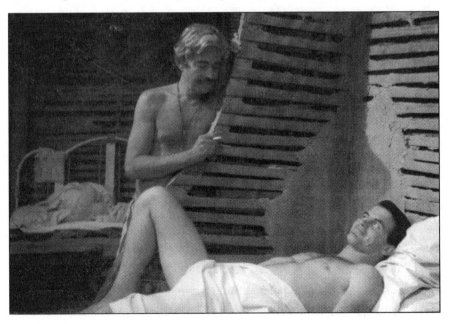

A scene not *in Tennessee Williams'* Vieux Carre, *but easily could have been, with co-player Patrick Taylor*

221

as a pariah. T*ime* magazine's review of *In the Bar of a Tokyo Hotel* had been particularly cruel, with the editor bordering the notice in black, as though it were an obituary. This led to a complete nervous breakdown, culminating with his brother, Dakin, confining him to an asylum. As I mentioned earlier, reviews can be very destructive. The London production of *Vieux Carre* was much better received with his friend Sylvia Miles as the landlady.

As Sean began to open up with me, I found out his father had recently died, from which he hadn't fully recovered. To support himself he was working at a health club, as well as distributing throwaway newspapers to local news stands. He would frequently stop by the Springer office during these deliveries, just to say hello. I liked that a lot. As far as I knew, he was a very handsome, masculine, twenty-four-year-old kid, who frequently went surfing when time permitted. Sometimes he would come sunbathe at our pool, and I would try not to stare at his firm, beautiful body. He was also quite handy with his hands, repairing the roof on the pool house, or doing any odd job I might ask him to do. And, as far as I knew, he was straight. I had rarely been one to make a pass anyway. I had had enough rejection as an actor without having it in my private life too. I liked the company of attractive people, but that was as far as it went. Besides, I told myself, in Sean's case, the friendship was more important. Of course, being as attractive as he was, he was constantly being hit upon by more aggressive types than me. But he wasn't naive and had to be aware of my growing attachment, despite my hands-off policy.

While this offstage drama was unfolding, *Vieux Carre* had its first preview. It was a disaster. Everything seemed to go wrong, plus the pacing was so slow the show ran nearly four hours, as well as there being numerous technical problems. The preview audience, consisting mostly of actors from Milton Katselas' class, were predicting immediate doom. We were all in a panic, particularly director Clyde Ventura. Day rehearsals were called and we worked late into the night. Slowly, the production was coming together, or it seemed to be. That was out of my hands anyway, and I had to concentrate on doing *my* best.

A week later we officially opened. Although there were still some rough spots, the production was enthusiastically received by the opening-night audience. "Bravos!" were heard in the curtain calls. A*nd* when I stepped forward for my personal bow—the applause meter rose considerably, with shouts of "Bravo" and even stomping of their feet! I was in shock. It was an appreciation, an affection almost, that I had never felt before. It was the most memorable night I had ever had in my long, frustrating career. I was stunned by the reaction. While most of the cast was out in the alley celebrating with the audience, I stayed, alone, in the dressing room, crying, with prayerful thanks. I finally joined the mob outside, immediately seeking out Jose Quintero. He greeted me with an enthusiastic embrace, saying all the special things I'd waited all my life to hear. I was *home*, at last.

Following the performance, Brenda Dickson, who was in the cast, was tossing a party in her luxurious apartment in Century City. Sean asked if he could ride over with me. In all the excitement I practically ignored David and Marlene, which wasn't intentional, but the ones we care the most about are usually the ones we're likely to hurt. Of course, the liquor flowed at the party and I had my share. When the soiree had ended, I drove Sean back to the Beverly Hills Playhouse to pick up his car. Not wanting this special evening to end, I parked in front of the theatre. We continued our conversation. He told me about his father's recent death, how close they'd been, his feeling of loss. I said my experience had been just the opposite, unfortunately. Then, for the first time, he voiced his feelings for me. If I were hearing correctly, his words seemed to be expressing more than just friendship. *Must be the alcohol,* I said to myself. *I've become a new father image.* I was so insecure that I couldn't believe he really liked *me.* He also said he had been fighting a drug problem, but he was sure he had it under control. Then he dropped the bombshell! "I'm bisexual, you know." No, I didn't know. Nor did I act upon this revealing information. It was the perfect opening of course, but not one I was ready to take advantage of. He leaned over and kissed me goodnight. Yes, it had been an eventful evening.

The notices for *Vieux Carre* began to appear. I was so starved for attention that I devoured each review. From the smallest publication to the biggest, my hunger was insatiable. I had poured my heart and soul into Mr. Nightingale and I desperately needed their approval. Miracle upon miracle, my prayers were answered: *The Los Angeles Times* said "THE STANDARDS ARE HIGH. RAY STRICKLYN SEEMS TO FEEL HIS PART TO THE BONE." Rick Talcove, writing in the *Daily News*: "A CONTINUOUSLY FASCINATING PRODUCTION. STRICKLYN ACHIEVES A RARE BLEND OF COMEDY AND PATHOS THAT ADDS UP TO SURE-LY HIS FINEST PERFORMANCE." "ESSAYED MARVELOUSLY BY STRICKLYN," added Bill Edwards in *Daily Variety.*

And the good news continued to pour in. Michael Kearns, writing for *L.A. Edge,* gloriously put it this way: "*VIEUX CARRE* WILL BE REMEMBERED PRI-MARILY FOR ONE THING: RAY STRICKLYN'S STARTLINGLY CONSUMMATE PERFORMANCE. IT'S A PITY TENNESSEE WILLIAMS IS NOT HERE TO SEE HIS LUMINOUS CREATION. HIS PERFORMANCE HAUNTS, TRANSCENDING TECH-NICAL ACTING PROFICIENCY TO CREATE MAGIC."

And Lee Melville, in *Drama-Logue,* brought me to my knees in grateful prayer: "THE FIRST TIME I SAW RAY STRICKLYN ON STAGE WAS A COUPLE OF DOZEN YEARS AGO IN A MESMERIZING, INSPIRING PERFORMANCE IN *COMPULSION.* THE HOLLYWOOD THEATRE WHERE IT WAS PRESENTED IS LONG SINCE GONE, BUT THE POWER AND SENSITIVITY OF HIS PERFORMANCE HAS REMAINED. HIS PERFORMANCE AS NIGHTINGALE THESE MANY YEARS LATER OFFERS ANOTHER TRULY MAGNETIC, MAGICAL MOMENT IN THEATRE. NEVER OVERSTATED BUT ALWAYS HONEST, STRICKLYN PROVES THAT SOME SUPREME ARTISTS NEVER LOSE THE GIFT."

I don't quote these reviews to boast. Over the years, hopefully, I've been able to see critical notices in a proper perspective. Somewhere between the pros and the cons lies the truth. But back in 1983, the *Vieux Carre* reviews saved my life. Literally. They were also quite humbling. Age and life had finally melded into my acting.

And at long last, I was no longer a juvenile.

* * * * *

With the success of *Vieux Carre*, I also obtained my first agent in years. Alex Brewis. Alex had a small independent agency, and was one of the few ten percenters who avidly covered the theatre scene. He had started Ed Harris' television career and appreciated good actors. In my case, it was like starting over again. My past career had little to do with the Ray Stricklyn of today. I was now a character actor, sporting a moustache that I had grown for the play, and my hair was turning gray. I was generally unknown to the new breed of youthful casting directors—I was a "new face" to most of them. Though many a time I wanted to reverse the questioning and ask *them* what they had done? It reminded me of a story Sylvia Sidney had told me. The actress had been one of Hollywood's premier stars in the '30s and '40s, and had continued to be active on the stage for years after that. In the '80s she was called in for an interview with some young upstart television executive. He asked, "What have you done? Do you have any film?" She answered with, "How much time do you have? A month? A year?" Understandably, she stormed out of his office. It was an insult. I've often thought there should be a school for casting directors to learn their craft too. Believe me, getting back into the business was even harder than when you're new and just starting out.

Now, however, I didn't have any unrealistic dreams about show business. The important thing was the *work*, not the rewards. *If* further good happened, it would be a pleasant and welcome surprise. This time I wasn't desperate, as I had been for too many years in the past. Of course, having the security of a weekly paycheck from John Springer was a great plus. Poverty for too long is deforming, it's humiliating. I knew that desperateness too well.

Yet I still had demons that I hadn't faced. Despite my newfound respect for myself as an actor, I was still drinking too much. But I wasn't ready to admit that, nor did there seem to be reason to be unduly worried. I never drank during the day, I wasn't an unpleasant or ugly drunk, I didn't drink on the job. I was in control—most of the time. *Most of the time*. That was the clue, but I wasn't ready to acknowledge that I might have a problem.

I lived for the Thursday-through-Sunday performances at the Beverly Hills Playhouse. The reviews, and word-of-mouth, had been strong enough that we were attracting sell-out audiences. Nightly, after the performance, Sean and I would go for a late supper, usually to Joe Allen's, a popular restaurant for film and theatre people. I always insisted on paying. While Sean would have a couple of glasses of wine, he wasn't a heavy drinker. I, however, was gulping down three or four martinis rather rapidly. I never seemed to be out of control, I was just unwind-

ing after a strenuous performance. I was on a high—from the performance—
and the continuing courtship of a very handsome and attentive young man.

One afternoon, Lynn Redgrave, a delightful person and a superb actress, had
stopped by the office to discuss a publicity campaign for her new television
series, *House Calls*, which was based on a Glenda Jackson-Walter Matthau movie.
During her visit, I received a phone call from Jeffrey Bloom, my young director
friend who had used me in *Dogpound Shuffle*. I said I'd have to call him back,
which I did in about forty-five minutes. After several years of marriage, Jeffrey and
Pam McMyler had been divorced, and he was now wed to a dynamic woman
named Carole. She was dark-haired, most attractive, very bright and witty and was
on her way to becoming a television producer. She'd also been married previously, to Dennis Wilson (of the popular Beach Boys singing group), as well as to
Christopher Stone. But the union with Jeffrey was *the* one and they were a strong
team, both professionally and privately. Anyway, Jeffrey was calling to ask me to
be in a television movie he was doing for ABC, which he'd written and would be
directing. The two-hour film, called *Jealousy*, would star Angie Dickinson and
David Carradine. He explained that it was only one scene as the sheriff in a small
community, but it was a good scene, with Angie and Susan Tyrrell, and I'd have an
effective monologue. He said he'd had some resistance from ABC casting executives, but he had been firm and insisted that I be cast. *That's* when friends
come in handy, if they push hard enough for you, which doesn't happen often.
The shoot was a very happy one and I was especially fond of Ms. Dickinson. A
nice lady.

Sometime later, I saw her at the opening of *Sweet Bird of Youth* at the
Ahmanson Theatre. She was with the director Richard Brooks (who thought I was
prettier than Debbie Reynolds, remember?). She couldn't have been sweeter. I
was particularly curious to know what Brooks thought of Lauren Bacall's starring
as the princess in Tennessee's play, since he'd directed the movie version. He was
a good friend of Bacall's, but he couldn't have been pleased with her performance, not after directing Geraldine Page, repeating her Broadway role, in one of
the great film performances. For my money, Bacall gave the worst performance I'd
ever seen by a major star. I'd also seen Shelley Winters attempt the role in a stock

production, and she had been equally bad. In Shelley's production, her Chance Wayne was played by a good actor named Terry Kiser. But he was so upset by the whole experience, that he'd given his notice on opening night. That was a time when I was desperately seeking work and had been submitted to possibly replace him (though I wasn't ideal for the role, by a long shot). I was supposed to meet with the director and Shelley after the performance. But as badly as I needed a job, I was so appalled by what I'd seen on stage that I went backstage at intermission, found the stage manager, and offered some excuse to cancel my appointment.

Meanwhile, back on the home front, David was preparing for his annual vacation in Mexico, joining his oldest friend, Hank Roberts, who had befriended him when he first arrived in Hollywood in the early '60s. Hank had been an agent for years, but had since retired and moved to Sag Harbor, New York, happily spending most of his time travelling throughout the world. Of course, David wasn't happy about my infatuation with Sean, even though we hadn't been lovers for years. There was still a possessiveness and, perhaps a fear that someone new in my life would drastically alter ours. But he was way ahead of me on that score. Yes, I was hung up on the young man, but I still had enough sense to know it was probably a fruitless pursuit in the long run. Besides the age difference, we really had very little in common, so far, besides *Vieux Carre* and the roles we were playing. But to David, Sean was a threat. Our mutual drinking didn't help the situation either. At that point in our lives I had been celibate for at least ten years. That's a long time. It also wasn't very healthy, mentally or physically, but those were the facts. Besides the play, Sean and I had been working on a scene from *Mass Appeal* for Jose's workshop.

David left for Mexico and the suppers with Sean continued. I had yet to make a pass at my young friend. But the impasse was about to change. Knowing David was away, Sean surprised me one night by asking if I would like him to stay over? Since he'd made the offer, I downed my last vodka and said yes. There was no sex involved, but after all the years of denying myself any kind of physical closeness, just to be near someone you genuinely cared for was an extraordinary feeling. I found myself waiting and wondering if the situation would occur again. It did the following weekend. Again, no sex, but I'd usually had so much to drink that just being held was enough.

But as Tennessee would say, the tables were beginning to "turn with a vengeance." I was becoming completely obsessed, being jealous if he had other plans, being possessive. All the things I'd hated when Dick St. John was pursuing me. I was acting like an adolescent, refusing to speak to him at the theatre, except in our few lines of dialogue in the play. Fortunately, I got hold of myself and we resumed our friendship. It was like a lovers' quarrel—without really having been lovers. The play was nearing the end of its six-month run, and I was dreading the final performance. Not only because I loved playing Mr. Nightingale so much and the approval of the critics and the audiences, but also because Sean and I wouldn't have that bond anymore. We shared three other intimate moments before *it* really happened. And he initiated that too. But doing the actual act was the worst thing that could have happened to our relationship. Although he'd said he was a bisexual, he now confessed that this was the first time he'd ever really been with a man. His guilt was immediate. I tried to console him, but the damage had been done.

From that moment on our relationship was on a different level. He was still attentive, but I sensed the relationship was entering its final phase. He said I was smothering him, giving him too many gifts and that my constantly picking up the tab made him feel less a man. The closing night of the play was particularly a traumatic one. All the cast was signing my company poster, and Sean wrote the most loving and tender letter on the back, telling me how much I meant to him. It was really very dear. But, in my neurotic state, I wasn't ready to accept him just as a friend. Our relationship had gone beyond that. I became angry, telling him it would be too painful to see him under those circumstances. I couldn't *just* be his friend.

Not only did *Vieux Carre* end the happiest and most successful time I'd ever had as an actor, it also ended a closeness that I had not allowed myself in many years. It was devastating to me. I felt like I'd had two deathblows at once. The loss sent me in a wallowing tailspin of self-pity and destructive behavior. My drinking accelerated. I'd make it to work each day, feeling like a zombie, but the minute I'd get home I'd start drinking, playing the theme music from *Somewhere In Time*, a

Christopher Reeve movie, over and over and over. Then I'd pass out without eating. Sean became a catalyst in a situation that had been building over the years, but one I'd refused to face or admit. David, of course, wasn't too sympathetic at first, but then he realized I was in serious trouble and pleaded with me to seek help. Michael Kearns, who was on the AA program, came and talked with me, but I was still in denial, and became angry with David for having Michael interfere.

Attempting to hold myself together for necessary work functions, I escorted Doris Roberts to some soiree. I had known Doris a hundred years before, during my New York Cromwell drug store days with Jimmy Dean; in fact, we'd met in that drug store. She was now a new client (starting her *Angie* television series, the first in a string of popular shows, including *Remington Steele* and *Everybody Loves Raymond).* She was also a good friend, and frequently David and I had been in her intimate circle of friends. On the drive home from the function we'd attended, I confessed the pain I was going through. She listened attentively and sympathetically, then strongly recommended that I join Alcoholics Anonymous.

Doris was very familiar with the program because her husband, a fine writer named Bill Goyen, had long been a member. I was frightened about taking such a step, not wanting to admit my disease. Generously, she offered to take me to my first meeting—on Sunday, January 19, 1984. First, however, we attended the morning funeral services for television producer Frank Glicksman *(The Long Hot Summer, Medical Center, Trapper John),* who, with his wonderful wife, Pearl, had become good friends with David and me. Following this sad occasion, we drove to the Cedar-Sinai AA meeting. I was very nervous as we entered the brightly-lit hall. I expected it to be a very gloomy place, with derelicts and bums, the cliche of how I viewed alcoholics. Instead, I was met by cheery, smiling faces, welcoming me. Also, almost everyone was stylishly dressed. It seemed more like a party—without booze, however. And, to my surprise, I recognized and/or knew many of the actors, directors and writers at the meeting. When the question, "Are there any alcoholics here today?" was asked, I hesitantly raised my right hand. And so, on January 19, 1984, I had my last drink. *One day at a time.*

The AA meetings were a godsend. They were often painful, yes, and it was difficult for me to "share"—to open up my gut and spill out my life story. But the people I met at the meetings were the most open, honest and understanding individuals I'd ever encountered. There was no room for sham or deceit. We weren't being judged. In listening to many others share, I came to realize that I was more fortunate than most. My traumas weren't nearly as devastating as those who had experienced murder, rape, drugs, jail sentences, fraud, incest, marital abuse, and disastrous driving accidents. And I was grateful that I had been spared those agonies. Still, our individual pain was all relative—and my life experiences had brought me to this point. We were stripped of our vanities, our arrogances. I attended three or four meetings a week, sometimes more, during my early days of recovery. When our friend Mary McCarty was in town, appearing in *Follies*, I kept remembering something she had said to David—"I've been up and I've been down. The important thing to remember is that neither place is permanent." Sage words, particularly pertinent, it seemed to me, to an actor. *Certainly this actor.*

The fact that I was finally trying to help myself began to ease the tension that existed between David and me. Sean was out of my life, at least physically. That doesn't mean I didn't still think about him. We'd seen each other a few times after the play closed, at Jose's house, and while our meetings were cordial, I generally steered clear of him, mingling with others at the gatherings. And though I wanted to embrace him, my hurt was still too fresh to talk with him rationally. Nor did I want to put myself in a possible situation where I might start drinking again. It was truly *one day at a time.*

During one of the AA meetings, I was told that I had a lot to be grateful for. That I was being given a second chance, not only with my career, but more importantly, with life itself. As the two were so interrelated, I vowed that I would do nothing to screw up this new beginning. Tennessee had said he was afraid if he got rid of his demons, he might lose his angels. I felt the reverse—if I got rid of my demons, I might find my angels.

* * * * *

If you're in show business, you're well aware of the annual Oscars, the Tonys, the Emmys, the Golden Globes, the Obies, and the Theatre World awards. Coveted prizes that all actors crave but few achieve. In Los Angeles, the most desired theatre award was from the Los Angeles Drama Critics Circle, followed by the annual *L.A. Weekly, Drama-Logue,* and *Robby* citations for "outstanding achievement."

The nominations were out for all the above, except the Los Angeles Critic Circle. My performance as Mr. Nightingale in *Vieux Carre* made every list, and, at their individual banquets, I won them *all*! Including Rick Talcove's and Bill Edwards' personal picks for the *Daily News* and *Variety*. It was quite a sweep, and I was indeed humbled by my good fortune. Thanks to AA, I took nothing for granted.

And when the Los Angeles Drama Critics Circle nominations were announced, sure enough, I made their list for "Distinguished Achievement by an Actor in a Leading Role." Jack Lemmon was also in the category, and you don't get much better than that.

Jack Viertel, a critic for the *Los Angeles Herald-Examiner*, was president of the LADCC, and he was producing the annual awards ceremony. As a reviewer for *Drama-Logue*, David was now a member of the organization. Viertel had a hunch that he would be a good choice to direct the ritual and David was approached. He first said no, but then thought better of it, saying, "Why not?" He had one stipulation, however—that the awards be presented in a theatre, not in a crowded restaurant as they had been in the past. The centerpiece of the evening would be a "Lifetime Achievement" award to a prominent theatre personality. This year they'd voted the honor to Robert Preston. David selected the Variety Arts Theatre, a beautiful old showplace in downtown Los Angeles, as the site for the presentations. In the past, the ceremonies had been a small, simple affair. With Galligan at the helm it would be an *event*. As Bob Preston had recently had an Oscar nomination for *Victor/Victoria*, David decided to aim for the big guns by asking Julie Andrews, who had starred in the film with Preston, to present him his award. Other members of the Circle said she wouldn't possibly accept the invitation, but she did. Then he asked another beauteous film star, Jean Simmons (who also co-starred with Preston in *All The Way Home*, and had recently had a personal Los Angeles stage success in Stephen Sondheim's *A Little Night Music*). She, too, accepted. Then he added entertainers like Donna McKechnie, Pamela Myers, and Laurence Guittard to entertain in song and dance, as well as the brilliant illusionist, Charles Pierce. It was shaping up to be a classy evening.

When the nominations had first been announced, I'd had a lovely wire from Bob Preston and his wife, Catherine, offering their congratulations. It read: "Take it from one who knows, the nomination is sweet, indeed."

The evening was progressing beautifully, first-class all the way. The final presentation was the "Best Actor" award. The superb actor Bruce Davison stepped to the mike to read the list of nominees. Then, he opened the envelope, and called out: "Ray Stricklyn for *Vieux Carre*!" I ran to the stage, received an embrace from Bruce and proceeded to thank Milton Katselas, Karen Kondazian, Clyde Ventura, Robert Wightman, who played opposite me, Eric Leonard, Jose Quintero, David, yes, even Sean, and most of all, Tennessee Williams, who had written such a beautiful role.

What a wonderful night it had been. Not only had I emerged victorious, but David had had a triumph too. After the ceremony, Julie Andrews grabbed him, exclaiming: "You should be directing the Academy Awards!"

The next issue of *Drama-Logue* ran a large photo of Bob Preston, Jean Smart

"Performers of the Year"— "Best Actor" winner with "Best Actress" Jean Smart, Lifetime Achievement honoree Robert Preston at the LA Drama Critics Circle Awards

(she'd won in the actress category for *Last Summer at Bluefish Cove*), and myself. Part of the accompanying story read:

> *TIME* MAGAZINE HAS ITS MAN OF THE YEAR, AND BOGIE HAS HIS 'WOMAN OF THE YEAR,' BUT WHEN IT COMES TO LOS ANGELES, THE MAN OF THE HOUR, THE WOMAN OF THE WEEK AND, CERTAINLY THE PERFORMERS OF THE YEAR ARE RAY STRICKLYN AND JEAN SMART. STRICKLYN MAY BE THE ONLY ACTOR EVER TO HAVE RECEIVED AWARDS IN THE SAME CATEGORY (LEAD PERFORMANCE) FOR THE SAME ROLE FROM ALL FOUR AWARD-GIVING GROUPS.

After so many years of rejection, my persistence had paid off. But heavy dues had also been paid before success was achieved. Rejection is a devouring enemy, the only haven from which is recognition. I was grateful to have been fleetingly recognized.

*   *   *   *   *

Perhaps the nicest reward I had from this sudden, unexpected acclaim was the response at my AA meetings. One bitchy comment, from an actor acquaintance upon hearing I'd won the award, was repeated to me—"He wasn't acting, he was just playing himself"—referring, I guess, to Mr. Nightingale having been an alcoholic. I took it as a compliment, after all, isn't that what good acting is all about? Using yourself? But there was nothing bitchy in the congratulatory hugs at the AA meetings. There was genuine good will and affection being offered. It meant a lot.

Also, through sharing at the meetings, I found peace regarding my father. Practically my last words to him had been "I hate your guts." Those four ugly words had resounded in my subconscious for years, with the guilt multiplying with every martini and vodka-on-the-rocks I drank. Now I could forgive him, and myself, for any wrongs that had been perpetrated. I also discovered that I *had* been like him after all. He'd given up on his dream to be an artist, and it had helped to destroy him. I had followed in his footsteps with my own career. Now I had been given a second chance. God willing, I could stop punishing myself.

* * * * *

David's staging of the Drama Critics awards was a start of a new beginning for him too. As his loving friends had said, "He's been bossing people around for years." Becoming a director seemed a logical next step.

The dreaded epidemic of AIDS was just raising its harrowing head, initially striking deadly fear in the gay community. The first person I knew who had contracted the disease was my *Vieux Carre* director, Clyde Ventura, who lingered for several years before finally losing the battle. Of course, there would be many more friends and acquaintances in the awful years ahead. Money was badly needed for research to fight this frightening disease, and thus S.T.A.G.E (Southland Theatre Artists Goodwill Event) was born, now the oldest and most honorable of all the fund-raising events. It was initially started by Michael Kearns and writer James Carroll Pickett, who approached David about staging a variety show to raise money for the cause. Once again, using the Variety Arts Theatre, David put together a magnificent entertainment, saluting the theatre music of Leonard Bernstein, and utilizing the talents of top Broadway and Hollywood musical players. Today, fifteen years later, the events have grown in size and importance. And David has directed every one of the evenings. He's received numerous awards for his efforts, including a commendation from Los Angeles' mayor, Tom Bradley. Eventually, he would quit his long tenure with *Drama-Logue* and the John Springer office to devote full time to his very active directorial career.

TAKE TEN

When I did *Vieux Carre*, a couple of critics had commented that I'd make an interesting Tennessee Williams, suggesting that I should maybe do a play about him. Being a procrastinator, I did nothing with the idea. I wasn't a writer. Tennessee died in 1983, shortly before we'd opened *Vieux Carre*, and Milton Katselas, who'd directed a successful revival of *The Rose Tattoo* in New York, as well as the L.A. production of *Camino Real*, wanted to do something to honor the playwright. He commissioned a sculptor to do a bust of Williams, which would eventually be placed in the courtyard of the Beverly Hills Playhouse.

Meantime, still basking in my recent glory, I had returned to the world of public relations with a renewed vigor. The difference now being my attitude and the fact that I was also beginning to have more acting interviews. One day I received a call from Eric Leonard, Milton Katselas' associate, asking if I'd be interested in putting together an evening saluting Tennessee, followed by the unveiling of the sculptured bust. Eric suggested I be Tennessee, but left the rest of the hour-long program up to me. I couldn't say no and the idea began to intrigue me. But *what* would the format be? I first decided that I'd do about fifteen minutes as Tennessee, perhaps reading his poetry, or some of the monologues from his plays. The rest of the time would be scenes from his plays, utilizing the talents of other actors. After discussing the idea with Eric, it was decided it was a little too similar to a special evening we'd had during the run of *Vieux Carre*. And a wonderful evening it had been too, with Maureen Stapleton playing Amanda in *The Glass Menagerie*, Eva Marie Saint as the fragile Alma in *Summer and Smoke*, and a radiant Julie Harris as Laura, blowing out her candles in the final moments from *The Glass Menagerie*.

I started doing research on Tennessee—and there was a wealth of material—but I kept going back to a most revealing interview he'd given to *Playboy* magazine in 1973, written by a wonderful writer named C. Robert Jennings. I thought it might prove difficult to get permission from the magazine, but I eventually tracked down Jennings' address—surprise—he lived in Los Angeles. But I didn't hear from him, so I kept searching for other material.

Then suddenly it dawned on me that earlier in the year (1984) we'd briefly worked with a woman named Charlotte Chandler, helping her with publicity on a book of interviews she'd done for Doubleday, *The Ultimate Seduction*. It was a fascinating group of interviews for, as Ms. Chandler wrote, "*The Ultimate Seduction* is not about sex, but about passion . . . sex was the ultimate distraction, work the ultimate satisfaction." It was a classy and diverse group she'd visited with: Frederico Fellini, Mae West, Pablo Picasso, sculptor Henry Moore, Henry Fonda, Juan Peron, and Tennessee Williams. I remembered her telling me that it was probably the last lengthy interview the playwright had given before his death, and that she had pages of excess material she hadn't been able to use in her book. I called Charlotte in New York, explained what I was trying to do, and she gave me permission to use her words. It was just a verbal agreement, no contracts were deemed necessary, as it was only scheduled to be a one-time event. Shortly after securing Chandler's okay, I finally heard from C. Robert Jennings. He thought it a splendid idea too, and gave me his blessings. I started adapting and combining the two sources. But as I was putting the material together, in a one-man play form, it kept getting longer and longer. No way, I decided, could I do this in just fifteen or twenty minutes. After discussing the situation with Eric Leonard, we abandoned the idea of doing any scenes, instead, going with an "hour visit with Tennessee Williams." "I have faith in you, Ray," Eric said.

I had loved the character of Mr. Nightingale so much, and it had been so successful for me, that I somehow wanted to keep the memory going. I decided to call the piece *Confessions of a Nightingale*. About four months later, Eric said the bust would soon be ready and the unveiling date was set for January 4, 1985. Invitations were sent out and the response was so overwhelming that Milton and Eric decided to add two extra performances. They, however, were busy with their own activities, and Eric suggested we bring in a producer for the event. Thus, David and Susan Obrow, with Mariko Ballentine as their assistant, were added to the project. Susan would go on to become Gordon Davidson's associate for the downtown Center Theatre Group, producing the top plays at the Mark Taper Forum and the Ahmanson theatres.

It was a formidable task I'd set for myself. I assumed Milton would be directing it, but his schedule was full of conflicts, so we could never coordinate our times. Of course, I really wanted Jose to stage it and, at first, he agreed, but he was equally busy. I also think he was a little wary of infringing upon Milton's territory. I was getting very anxious; the time was slipping by and I still had no director. Finally, I decided I'd just have to do it myself. And so I started the lonely, scary task of directing myself in a one-man show. But, to bolster my wavering nerve, I reasoned that it was only for one weekend, there wouldn't be reviews, so I'd just have to do the best I could under the circumstances.

Memorizing the script for an hour-long show, with you as the only actor, was a mammoth job. I'd hole myself up in my bedroom, learning it page by page, until I'd finally gotten through the whole script. I remembered a method of working that I had read the great Walter Huston once used. He said when he'd get a long play script, he would learn the words as soon as he could, repeating the words over and over until they were firmly entrenched in his mind. If I remember the method correctly, he'd have the words so at his fingertips that he could say them while tap dancing, while standing on his head, while being distracted. He could race through a script, saying the words by rote, in other words, nothing could throw him. Then, he felt, he had the freedom to do anything he wanted with the material. And that's what I tried to do with *Confessions of a Nightingale*. With great assistance from Jackie Hyde and Marlene, I learned the long script. Once I'd memorized all the words, I needed some kind of feedback, so I started doing portions of the piece at various outlets, trying it out. I did a reading at a bookstore for a poetry group, I took it to Jose's class, and I took it to Clyde Ventura's group at Theatre West. The results were very promising. The January 4 performance was fast approaching, with Milton arranging for actress Eva Marie Saint and playwright Jerome Lawrence to be the official unveilers of the bust.

The hour was at hand.

* * * * *

In my dressing room backstage at the Beverly Hills Playhouse, I was alternately excited and frightened. Dressed in my off-white suit, with sneakers and no socks, wearing a pair of horn-rimmed glasses, I sat frozen in my chair. I lit one cigarette after another. *What was I doing?* Did I really think I could hold the attention of an audience all by my myself for a solid hour? I'd thought of that daunting prospect before, of course. My one salvation was that during my AA meetings I noticed that we all sat spellbound, as a speaker would reveal his/her story, sometimes for more than an hour. *Those* stories held. And they weren't even actors. Or were they? Their dramatic tales were often better than any script. If you kept it simple and honest, it was possible to be compelling. I stubbed out my umpteenth cigarette, picked up a glass of prop white wine and headed toward the stage. There was no turning back now.

I nervously stood in the wings as Karen Kondazian stepped to the front of the theatre, welcoming the audience, telling a story about Tennessee Williams coming to see her perform in *The Rose Tattoo* on that very stage. Afterwards he'd stayed for a Q&A with the audience. This seemed to lend immediacy to the evening. Then she said, "Tonight, ladies and gentlemen, Mr. Williams is with us again. Please join me in giving him a warm welcome ... "

The houselights dimmed, a spot came up on a white wicker chair, center stage, and "Tennessee Williams" entered. Indeed, he was given a very warm welcome. Raising his hand, he spoke:

> Thank you, thank you. You act as if you think something wonderful is about to happen. Keep it up! Enthusiasm is the most important thing in life ....

For an hour he chatted, regaling his audience with bawdy stories—"I once asked Tallulah Bankhead if a certain leading man of hers was gay. She said, 'How could I possibly know, darling, he never sucked my cock!'"—He continued with horror stories, with wit and wisdom. Finally, the hour was over as he spoke his last words:

> And in the final analysis, isn't all of life just an attempt to escape loneliness? The search for another warm body, with a warm mind—ah!—that's the ultimate sex if it can ever be achieved. That's when the nightingale really sings!

The stage lights dimmed. The End.

There was utter quiet for a moment. Then, the footlights came up and I made my entrance for the curtain call. In one sudden, spontaneous moment, the entire audience were on their feet, shouting and screaming their approval! I didn't know what hit me, the roar was so deafening. I said a silent prayer and walked off stage, in a daze. *Did that really just happen?* I started to weep. David was the first to reach me backstage, quickly followed by Jose Quintero. He, too, was in tears. He had been so close with Tennessee, he said, that he could barely control his emotion during the performance.

And so began the most rewarding, the most successful, and the most frustrating experience in my career. During one night, during one performance on January 4, 1985, my life would be changed forever.

* * * * *

The response to *Confessions of a Nightingale* was so immediate that Eric and Milton said I must continue doing it, much to my delight. And so, for the next year, I would don my white suit and become Tennessee Williams on the stage of the Beverly Hills Playhouse, playing four performances each weekend.

A few days after the first performance, I was in my Springer office reading the morning copy of *Daily Variety. A*s I turned a page, I suddenly noticed a full-page ad. It was an "Open Letter to the Industry"—urging them to see *Confessions of a Nightingale*. It was signed by Eva Marie Saint and her husband, director Jeffrey Hayden. I was stunned. What a dear gesture, particularly from two people I barely knew. Of course, I'd been a fan of Eva Marie's for years—from the moment I first saw her sitting in a field of yellow daisies years ago at the Westport Playhouse. I immediately tracked down their phone number and called to thank them. It was the beginning of a mutual admiration society.

That ad, and the word-of-mouth, started the ball rolling. The press began to cover the weekend performances, with George Christy in *The Hollywood Reporter* leading the way, devoting his whole, widely read column to my "little show." Every performance was selling out. Next the reviews started appearing. Ray Loynd, a critic for the *Los Angeles Times*, wrote: "RAY STRICKLYN SCORES A SUBLIME ACHIEVEMENT. HIS PERSONIFICATION GOES BEYOND MERE PHYSI-CALITY TO EXPOSE THE AUTHOR'S VERY SOUL. AN ACTOR, FINDING THE ROLE

OF HIS LIFE." *The Hollywood Reporter* raved: "A BRILLIANT PORTRAYAL. STRICKLYN'S STUNNING SOLO PERFORMANCE IS ONE OF THE BEST OF ITS KIND. HE'S CREATED A THRILLING EVENING, A RIVETING, VIRTUOSO CHARACTERIZATION. A SPELLBINDING DANSE MACABRE." And Dick Lochte, writing for *Los Angeles* magazine, put it this way: "A CLASS MENAGERIE. RAY STRICKLYN'S TOUR DE FORCE PERFORMANCE IS TOTALLY CAPTIVATING AND REMARKABLE. HE DOESN'T SEEM TO BE ACTING AT ALL. A TURN THAT VERGES ON THE MIRACULOUS." There were dozens more, all glowing. Ernest Thompson, who'd won the Oscar for his *On Golden Pond* screenplay, hurried backstage to exclaim, "This will make you a star."

I increased my AA meetings to an almost nightly affair. I humbly gave thanks for the good coming my way. I had been sober for a year now and I wanted to make sure I'd make it to the second year, one day at a time.

George Anderson, who was associated with the Alley Theatre in Houston, caught a performance and went home raving. The Alley invited me to do a special "one-nighter" on a Monday evening, paying me a thousand dollars for the performance. Of course, I hadn't played there since the debacle over *Camino Real*. There was one major difference now. Nina Vance had died (*The Los Angeles Times* asked me to write an article about her) and the new artistic director was none other than my old childhood chum, Pat Horn, now known by her married name, Pat Brown. For several years Pat and her husband, Jerry, had had their own theatre in Long Beach. I had seen them during that period, and we'd tried to coordinate my doing *Look Homeward, Angel* for them, but, for some reason, it never came to fruition. Now she was head of the Alley. Of course it was great seeing her again. This was the first time, however, that I'd be playing my intimate show in so large a theatre. But it worked, so that was a great relief. Afterwards, the backstage area was jammed with family—Mary Ann and Clayton, of course, as well as dozens of "kids" I had gone to school with—forty years earlier! Even my old junior high sweetheart, Billie Joyce Tinsley, showed up. Sadly, after several good years as artistic director at the Alley, Pat Brown was fired from her position. I never heard her side of the story, but the charges were "misappropriation of theatre funds." She moved from Houston and I've not heard of or from her since. I'm sorry about that, for I had great affection for her. My one performance of

Confessions would be my swan song at the Alley Theatre. I returned to Los Angeles and continued my weekend performances in Beverly Hills.

Because of the outstanding press, Charlotte Chandler flew in from New York to see what her "interview with Tennessee Williams" had wrought. She was as surprised as she was pleased.

Charlotte Chandler was a mystery woman. Although I knew she'd written a bestseller about Groucho Marx, *Hello, I Must Be Going*, and her collection of outstanding interviews in *The Ultimate Seduction*, I knew little about her personally. Nor was I to find out. She seemed to have money, always staying at the Beverly Hills Hotel, where she was catered to like a queen. She also seemed to know every important heavyweight in the motion picture business—particularly the power moguls—the executives, the producers, the directors. Her rapport with these people was beyond having, perhaps, interviewed them. They, too, seemed to cater to her. Although I'm not good at guessing ages, I presumed she was in her mid-to-late fifties. Her appearance, however, would cause a stir. She was quite tall, appearing even more so with her gnarled mousy hair piled on top of her head, which, when rarely unfurled, would reach her waist. She also spoke in a whisper. You had to lean forward to catch her words. As I was to find out in the months and years ahead, her game was *power.*

"The show must come to New York," Charlotte enthusiastically stated. I was wary about that, but also excited that there might be a remote possibility. She returned East. Before long, she was calling me almost daily, whispering the latest "happenings" regarding *Confessions of a Nightingale*. Milton Goldman, her dear friend, and one of the powerhouse agents at ICM (International Creative Management), wanted to handle the project. He could move mountains, if he chose, she said. Also, Mitch Douglas, who was ICM's literary agent, would be handling the script negotiations, contracts, etc. Douglas had been Tennessee's representative for a period, so that was a plus in our favor. Next there were calls telling me that various New York producers would be flying to Los Angeles to catch a performance. "Was this really happening?" I asked myself? It all seemed surreal.

Over the next few weeks, four different producers had come from New York to view the play. All expressed interest, she said, but their main complaint was the length of the show. One hour just wasn't long enough for a full evening in New York. I would have to lengthen the script to at least ninety minutes (to be played without an intermission).

Fortunately, I had the luxury of the Beverly Hills Playhouse to experiment with new ideas, slowly adding additional material each weekend. Then, one day, Milton Goldman called to say a deal had been made with producer Jack Lawrence, who was a millionaire songwriter—having written such hits as *Tenderly*, Sinatra's *All or Nothing at All,* and the Ink Spots' smash recording *If I Didn't Care,* among others. He'd also written the musical, *I Had a Ball,* which had starred Buddy Hackett and Karen Morrow. He now owned two theatres in New York both in the same complex at 359 West 48th Street. He'd renovated the old church building into a beautiful showcase theatre. The large theatre was for Broadway productions, the smaller 300-seater was designated an Off Broadway space. He had planned to name the Broadway house the Tennessee Williams Theatre, in honor of the playwright. The Williams estate had opposed that, but after arbitration, he'd finally won the legal battle. The smaller theatre was the Audrey Wood Playhouse, dedicated to Tennessee's brilliant agent for all those successful years (before they had a devastating breakup). At this point, the theatre hadn't been officially renamed, so the marquee read as the Jack Lawrence Theatre. I would be appearing in the Audrey Wood space.

I was about to enter into the complicated world of contract negotiations—not as an actor—but as a "playwright." I was certainly a naive novice in that area. Mitch Douglas phoned to say—at Charlotte's insistence, no doubt—that she didn't want to share billing with C. Robert Jennings. It wouldn't be "classy," I was told, to have *Playboy* magazine involved in any way. The West Coast program had read: *Confessions of a Nightingale,* created and arranged by Ray Stricklyn from interviews by Charlotte Chandler and C. Robert Jennings. That was the proper wording, I felt. I *had* created the piece, I *had* adapted their words (Tennessee's, actually). Neither Charlotte nor Jennings had had any input in what materials of theirs I used. I had adapted it to fit my needs as an actor.

An ultimatum was issued by Mr. Douglas. C. Robert Jennings' material had to go. In many ways, it was the best material, the most powerful. But Douglas and Chandler stood firm—either Jennings goes or the production will not go forward.

All I wanted to do was act, but now I was forced to enter the complicated world of negotiations. Nor was I capable in such matters. I went to a literary agent at William Morris, seeking help. The agent offered to handle my end of the contract. This didn't set well with Miss Chandler either. "It only complicates matters," she argued. "We should keep it in the family." Meaning, of course, her "ICM family."

I hated myself for it, but I made the decision to go along with their agenda. It was either that, I was told, or a cancellation of the New York production. Also, they were threatening to not even let me continue doing the play at the Beverly Hills Playhouse, saying I didn't have a contract, nor were any royalties being paid to Miss Chandler. It was a mess. I had entered the ugly, cutthroat world of New York show business. I hated it. But it was to get worse. The new demand was that the billing should read "by Charlotte Chandler and Ray Stricklyn, adapted from Miss Chandler's *The Ultimate Seduction.*" And that was decided upon only after she'd tried to talk me out of having my name on it at all, other than as an actor. "Oh, Ray," she'd whisper, "you don't really care about the writing, you just want to act." For once, I stood firm, insisting that I be listed as coadapter—even though my name had now been relegated to second position. Naively, I assumed we could split the writers' fee fifty-fifty. Wrong again. She was demanding 60 percent, with Jack Lawrence, as producer, receiving 25 percent. That left me with 15 percent. *I had created it, for chrissakes!* But no matter how much I screamed at them, it was a take-it or leave-it situation. They knew how badly I wanted to act, and that was my downfall. I felt like I had been raped.

And so, under the worst possible conditions, as far as I was concerned, the contracts were finally signed for me to make my first New York appearance since *The Grass Harp* back in 1953. It was true, I did care about the acting most, but the whole negotiations seemed so morally corrupt to me. I suppose it's not an unusual behind-the-scenes situation, and the one with the power ends up being the "winner." I finally gave up—reasoning that the show probably wouldn't run anyway—and I must now concentrate on being an actor and hope for the best.

Understandably, Bob Jennings was furious at this development. I couldn't blame him and I felt horrible about it. It turned out he was also a fellow AA member, which I hadn't known, and that made me feel even guiltier. He blamed me and rightly so. He was threatening to sue, though there were no legal contracts between us. Morally, of course, he was right. But a higher power than ICM or Charlotte Chandler would settle the whole ugly mess. Bob Jennings had AIDS and would soon be dead. I hated New York show business.

While all this insanity was transpiring, I tried to keep mine by adapting the new material Charlotte was supplying to replace the Jennings material we were deleting. She *did* become more involved now, sending me reams of new ideas and suggestions.

I had wanted to keep *Confessions* running at the Beverly Hills Playhouse for a full year, which I did, thanks to the generosity of Milton Katselas and Eric Leonard. We closed on January 4, 1986. It had been a wonderful, exciting experience—until New York entered the picture.

* * * * *

Another phase of my life was about to come to an end as well. In early 1986, John Springer decided to close his West Coast office. I had planned to take a leave of absence during the New York engagement, but assumed I'd be returning to the PR world once that was over. After all, it was my security blanket. Alas, that was not to be. I was now, like it or not, a "full-time" actor, and that was a pretty scary proposition. David and I were terminated, and John got rid of the office space, though he kept Kim on for another year, working out of her apartment. It was the end of an era. My part-time job had lasted for twelve years. Little did I realize that my next one would last even longer.

* * * * *

No longer having to report to the office every day, I now spent most of my time at home, on long distance with Charlotte, Mitch Douglas and/or Milton Goldman. I tried to put the unpleasantness of the contract negotiations out of my mind—the damage was done—and I needed all my energies concentrated on positive images. Now Charlotte was all sweetness and light, my "new best friend." She'd arranged everything *her* way, so she seemed quite contented. Being a Libran, I can't stand dissensions, and I will do almost anything to avoid confrontations, usually at my own expense. Not a trait I am happy with, but that's the way I am.

There were other major changes happening, however. Although I had directed myself in the L.A. production, I had never been listed as such. Nor did I want to be. Understandably, producer Jack Lawrence insisted on hiring a New York director and he selected John Tillinger, who was enjoying a critical success with several Off Broadway productions, notably the works of playwright A. R. Gurney. That seemed a wise decision. A bigger problem was the set. My Los Angeles staging was very simple—it was a theatre stage with just a few set pieces, primarily the large peacock wicker chair, a small table, a desk and chair, and an old steamer trunk. Tennessee was chatting with the audience, as he had done many times in real life. It was simple and direct. Producer Lawrence, however, had other plans. His adopted son, Richard Lawrence, was a set designer, and a good one too. Without consulting me, though, they switched the setting from a near blank theatre stage to Tennessee's home in Key West, Florida. This changed the whole original concept of the show. I'd always been leery of one-person shows where the actor is talking to some imaginary person. That's why I made mine a direct visit with the audience. But by the time I got to New York, the set had already been built. It was a stunner too, and expensive. I was told they'd spent close to $50,000 on it. They seemed very proud of that. But as far as I was concerned, it was an unnecessary waste—the money should have been used, I thought, for promotion and advertising. From their vantage point, however, it was an opportunity to show off Richard's talent for set designs. I also tried to get them to hire John Springer to do the publicity, but I had no control of that either. John was upset, thinking I had the power to insist. But Ray Stricklyn had *no power* in this production. I was a hired actor, period. As I was still in Los Angeles, I didn't know any of the above was going on, however. I would find out soon enough.

Once again, it was time for the Los Angeles critics to bestow their annual awards for the 1985 season. My great good fortune continued. Again, I received *all* the acting awards, from *Drama-Logue* and *L.A. Weekly,* the Robby, as well as a new one, the Media Award from AGLA (the Alliance for Gay & Lesbian Artists in the Entertainment Industry). And once again, I'd received a nomination from the L.A. Drama Critics Circle.

This time, however, David wouldn't be staging the affair, as it was being held in the Blossom Room at the Hollywood Roosevelt Hotel, the site of the very first

Academy Awards presentations. The special honored guest this year was Jose Quintero. How marvelous! That made the upcoming evening even more special. Charlotte and Jack Lawrence were urging me to come to New York immediately. I stood firm, for once, saying I wanted to attend the awards ceremony. Charlotte said I probably wouldn't win since I'd had that distinction only two years earlier. She may be right, I thought, but I was still honored to be nominated, plus I wanted to be there to salute Jose. I stayed. I attended. And I won! When actor Perry King announced my victory, I received a standing ovation. It was a most moving tribute from my peers. I was deeply touched. The *Los Angeles Herald Examiner*, in writing about the event commented:"Obviously, the most popular win was Ray Stricklyn's."

I was now ready, or as ready as I'd ever be, to face New York.

* * * * *

It had been decided not to mention my awards in any of the pre-publicity. There had long been a superstition that any show originating in Los Angeles, no matter how well it had been received there, would be a failure in New York. It wasn't just a superstition either, as very few West Coast productions had repeated their success, at least critically. There's always been a rivalry between the two cities. New Yorkers can be very snobbish in their attitude—if it's not from New York, it can't be very good. Hollywood may be the home of that lower art form, the movies, but "good theatuh" is strictly Gotham's domain. That goes for performers too—if you're a Hollywood actor, you're not as good as a New York actor. Hogwash, of course.

We were set to open at the Audrey Wood Playhouse on September 23, 1986, following nine preview performances. Our rehearsals were satisfactory, though nothing new was really discovered. John Tillinger's direction consisted of having me move a few more times than I'd done in Los Angeles. But, as he said, he didn't want to fool around with what had worked so well. I was grateful for that. The magnificent, if unnecessary, set was beautifully lit by Natasha Katz, who went on to a prominent career in her field.

I must say, it was exciting to walk by the theatre and see my name on the marquee. That's a little perk that means a lot to an actor. The afternoon of the opening, I had finished my run-through, and I was standing in the backstage area connecting the Audrey Wood to the larger Lawrence theatre. Someone said, "Hi." I turned around and it was Lily Tomlin. "I just wanted to wish you luck," she said. "I know what it's like doing a one-person show." She had been at a meeting in the Lawrence theatre, but took the time to seek me out and wish me well. That was nice.

Another nice lady, but one I slightly knew, was Donna McKechnie. She really took care of me during my first weeks in the city. Donna had returned to her Tony-award-winning role in *A Chorus Line* and was, once again, the toast of Broadway. Every evening, on her way to her theatre, she'd stop by my dressing room to bring me some goodie or a remedy that would give me energy or keep me from catching a cold. We had first met when she danced and sang in David's very first AIDS benefit, the Leonard Bernstein tribute. She'd stopped the show in that one too, in a sensational number David had staged from *West Side Story.*

The September 23 opening seemed to go well. I was in such a daze I don't recall too many details. I know I was exhausted from the nine previous previews, plus added rehearsals, and I was coming down with a cold. I remember receiving a standing ovation opening night, which, I was told, from jaded New Yorkers, meant something. Whatever the reason, you can't beat that response. I recall there was a party afterwards at some restaurant Jack Lawrence had rented for the night and I sat with Sandy Duncan and her husband Don Correia. I remember Douglas Fairbanks Jr. being there (I didn't tell him that I'd raised the Iwo Jima flag behind him on *The Ed Sullivan Show* a thousand years ago!) and, of course, David had flown in from California, as had our friend, Lee Melville. Hank Roberts had come in from Sag Harbor. It was a warm feeling, having dear friends around, but it was a night that I was glad to see over. The mounting nerves and tensions had taken their toll and I was totally exhausted.

Then the agonizing wait for the reviews to appear. *The New York Times* and the *Post* were the first to appear. They were favorable. Mel Gussow, in the *Times,* said: "TENNESSEE WILLIAMS LIVES ON IN HIS MASTERLY WORKS, AND WITH THE HELP OF ACTOR RAY STRICKLYN WE REMEMBER THE DISTINCTIVE WILLIAMS MANNER." *The New York Post* added, "BY ALL MEANS GO TO THIS ILLUMINATING CONFESSION." I breathed a little easier. One notice, particularly, had actors, strangers to me, coming up asking if I knew how fortunate I was that John Simon had liked me. He was, perhaps, the most feared critic in New York, frequently writing devastating comments about actors in his *New York* magazine reviews. He'd written: "RAY STRICKLYN DOES A FINE JOB AS WILLIAMS. ALL THOSE SMALL MANNERISMS, TICS, IDIOSYNCRATIC INTONATIONS, HESITANCIES, SHIFTS OF MOOD ARE FRAUGHT WITH AUTHENTICITY. THIS IS HOW A MAN FIDDLES WITH HIS HAIR OR TOSSES HIS TORSO. THIS IS HOW A WRITER CONTRACTS AND STRETCHES INSIDE THE UTTERANCES, HOW HE RUMMAGES IN THE PAUSES BETWEEN THEM. THIS IS WHAT FEELING AND THINKING ONE'S WORDS LOOKS LIKE. THE AUTHORS HAVE ORGANIZED THEIR MATERIAL WITH IMPRESSIVE SKILL." There were dozens of other reviews that appeared, decidedly mixed in their opinions, with two being particularly negative—the *Village Voice* and *Variety*. They hurt, believe me. I'm sure there were other negative ones, but I never read them. The publicist was considerate enough to put the reviews in two separate envelopes—one with positive notices, the other "to be read when you're feeling good about yourself." I never opened it. Why? I would allow the negative ones to practically paralyze me, so I saw no constructive benefit in reading them if I could avoid it.

About a week after we opened, the important *Time* magazine notice hit the newsstands, with a full-page review and a color photo. Critic William A. Henry III wrote: "UNMISTAKABLY A PERFORMANCE, AN INGRATIATING SALTY INTERPRETATION OF WILLIAMS. THE FLAVOR IS AUTHENTIC AND STRICKLYN'S PSYCHOLOGICAL INTERPRETATION ENGROSSINGLY SUCCEEDS, GIVING POIGNANT LIFE TO WILLIAMS' YEARNING." That particular review would prove a valuable one in the very near future.

The show wasn't a smash hit, maybe, but we weren't a total disaster either. I knew, going in, that *Confessions of a Nightingale* wasn't a typical commercial property, and I saw it as a "special event." Although we easily could have run longer, producer Lawrence closed the show after sixty-six performances. Certainly, it was an inexpensive show to operate, plus he *owned* the theatre, and he was only paying me a thousand a week. But he was now bored with it, plus he and Richard were planning an extended trip to Europe and that seemed to be their number one priority.

But, oddly, I wasn't too unhappy to see the engagement end. I was sick with a cold half the time, which was very debilitating, and I also missed David and Brewster and Baybay. Milton Goldman was always most considerate, taking me to lunches at the Russian Tea Room, where he was always given the very best table and was treated like a king—with celebrities popping by the table to say hello. Kim Novak, for one. And John Springer was with critic Rex Reed one day, and we joined them for a spell. I was a great admirer of Reed's writing, having read all his books of celebrity interviews.

During the run of the play, however, one very positive thing happened. Because of the *Time* review, Milton Goldman had had a call from the Cleveland Play House. They had a special-event series where they brought in famous stars for a performance. Frank Langella had been announced to do a one-man piece, but for some reason, had to back out at the last moment. The event coordinators in Cleveland happened to read the *Time* notice, and asked him about my availability to replace Langella. The performance was on a Monday, which was my day off, so after arguing with Jack Lawrence, he finally consented to my doing it. The good news, thanks to Goldman's negotiation, was that they would pay me $6,000 for the performance. Now, *that* was a good fee! It also made me aware that perhaps there was a life for *Confessions* after New York. I flew to Cleveland, did the performance, and the management asked me if I would like to come back for an extended run once I'd closed in New York. Suddenly, all wasn't so black after all. Also, ICM's Mitch Douglas was closing the deal for *Confessions of a Nightingale* to be published by Samuel French, Inc. Now I was going to be an in-print playwright—well, a coadapter, anyway.

Following my closing, Milton Goldman tossed a "farewell" party for me at a restaurant. Of course, it was really done for Charlotte, but, whatever, it was a pleasant evening. He'd invited several of his celebrity friends—Douglas Fairbanks Jr., Joan Bennett, Vivian Blaine (she'd seen the show in Cleveland), Sylvia Miles, and Anne Meara. I'd asked a handsome young singer from Los Angeles, Brian Lane Green, who was starring on Broadway as Huck Finn in *Big River*, to be my guest. If I'd allowed myself a new fantasy, I would have been his Tom Sawyer, but, wisely, there would be no more Sean's in my life. The next morning I flew home to Los Angeles. And happy to do so.

* * * * *

On the home front, David's directing career was progressing steadily. Thanks to Eric Leonard and Milton Katselas, he'd staged a superb production of Leonard Bernstein's difficult musical, an opera almost, *Trouble In Tahiti*, at the Skylight Theatre. He had Laurence Guittard and Eileen Barnett as his leads, and a young girl named Dale Kristien in the supporting cast. She would be heard from in the years ahead—when she starred opposite Michael Crawford in the Los Angeles production of *The Phantom of the Opera*. He did have a knack for casting. Another production would be *Gift of the Magi*, done at the Coast Playhouse, with a sterling cast including Bill Hutton, who'd starred in the original Broadway production of *Joseph and the Amazing Technicolor Dreamcoat*, Dale Kristien, Jane Carr, B. D. Wong, and Lindy Robbins. He co-created, with Billy Barnes and Ron Abel, a delightful musical revue entitled *Blame It on the Movies*, which would move on to Burt Reynolds' theatre in Jupiter, Florida, before he restaged it for an Off Broadway engagement. As recently as 1998, he revived it for the Pasadena Playhouse's main stage. A real audience-pleaser. He would also do a sequel, which would be equally popular. Interspersed with these activities, of course, were the annual AIDS benefits. For the Mark Taper Forum he'd also do Lanford Wilson's *A Poster of the Cosmos*, with Brian Kerwin, as well as staging *An Evening with Noel Coward*, a special event at the Taper, with an all-star cast, including Frank Langella, as Coward, Tyne Daly, Nathan Lane, Roger Rees, Jane Carr, Linda Purl, Lu Leonard, Roscoe Lee Browne, Karen Morrow, etc. He'd also direct the 25th Anniversary Salute to the Center Theatre Group, honoring Robert Fryer and Gordon Davidson, as well as the dedication ceremonies for the reopening of the Ahmanson Theatre, headlining Gregory Peck, Charlton Heston and Lynn Redgrave. Along the way he'd pick up several *Drama-Logue* awards: one for his direction of *Lettice & Lovage*, toplining Jane Carr and Mary Jo Catlett, for the Pasadena Playhouse; another citation for an original musical he created, *The Gay '90s Musical* (which was recorded by the Varsese Sarabande label); as well as another new musical, *Lullaby of Broadway: The Life & Lyrics of Al Dubin*, with a book by our close friend Joel Kimmel. He also staged a unique version of *Cabaret*, with an all-Asian cast, which led to his going to Singapore to stage *The Fantasticks* for the Singapore Repertory

Theatre. So, as you can see, he's kept very active over the years. And, hopefully, will continue to do so.

* * * * *

Although I was glad to be home from the chaos of New York, my stay was brief. It was time to hit the road. I fulfilled my seven-week return engagement at the Cleveland Play House, then *Confessions* was booked for a two-month stand in Chicago, arranged by Charlotte. The show received unanimous raves—this is what New York should have been! *The Chicago Tribune's* Richard Christiansen wrote: "THE MATERIAL IS GIVEN FRESH POWER BY STRICKLYN'S DELIVERY, CREATING MOMENTS OF GREAT POIGNANCY. THE ACTOR HAS DONE A TRUE AND FAITHFUL JOB OF RECREATING WILLIAMS. THROUGH DETAILS OF VOICE, GESTURE AND BODILY MOVEMENT, HE PAINTS A CLEAR PHYSICAL PORTRAIT, AND, MORE IMPORTANTLY, HE CAPTURES THE SPIRIT OF DEFI-ANCE AND VULNERABILITY. HE HAS MASTERED THE QUICK CACKLE AND THE RUSH OF WORDS, SHIFTING FROM TEARS TO LAUGHTER WITH SUDDEN, STARTLING EFFECT."

And the *Windy City Times* commented: "RAY STRICKLYN'S GREAT TRIUMPH JOINS THE RANKS OF THE CLICK SOLO SHOWS OF HENRY FONDA, JULIE HARRIS, HAL HOLBROOK AND JAMES WHITMORE. AN EXTRAORDINARY, BRILLIANT ONE-MAN PERFORMANCE. DON'T MISS IT."

But it was the review of the *Chicago City Star* that I particularly liked, not just because it was a lovely notice, but because it captured what I had tried to do when I was first putting the show together—to give an essence of Williams, not a clone-like impersonation. The notice read: "IN A ONE-PERSON DRAMATIZA-TION YOU CAN MARVEL AT HOW MUCH THE ACTOR LOOKS AND SOUNDS LIKE THE INDIVIDUAL, BUT WHEN IT HAPPENS IT TURNS THE PERFORMANCE INTO A STUNT RATHER THAN THEATRE. WE MARVEL AT THE IMITATION. THERE IS ABSOLUTELY NO PROBLEM OF THIS KIND AT ALL WITH RAY STRICK-LYN'S PERFORMANCE. IT IS VERY POLISHED AND RINGS ABSOLUTELY TRUE FROM OPENING TO CLOSE. THE REASON IT DOES IS BECAUSE OUR VISION OF WILLIAMS IS BEING CREATED RIGHT BEFORE OUR EYES."

I played large theatres, I played small theatres, and I played colleges. For a solid year I was booked—San Francisco, Pittsburgh, North Carolina, South Carolina, Denver, Texas, San Diego, Long Beach, St. Louis, and Palm Springs. Even Independence, Kansas, for the William Inge Festival, with many noted playwrights in my audience—Robert Anderson, Horton Foote, Jerry Lawrence, and John Patrick.

The only negative experience was in Washington, D.C. First, it was during a heat wave and the air conditioning wasn't working in the theatre, so that was a misery for both audience and actor. All the reviews were favorable—except one—the most important one—*The Washington Post*. Critic David Richards wrote a scathing notice. The theatre management tried to console me, saying he'd done the same to such great actresses as Colleen Dewhurst when she did a one-woman play, *Carlotta*, based on the widow of Eugene O'Neill, and Zoe Caldwell had fared no better when she tackled a work on Lillian Hellman. Maybe Mr. Richards just didn't like one-person shows. Whatever his reason, he didn't like the play or me. I also wondered if his nasty notice had anything to do with Charlotte Chandler? She had flown to Washington for the opening, commenting that Richards "owed her a favor." What, I don't know. Whatever it was, he returned the favor with vitriol. I couldn't wait to get out of Washington, D.C.

Playing New Orleans was a particular treat. Of course that was Tennessee Williams territory. It's where he created *A Streetcar Named Desire,* for one, which, to me, is still the greatest American play ever written. The city had formed a "Tennessee Williams Festival," to be held each year. I helped open the festival and it was a great success—at least ten years ago now—and it's still going strong. I've played it four separate times over the years, and it's always been a favorite spot to don my white suit one more time. Tennessee's brother Dakin would show up at these, which always made me nervous. He had first seen the show in Chicago, seated on the front row, no less. Since he was known to be a bit of an eccentric, I was sure he'd stand up in the middle of the show exclaiming that "that's not the way it was!" He didn't, thank God. While he was complimentary about my performance, he did quibble, however, with some of the material, saying it was another of Tennessee's "distortions of the truth." I tried to explain that I was doing the playwright's life, so I had to go with his version of things, right or wrong. He didn't like that too well, but I didn't alter anything.

Perhaps the two most exciting engagements were being invited to be the official U.S representative at the prestigious Edinburgh International Festival in Scotland, as well as the International Israel Festival in Jerusalem. Hundreds of shows were presented from all over the world. The Edinburgh performance elicited a wonderful review from John Peter in the *London Sunday Times*: "THE BEST THING IN THE OFFICIAL EDINBURGH FESTIVAL IS A ONE-MAN SHOW FROM AMERICA WITH RAY STRICKLYN. THIS IS A REAL TOUR-DE-FORCE, WILLIAMS IS ALL THERE. THE DRAWLING, GRITTY VOICE, THE WISE, BITCHY HUMOUR, THE VULNERABILITY, THE DIGNITY, THE ESSENTIAL TOUGHNESS." Charlotte showed up there too, but insisted I pay her fare out of my fee! Oh yes, she endeared herself to me every step of the way. Lee Melville also flew over, covering the event for *Drama-Logue*.

I was worried about how the show would play in Jerusalem. First of all, I didn't even know if they knew who Tennessee Williams was, plus I was concerned about a possible language barrier. Both worries were unfounded. English was the second language, so that wasn't a problem, and I was told by young actors I met that Tennessee's works were used all the time in their classes and/or for audition material. He was universal. The theatre I was in was fascinating—reputed to be the oldest in Jerusalem—and built inside a huge cave. It seated around 300 people and the acoustics were extraordinary. Another surprise was in the curtain calls. They didn't applaud—instead they stomped their feet in unison. That was a first.

Finally home, once again, I decided it was time I concentrated on trying to get my television career reinvented. Since Alex Brewis, my agent, wasn't franchised to handle theatre, I had reluctantly left him. I needed new representation. My friend Jeffrey Bloom suggested that I see his agent, Nicole David, who was one of the most powerful in her field. He set up a meeting. It wasn't successful, and it was obvious that she was only seeing me as a favor to Jeffrey. I'd naively thought because of the reams of press I'd received in Los Angeles, plus my awards, then the New York production, that there should be interest. Wrong. Practically her first words to me were, "Well, you'll never be a star." I am when I'm Tennessee Williams,

I wanted to tell her! Instead, I said, "Maybe not, but I should be a working actor." I then mentioned how fond I was of Ed Harris, who was her client, but she responded with, "I'm not even sure Ed's going to be a star." I was happy to leave her office. I then contacted another major office, and while they were much nicer, the turndown was similar: "Oh, Ray, I know you're a fine actor, but how much money could you bring into the office? We just turned down Ernest Borgnine because we figured he wouldn't generate more than a million a year. How much could you bring in?" I almost laughed; in fact, I think I did. Hollywood was still Hollywood, only the stakes were even bigger now. With rare exceptions, if you weren't a Robert Redford, the powerful talent agencies weren't interested.

As he had so many times in the past, David came to my rescue. Marion Rosenberg was an up-and-coming dynamo in the agency world, having previously been in the production end of the business. She'd been an associate producer on the Oscar-winning *Deer Hunter* film, which had starred Robert DeNiro and Meryl Streep, and, I was to find out later, had worked with producer Elliott Kastner when I did my small role in *Dogpound Shuffle*. She was English and she had class. She also liked stage actors, a novelty amongst Hollywood agents. David had gotten to know her because she represented Brian Kerwin when he was handling his publicity at John Springer. He called Marion, asking if she had any interest in me. She did. And so, at last, I had my first top-drawer agent since Paul Kohner. Her young associate was a man named Matthew Lesher. Unlike Nicole David, they both agreed that I should be a working actor. And I would become one.

But first, I would do *Confessions of a Nightingale* one more time. Susan Dietz, the artistic director at the Pasadena Playhouse, asked me to be part of a new series they were planning for their main stage—"Great Performances," it was called, with each show running one week. It was a prestigious event. Peggy Lee, singing from a wheelchair, opened the series. She'd hurt her back and wasn't able to stand. Of course, her voice was still wonderful. And she was also an old pro. Opening night she didn't get her expected standing ovation, but she had balls, telling the audience, "I'd stand for you, if I could." She got her standing ovation. I saw her in the lobby afterwards and she kept staring at me, but I don't know if she ever figured out I was the same Ray Stricklyn "with the shaved eyebrows" who had once handled her publicity. The delightful musical comedy team of Betty Garrett and Dale Gonyea followed Miss Lee. My turn was next. It was a smashing return to the L.A. area, and I loved playing in that beautiful old theatre, with 700 jam-packed seats. I received my standing ovations, nightly, I wanted to tell Miss Lee. The wonderful comedian Dick Shawn closed the series. He was absolutely brilliant. He died shortly thereafter, on stage, but in a different theatre. That's the way to go, I thought. Except I was greedy. I wanted mine to be right after the standing ovation! When the critics were all picking the "Best of 1987," The *Los Angeles Times* reviewer, Ray Loynd, led off his selections with, "REACHING IMPRESSIVE SOLO HEIGHTS, RAY STRICKLYN WAS MESMERIZ-ING." The Pasadena Playhouse week had been rewarding in another way too— they paid me $10,000.

Susan Dietz would later bring me back to the Playhouse for a three-week run in their smaller theatre. The marvelous Gena Rowlands graciously hosted my opening. Gena, whom I didn't know, had first seen the play in its original version at the Beverly Hills Playhouse. At that time she wrote me a lovely note, with a

The wonderful Gena Rowlands graciously hosted my Confessions of a Nightingale *opening*

postscript from John Cassavetes, who I hadn't seen since 1956, when we filmed *Crime In the Streets*.

* * * * *

Attending one of the Pasadena Playhouse performances were Esther and Richard Shapiro. They came backstage. I knew their faces looked vaguely familiar, but from what? Their names had a familiar ring too. Pretending I knew who they were, I stupidly asked, "Well, what have you been up to?" There was a slight pause, then Esther said, "Well, *Dynasty* keeps us pretty busy." Oops! Those Shapiros! Of course they had created the number one show on television and were executive producers with Aaron Spelling. "We'll be in touch," they said, exiting. They had been the couple who came backstage to see me when I did *Kataki* in Laguna Beach almost twenty-eight years ago!

And hear from them I did. Esther called saying they were producing a new series, *The Colbys,* which would be a spinoff from *Dynasty*. "It's high time you started making big bucks," she laughingly said. "We're creating a role just for you. You'll be a southern psychiatrist named Dr. Parris, and we'll guarantee you at least seven episodes, probably more, as there may be crossover to the *Dynasty* story line." *The Colbys* was a high-profiled, very expensive program on the ABC schedule. A top cast had been assembled, headed by Barbara Stanwyck and Charlton Heston, long two of Hollywood's leading stars, as well as starring roles for Stephanie Beacham, Emma Samms, John James, Katharine Ross and Maxwell Caulfield. Just before the scheduled start of the series, ABC-TV, Aaron Spelling, and the Shapiros tossed a lavish party at the Beverly Hilton Hotel to introduce the casts of both *The Colbys* and *Dynasty* to the press. I escorted Marlene's beautiful daughter, Nancy Milo, who looked every inch a star herself. Each actor was introduced separately—John Forsythe, Linda Evans, Diahann Carroll, etc.—I was introduced as "the distinguished stage actor who's recently had such success as Tennessee Williams." Only Joan Collins and Michael Nader failed to show at the party. I was eager to meet Barbara Stanwyck, certainly one of the legendary ladies of the silver screen. She was most gracious when Esther Shapiro introduced me, welcoming me to the cast.

Although I was not a witness to any tension on the set, there were stories floating around about initial friction between Charlton Heston, Miss Stanwyck, and Maxwell Caulfield. It seems Maxwell was often late, causing the two venerable stars to take him to task. Maxwell I knew. I handled his publicity when he starred in *Grease 2*, with everyone predicting great stardom for him. He had created a stir in a couple of New York plays prior to his film debut. He, of course, was extremely attractive with a taut, magnificent physique, which he loved to show off. He was also English, a good actor, and very young, barely in his twenties. When he first came to the Springer office, he had just married British actress Juliet Mills, who was twenty-odd years older. No one thought the marriage would last, but it has. But Maxwell could also be very arrogant, thinking he was a star before he became one. I liked him though, and we got along quite well. Unfortunately, when *Grease 2* was released it was a big bomb, and the press quickly lost interest in him. His co-star in the film, however, went on to become one of the big new stars of the 1980s and 1990s—Michelle Pfeiffer. *The Colbys* was a new start for him. He and Juliet had asked me to be in a play with them in George Orwell's *1984*, but I was unable to do it because of my *Confessions* schedule. Most of my scenes on *The Colbys* would eventually be with Maxwell and Emma Samms, a beautiful young English actress.

When I'd initially discussed my role of Dr. Parris with Esther Shapiro, she told me to play him "just like you play Tennessee Williams." So, I envisioned him as an eccentric southern doctor dressed in an unpressed old white suit, a real eyesore amidst the posh and lushness of everyone else on the series. I thought it would make an interesting contrast. In my debut script, Miss Stanwyck's character had called me (I was an old friend) asking for help with Fallon (Emma Samms). Fallon thought she had been abducted by aliens and the family thinks she's lost her mind. Stanwyck wants me to "save" her, amidst protests from other family members. As you can see, this plot line is pretty far-fetched. The first script I was in was centered around introducing my character, so I had a lot to do. My first scene was a big confrontation with the whole family, a monologue almost, with me telling them they mustn't interfere with my treatment. It went well. The director was Curtis Harrington, who had been at Fox years ago when I was there, as an assistant in Jerry Wald's production unit. He was also an acquaintance of my English friend Edward James. During a break in the filming, Curtis told me he had known Charlotte Chandler years ago in Paris, only she had a different name then. Another reliable source said she was an heiress to the Singer Sewing Machine fortune.

A few days after I'd finished my first episode, I had a very nice note from Miss Stanwyck, again welcoming me to the series, but adding, "You've brought us a little class." That was thoughtful. She seemed to like me and once we had a long chat about Henry Fonda, whom she adored, and vice versa. Unfortunately, she wasn't in the best of health, and eventually asked for her release from the series, which was granted. And though I was very happy to be working, I wasn't pleased with the way Dr. Parris evolved either. By the time I'd shot my first scene, I was no longer a disheveled southern doctor. Instead, I had become as beautifully dressed and as rich as everyone else in an Aaron Spelling series, speeding around in an expensive foreign sports car. The only quality that set him apart was my accent. I did my seven episodes, then crossed over to do a *Dynasty* segment before the character was written out. The series went off the air not too long after. Still, it had been very good exposure.

The promising news, however, was that the Shapiros said they wanted to

A running role as Dr. Parris on the ABC series The Colbys, *here with Emma Samms*

produce *Confessions of a Nightingale* as a film or television special under their production banner. They certainly had the clout and the money, so I kept my fingers crossed. Of course, Charlotte became involved and met with them several times. We were kept dangling for a couple of years before I knew it wasn't becoming a reality.

Over the years we had had several nibbles to film *Confessions*, but Charlotte had always nixed them, thinking we could get a "better deal" elsewhere. It was most frustrating. Finally, as late as 1994, it looked like it would really happen when Bridget and Jerry Dobson took a five-year option on the show. The Dobsons were very successful writers/producers in the daytime soap opera world, having created *Santa Barbara*, for one. They had entered my life through David, as he'd directed a workshop of a stage musical Bridget had written, *Slings and Eros*, which was quite delightful. Anyway, they optioned the script for $50,000, with ICM's Mitch Douglas again handling the negotiations for Charlotte. It took months for the deal to go through, costing thousands of dollars in legal fees for the Dobsons, before Charlotte finally signed the contract. Of course, she kept most of the fee. But, at this point, I just wanted to film it, even though I had been screwed once again. However, the Dobsons lawyer had neglected to put anything about distribution rights in the contract, which was very important. Douglas indicated there would be no problem, just add the clause, and he'd have Charlotte sign it. She refused to do that, however. I never found out why, either. I called her, pleading with her, but she'd only whisper that she was "considering" it. I became angry and told her I'd never speak to her again if she fucked this up. Of course, that was no threat to power woman. And so, *Confessions of a Nightingale* remains unfilmed. I offered to give my pittance back to the Dobsons, but being very honorable people, they said it was their lawyer's mistake, not mine. The whole mess became a tax write-off for them. I've not seen nor spoken to Miss Chandler since. I decided it was dear C. Robert Jennings getting his revenge from the grave.

* * * * *

With *The Colbys* now a job in the past, Matthew Lesher, at Marion Rosenberg's office, phoned to say NBC-TV wanted to see me about possibly appearing on the daytime soap opera, *Days of Our Lives*, which had been on the air for umpteen years. Although I had never been a soap watcher, this particular one had been a favorite of my mother's, so I'd occasionally seen it when I was visiting her in Houston years before. I met with the casting director and she said they were writing in a character named Howard Hawkins, a poor, homeless man, who is befriended by Jennifer on the series. I read for the role and was signed. At that point they weren't sure how long the character would be involved in the story line.

Of course the plots can become pretty outrageous and my poor homeless man, whom you felt very sorry for, suddenly became a con artist, then a millionaire through his shady dealings. It was all quite far-fetched, but it was also fun to now be the villain. Most of my scenes were with Matthew Ashford (as Jack Deveraux) and Melissa Reeves (Jennifer), the good guys, while my fellow conspirators in crime were the very handsome J. Eddie Peck and a wonderful black actress named Charlayne Woodard. I came to have great admiration for the soap actor—certainly it's "instant acting"—and not an ideal way to work—but it was a valuable experience. I only appeared in about three episodes a week, but that was plenty for me. I ended up doing the show for almost a year before my character suddenly disappeared. The last time you saw Howard Hawkins, he was holed up in a hotel room, having bilked someone out of a million dollars. I guess he got away with it, for what happened to him was never explained. Suddenly he was gone.

I was constantly surprised that so many people watched the show. I would have almost immediate recognition wherever I might be. "Howard Hawkins?" they'd ask. Some could be quite vocal in their anger at the way I was treating their heroine, Jennifer. The show also helped when I was touring with *Confessions*. The box office always seemed to jump up if it was publicized that I had been a "star" on *Days of Our Lives*.

Once again, my friend Jeffrey Bloom had a role for me. He was writing and directing a new series for ABC called *Juarez*, taking place on the Texas border. A new young actor named Benjamin Bratt was the star (he's now on *Law and Order*). Jeffrey had written a wonderful character for me to play—a very seedy, low-life type, whose dealings were less than lawful. Sort of like the characters Sydney Greenstreet played so beautifully in all those Warner Bros. movies in the '40s. It also looked like it might develop into a running role, so that was also a plus. The series, however, dealing with the border patrol and immigration problems, never reached the air (as far as I know). They shot three episodes, and then the network yanked it from their upcoming schedule. That was a major disappointment for all concerned. I had a very good piece of film—except no one ever saw it.

But I seemed to be on a television roll. Next, I was signed for a very good part in five episodes of the *Wiseguy* series, which was filmed in Vancouver, starring Ken Wahl and Jonathan Banks. I played Senator Pickering, a no-nonsense southern politico, who ruled in the Senate. Eventually, I pulled a filibuster, which lasted for hours, saving the day in a very complicated plot development. I was very proud of my work on this.

I was pleased the way my career seemed to be going. Between the television shows, I'd usually have a booking of *Confessions* somewhere, and that success always kept my morale up. The stage was my artistic satisfaction, the television a financial plus. Over the years, I'd occasionally be offered other plays, either in Los Angeles or at some regional theatre, but I had always turned them down. My success as Tennessee made everything else pale by comparison. In some ways, that success became a trap. But I reasoned that while I may not have control over the television parts I might be offered, I did have a choice as to my stage life.

During my Springer days, director Warner Shook had staged a stunning reading of William Inge's *Bus Stop*, with Brian Kerwin in the male lead. Somehow, he never got that production going. Now, all these years later, he was finally doing it for the Pasadena Playhouse's main stage. I called Warner and asked him if I could play the tragic professor, who has been run out of town after being accused of molesting a girl student. It was a strong role and one I wanted to try. I was cast. Warner decided on a young actress named Lea Thompson for the leading role of Cherie (played so marvelously on stage and film by Kim Stanley and Marilyn Monroe). She had just scored in a couple of Michael J. Fox *Back to the Future* movies (and today as the star of the *Caroline In the City* sitcom), and was a promising new talent. But I thought Warner made a major mistake in his casting of the male lead, Bo. It was a difficult role—the audience must like him, otherwise he can be a pretty obnoxious, dumb cowboy, quite abusive in his treatment of Cherie. Brian Kerwin had had just the right amount of innocence and charm to make the role work in Warner's original reading. The actor he selected for the Pasadena production, however, was very dark—both in appearance and projection. He'd just finished playing the heavy dramatic lead in Lanford Wilson's *Burn This* at A.C.T. in San Francisco and he brought that searing intensity to Bo. He was obviously a good actor, but this quality was very wrong for Bo. Others, however, liked him, so that was just my private opinion. It turned out to be a good production, but not as exciting as it should have been. Some of the critics thought the play now dated, particularly in a political climate where abusiveness to women and child molestation were a definite no-no. The reviews were mixed, though Travis Michael Holder, writing in *The Tulucan*, really liked me: "A STANDOUT, AS ALWAYS, IS RAY STRICKLYN. HE IS INSPIRED CASTING. NEVER HAVE I SEEN SHAKESPEARE'S BALCONY SCENE (AS PLAYED IN *BUS STOP*) WORK SO WELL—THANKS TO THE SKILL AND IMMEASURABLE TALENTS OF MR. STRICKLYN. ONE OF LOS ANGELES' BEST NATURAL RESOURCES."

* * * * *

The years were rolling past and I continued interspersing my television work with touring *Confessions of a Nightingale*. I played dates in Florida, St. Louis, New Hampshire, Kansas, as well as return engagements in Los Angeles at the Canon Theatre and the Westwood Playhouse. The performance in Santa Barbara was amusing in retrospect. I was only into the show about ten minutes when I noticed two elderly ladies, both on walkers, slowly exiting up the aisle. It seems they had been offended by the talk of homosexuality. The next day the critic chastised them: "Ladies, you should have stayed, you might have learned something. After all, you were getting Tennessee Williams, not John Wayne."

I was especially pleased when audience members would seek me out after a performance, saying how moved they'd been, and my show had whetted their appetite to learn more about Mr. Williams—by reading his plays, renting the movies of his works. In *Confessions*, Tennessee, talking about his near-death experience, says: "I no longer believe in being frugal with money, time or energy. I never know where I'll be tomorrow, or even if I'll be." This prompted one woman to write me saying the play had changed her life. She'd had a serious falling-out with her daughter, now living in Europe, but she was leaving immediately to join her in an effort to make up for lost time. She knew too, that she didn't know where she'd be tomorrow—or even if she would be. Moments like that were very moving.

After the *Juarez* television fiasco, Jeffrey Bloom had continued writing for various other series, doing a number of scripts for Peter Falk's *Columbo*. Now he had a new series, *Veronica Clare*, which he was also producing for the Lifetime cable network. He said he'd had the script written just for me—the title character, a real tour-de-force—as a wealthy southern gentleman who turns out not to be so gentlemanly—having killed his first wife, then years later, his young bride. Lois Chiles played my daughter. We had met when we were both in Jose Quintero's workshop and I had always been very fond of her. It was the best role, I think, that I ever had in my television career. What a lovely gesture of friendship and trust from Jeffrey and Carole Bloom.

I followed that with another guest villain lead on the *Silk Stalkings* series, and then I had one of my happier television experiences. Director Peter Hunt cast me for a featured role in his two-hour movie-of-the-week, *Danielle Steel's Secrets*. I was playing the director of a new television series, with the distinguished Christopher Plummer as my producer. What a wonderful man he was—is. I spent a good deal of time with him between scenes. He seemed quite interested in hearing about my Williams show, saying he was contemplating such an effort himself, but he didn't know if he still had the stamina to sustain it. A few years later, of course, he did his critically acclaimed *Barrymore*. *Secrets* was such a joy because of Peter Hunt also. During the shoot he kept building up my part, adding me to scenes I hadn't been written in. In other words, he knew how to treat actors, particularly stage actors, whom he loved. Besides Mr. Plummer, he'd also cast Linda Purl, a beautiful actress with extraordinary gifts. She is a major actress—and should be a major star. Mr. Hunt also had me bring *Confessions* to his prestigious Williamstown Theatre for a special performance. Not too long after, he cast me in another television movie, *Hart to Hart Returns*, a reunion script for Robert Wagner and Stefanie Powers. I had a powerful scene with Stefanie as a brilliant scientist wrongfully imprisoned. Another pleasurable television experience was on the *Harry and the Hendersons* comedy series. I had been cast to play a doctor on the Bruce Davison sitcom, but it was only one scene and not a particularly rewarding one. However, a job was a job. But after we'd been in rehearsal for a couple of days, I received a call from the casting office saying they'd decided to delete the scene. They were most apologetic and said "they'd make it up to me." Sure, I thought. Bruce, who is such a fine actor, called me to say he was sorry it hadn't worked out, then added, "I told them the scene was a waste of your talent." Well, in about a month, the casting director called me back to say they'd written a special guest-starring role for me—and not just for one episode, but a two-parter. Now I was even a bigger fan of Bruce Davison.

* * * * *

Back in 1987, when I was about to open in Chicago, I had a very bad cold. The producer sent me to her doctor where she prescribed the usual dosages of flu medicine. During the visit, however, she took some x-rays. She then asked me about my smoking habits because, she said, there were the beginning signs of emphysema. I paid little attention to her diagnosis, however, and kept on smoking. Also, I didn't seem to be suffering in any way.

However, around 1992, I'd been asked to do my show in Valdez, Alaska. It was

At the prestigious Edward Albee Theatre Conference in Valdez, Alaska with (left to right): Lee Melville, Patricia Neal, Eva Marie Saint and Jeffrey Hayden

to be the start of an annual event saluting noted playwrights. The first year was honoring Edward Albee, the brilliant writer of such scripts as *Who's Afraid of Virginia Woolf?, A Delicate Balance*, and *The Zoo Story*. It was a most prestigious event to be associated with. However, I began to notice, when walking up the slightest incline, I would become completely exhausted, breathing heavily, having to stop several times before reaching my destination. Must be the altitude, I thought. I got through my performance okay, and that was what I was most worried about. Once back in Los Angeles, I continued having what I thought were minor symptoms—being overly tired, shortness of breath. But they weren't consistent attacks, and I put it out of mind. Of course, I kept on smoking.

TAKE ELEVEN

The 1990s were speeding by much too rapidly. It's true, once you reach a certain age, about time flying. The months turn into years before you even realize it. I found it impossible to believe that I had reached the mid-sixty mark. It seemed only yesterday that I had been a kid in my forties. But the calendar and the clock don't lie.

Throughout my life I had had few health problems, other than a penchant for colds. Besides my appendectomy and having my broken leg set, I'd spent no time in a hospital. I found that quite amazing, considering I had done little to take proper care of myself. I didn't exercise enough. I didn't eat proper foods, I drank too much and, worst of all, I smoked four packs of Kool cigarettes a day. Not a very healthy regime. Yet the fates had been good to me. My problems had been more mental than physical. But through it all, I had somehow managed to cope.

The neglect, however, was about to catch up with me. Although I had been warned about the beginning signs of emphysema almost ten years earlier, I had paid no attention to the Chicago doctor. Now I found my energy level depleting rapidly, a general fatigue sapping my strength. It was time to pay a visit to a doctor.

The news was not good. The emphysema was much more pronounced. I had lost 50 percent of my breathing capacity. "If you take care of yourself, if you stop smoking, we can, perhaps, add five years to your life," the doctor said. Understandably, his news depressed me terribly. My life was over, I knew. It was very easy to get down and out, particularly for someone wallowing in a negative attitude. So I began withdrawing from life, not wanting to leave the house or see friends. Why bother to quit smoking now, I foolishly reasoned? The damage had already been done.

Occasionally I'd be offered a television job, but I was so lacking in energy, both mentally and physically, that I had little desire to work. I did accept a small role on a *Cheers* episode, playing the town constable, attempting to marry Kirstie Alley to Roger Rees. But the long hours on the set were agonizing. Later, I accepted a guest lead on Fran Drescher's *The Nanny*, but the day before the shooting I had to withdraw. I'd caught a cold, which was disastrous when coupled with emphysema.

For two years I wallowed in my self-pity, rarely leaving the house or seeing anyone, other than David and Marlene, who still lived next door. Slowly, I began to emerge from my self-imposed exile. As Tennessee Williams had said, "Prolonged depression is almost as difficult as prolonged happiness."

* * * * *

There was about to be another dramatic change. David decided it was time we moved again. Certainly we had outgrown the duplex on North Genesee. We had so many things. Well, David did. He had a massive monkey collection, as well as expensive crystal paperweights. The big earthquake had smashed most of our fine cut china. We also had a huge library, with hundreds of books, mostly dealing with film and theatre, and, of course a giant record and CD collection. Moving, however, was the last thing on my mind, particularly in my precarious state of health. But we talked with a couple of real estate brokers, just in case. Since we didn't want to sell the duplex, securing a loan wasn't easy, but thanks to my good credit, one was finally secured. We found a large house, located in the Wilshire Boulevard area, on Lindenhurst Avenue. It was a big responsibility, but it was also the first time we'd really had room, with three bedrooms and three baths to boot. The escrow closed at the end of 1995. Now we had room for house guests and dear Uncle Hank (Hank Roberts, that is) was our first visitor. He'd moved from Sag Harbor to the Las Vegas area, and between his travels, has frequently stayed with us. A dear friend. Also, Mary Ann and Clayton made a rare visit from Houston. I loved having them so near. And Donna McKechnie stayed with us for a week when she was here to do David's latest AIDS benefit, this time saluting the music of Alan Jay Lerner, Frederick Loewe and Burton Lane. There was also a small guest cottage in the back of the house, and our friend Lee Melville would eventually use it a couple of times a week. He had long since retired as editor of *Drama-Logue*, and was now running a lucrative family business in Hesperia, California, a small community en route to Las Vegas.

* * * * *

With the expense of a new house, it was time I tried to return to work. I was feeling better. Although I now considered myself in semi-retirement, I suddenly had a new rash of offers to do *Confessions of a Nightingale*. That started after David secured a booking at Pepperdine University in Malibu, which has to be the most beautiful campus in the land, overlooking the Pacific Ocean. The large Smothers Theatre was packed and the reception I received was most gratifying. Dear Eva Marie Saint and Jeff Hayden came to see it again, as did Shirlee Fonda, Robert Fryer, Linda Purl, Jacque Mapes, Naomi Caryl, Jonathan Kanes, Harry Prongue, Virginia Wyngarden, and a host of friends, old and new.

This led to other dates in Pittsburgh (arranged by Jeff Hayden, at a healthy fee), in Cambria, a return engagement to Palm Springs, and a request to play the Edward Albee Festival in Valdez, Alaska again. This was very flattering, as Edward was most particular about who and what was performed at the theatre conference. The honored playwright was Robert Anderson (*Tea and Sympathy, I Never Sang for My Father*, etc). I suggested they bring in Eva Marie and Jeff, who do a lovely evening based on the works of Willa Cather. Playwright A. R. Gurney would also be there, represented by his play, *Sylvia*. A highlight of this year's festival was the guest appearance of another Oscar-winning actress, Patricia Neal (*Hud*). Her 45-minute presentation on her dramatic life was spellbinding. She also surprised us with a wonderful rendition of Stephen Sondheim's song, "Send In The Clowns." When I told her I'd played Gary Cooper's son in *Ten North Frederick* she showed more than routine interest. Cooper, of course, had been the love of her life and their long affair had ended sadly when he returned to his wife. In fact, some of the critics had commented that the film's plot line was very similar to their well-documented relationship.

Following the Alaska date, I had one more scheduled appearance before the end of the year—a three-week engagement in the "Great Performances" series at the Sacramento Theatre Company.

But first, there were dozens of odd jobs to do around the new house. While I had been on tour, David had planted additional trees and flowers, with lush plants lining the front patio. Brewster and Baybay were adjusting to their new surroundings. They too were getting along in years—almost fifteen now. They'd lost their hearing and their eyesight was failing, but they were as dear as ever, sleeping with me nightly. They'd also been joined by a new addition to the family—a feisty black kitten named Dagmar.

While unpacking various boxes, I came across pictures of friends, old and new. What a flood of memories that brought on—particularly when I came across photos of Jacquelyn Hyde, Gertrude Flynn, and Sarah Hardy. All three were gone now. Both Jackie and Sarah succumbed to cancer, while dear Gertrude, in her eighties, outlived them both, though suffering with Alzheimer's disease in her last years. I came across wedding photos of Phyllis and Rock. He, of course, was taken by AIDS, and Phyllis, who we'd seen many times over the years, was contemplating building a new home in West Palm Beach. Marlene, approaching eighty, but with more energy than most, was still living in our little duplex on Genesee. Carole Cook and Tom Troupe were as active as ever in their respective careers. David had directed them both in a revival of *The Lion In Winter* at the Pasadena Playhouse. Jose Quintero and his friend Nick were now living in Florida, following Jose's bout with lung cancer. But he was still teaching and I envied all his new young students, wondering if they were aware of his genius? And Sean? He seems to have disappeared completely. I've often wished I could see him again, to make amends for our aborted friendship. I hope he's well.

The photo supply seemed endless—a reminder of the old pool parties—with such dear and longtime friends as Al and Erma Chavez, David Morgan, who has befriended us many times over the years, our writer friends, Brian Taggert and Joel Kimmel, both so witty and talented, Kim Garfield, still active in public relations, our Palm Springs pal, Michael Larsen, Jeffrey and Carole Bloom, who I owe so much, are still battling the television wars, Mary Jo Catlett, one of my favorites, both as an actress and a friend. She lights up a stage, and a room for that matter. The wonderfully gifted Bill Hutton, Kirby Tepper, and, through David, newer friends, like Dorris Halsey, Ron Abel, Naomi Caryl, Jamie Anderson, Linda Purl, John Beaird, Ando Iovino, Kay Cole and her husband, Michael Lamont, John McDaniel, Ronn Goswick, Jacque Mapes, Robert Fryer, Harry Prongue, P. K. Strong, Susan Obrow, Lars Hansen, and Florence Fink.

At the bottom of one large cardboard box were dozens of old playbills, reminders of hundreds of shows I'd seen over the years. They brought back a flood of memories, of individual performances that I've particularly cherished. Of course Laurette Taylor's luminous Amanda Wingfield in *The Glass Menagerie* was the first truly great performance I witnessed, and certainly Geraldine Page in *Summer and Smoke* and *Sweet Bird of Youth* would be at the top of my list. Kim Stanley was always fascinating to watch, be it in *Bus Stop, The Far Country*, or *The Three Sisters*. She, along with Taylor and Page, was a truly great actress. I was also stunned by Sandy Dennis' Alma in *Eccentricities of a Nightingale* (Tennessee's rewrite of *Summer and Smoke*) at a theatre in Long Beach. Marlon Brando's Stanley in *A Streetcar Named Desire*, so full of power and electricity, was the most exciting male performance I think I ever saw, though Ed Harris' explosive Chance Wayne in *Sweet Bird of Youth*, in a small L.A. theatre, would be way up there, too. I loved Ruth Gordon's eccentric and delicious performance in *The Matchmaker*, and Michael Moriarty's performance in *The Night Thoreau Spent In Jail*. For sheer star power, I can't forget Ethel Merman's *Gypsy*, Barbra Streisand's *Funny Girl*, Katharine Hepburn's *Coco*, or the mere shimmering presence of Marlene Dietrich in her one-woman show, and, of course, the unforgettable Judy Garland when she returned to the Palace and sang and sang and sang. And I will always remember the brilliance of Harold Prince and Michael Bennett's staging of Stephen Sondheim's *Follies*, with Dorothy Collins breaking my heart when she sang "Losing My Mind." Or witnessing the birth of two great plays, Arthur Miller's *Death of a Salesman* and Edward Albee's *Who's Afraid of Virginia Woolf?*

As far as movie performances go, I have so many favorites, but ranking right at the top would be Vivien Leigh's Blanche du Bois in *A Streetcar Named Desire* and her Scarlett in *Gone with the Wind*. Bette Davis painted so many fine portraits, but my particular favorites were *All About Eve* and *The Letter*. And you know I'd add Geraldine Page's performances in just about anything, but particularly *Sweet Bird of Youth, Summer and Smoke, A Trip to Bountiful* and *Interiors*. Mr. Brando, I think would head my actors' list for two performances, *Streetcar* and *On the Waterfront*. I thought the love scenes in the latter, with Eva Marie Saint, were extraordinary. My favorite Laurence Olivier performances were in *The Entertainer* and *Wuthering Heights*. The late 1940s found Olivia de Havilland at the peak of her career, with wonderful work in *The Heiress* and *The Snake Pit*. Montgomery Clift moved me tremendously in *A Place in the Sun* and *From Here to Eternity.* Certainly Jack Lemmon has had a remarkable career, topped by his comedic turn in *Some Like It Hot* and his devastating work in *Glengarry Glen Ross.* Walter Huston was brilliant in *Dodsworth* and *The Treasure of the Sierra Madre.* And Liv Ullmann destroyed me with her performance in Ingmar Bergman's *Scenes from a Marriage.* I can't forget Ingrid Bergman's radiance, particularly in *Casablanca* and *Notorious,* or the greatest "comeback" of all time—Gloria Swanson's Norma Desmond in *Sunset Boulevard.* I could go on and on, but I won't.

* * * * *

Before the year ended I did one more television show, a very funny episode of *Seinfeld,* the most popular program on the tube. I was flattered when Jerry Seinfeld personally cast me, playing an *Andrea Doria* survivor in an amusing exchange with Jason Alexander. Amazing how many people saw that segment. But again, the long hours on the set proved very difficult for me.

* * * * *

It was now December 7, 1997. That evening was to be my final performance of *Confessions of a Nightingale* at the Sacramento Theatre Company. With effort I had finished my three-week engagement, but the run had taken its toll. My irreversible emphysema made it difficult to do the nightly performances, eight shows a week. The strain was devastating. But, somehow I managed. The show must go on.

When I returned to Los Angeles shortly before Christmas, I was totally exhausted. My breathing had become even more erratic, if I could catch my breath at all. It's a very scary sensation not being able to breathe. The least little bit of exertion would bring on an attack—heavy, short-winded wheezes, attempting to get oxygen into my lungs. Just walking from one end of the house to the other was a major chore, and the simple tasks of lifting groceries or taking a shower or walking the dogs became increasingly difficult.

Then, early on a Saturday morning, my breathing was considerably worse. With Marlene at my side, I was rushed to Cedars-Sinai Medical Center, where I remained in intensive care for four days. I now only had 30 percent of my breathing capacity. Dr. Soffer also asked if I wanted to remain on a life support system or have the plug pulled. That was a jolt, though I suppose it's a question asked. I responded with a weak, "Pull the plug." It was shocking for me to realize that cigarettes had been my most constant companions for over fifty years! And yet the cigarette companies continue to argue that smoking is not addictive. Indeed.

"An actor finding the role of his life," wrote a critic, how true! As Tennessee Williams in Confessions of a Nightingale

EPILOG

Has it been a wasted life, as I've sometimes wondered?

I'll have to give a yes and no to the question. Being a Libran, I do have a tendency to weigh the pros and cons of just about every situation. The scales are loaded on both sides, though tilting precariously.

Certainly the 1950s were promising. Full of youthful vigor and ambition, believing I would climb to the heights in my quest for success. The 1960s, however, were a disaster, filled with self-destructive behavior. A decade lost, never to be fully recaptured. Those were perhaps the most crucial years as far as my career was concerned. Just when I was on the threshold of achievement, my feelings of guilt and unworthiness sent me plummeting, both professionally and privately. The 1970s found me slowly digging myself out of the mire I'd created the decade before, though the two combined comprised almost twenty years of self-punishment. The 1980s were the good years, the mature years, the productive years, regaining my self-respect as a man and as an actor. And the 1990s? The mellowing years, attempting to accept the positive as well as the negative. Mixtures of regrets, yes, but intermingled with a sense of accomplishment—against all odds.

I've tried to face the hard truths of my life—the good, the bad, and the ugly. I pledged myself to an actor's life. The wisest choice? Debatable. But it was the inevitable road I was destined to travel, often at great expense, forsaking a personal life in search of an illusive dream. A scrapbook full of glowing reviews fade in time, a deep friendship does not. Fortunately, I found the latter with David. Although it may not have been a conventional relationship, with many ups and downs, it has been a consistent force, surviving for over thirty years. The angels were with me there. I'm proud of that.

I'm not proud, however, that I've often lived a selfish life. But that's a demon shared with many another actor. It's part of our makeup, our need, and our desperateness to be liked. I've also been arrogant, vain, stubborn, weak and lazy. Not commendable qualities. But through it all, I like to think I've been an honest person. Not always with myself, perhaps, but I've strived to be with others.

An angel was with me when I joined AA, perhaps the most important day in my life. It's the one demon I licked. I'm proud of that accomplishment—fifteen years of sobriety, one day at a time. In later years I didn't attend the meetings, which are very important, but I did manage to stay sober, which is more important. I wish I could say the same about my cigarette addiction. I've been a failure there, as my present health clearly and sadly reminds me. A most destructive demon.

As for my homosexuality? I'm not proud of it nor am I ashamed of it. It's part of who I was. I say was because it is a segment of my distant past, another lifetime. It caused me pain and, on occasion, it brought me joy. But I don't think I ever really lived a "gay" lifestyle. I tried to be discreet and, for the most part, I think I succeeded, except when I allowed alcohol to rule. When I first started to put these words to paper, I had no plans to discuss the subject at all—too private, I thought. But not discussing it would have been dishonest, a lie. It's not as though I'm "coming out" at this late stage of my life. As Carole Cook succinctly put it, "You don't think you'd be surprising anyone, do you?"

Do I think my sexual orientation hurt my career? Probably. I wasn't aware of it being a detriment in my early years, but I'm sure in some quarters it was a negative factor. The 1950s and 1960s were homophobic decades. Of course, now, as a character actor, I don't think anyone gives a damn. But we're also living in a different age, times have changed. Certainly my most successful stage roles— *Compulsion, Naomi Court, Vieux Carre* and *Confessions of a Nightingale*— were all homosexual characters. In those cases it worked for me, not against me. Nor did it seem to affect my television work—being cast in only so-called "straight" roles—be it a doctor, a senator, a sheriff or a villain. And, ideally, that's the way it should be. It's the performance that should count, not a bedroom preference.

As for my aborted movie career? That's really for others to judge. Personally, I think I demonstrated "promise," nothing more, nothing less. But I was always a pro. I did my job. In the "Who's Who" books on film history, I'm listed in some as a "second lead." I suppose that's an accurate description. I only appeared in seventeen films. I starred in a couple, co-starred in a few, supported in some, and did my share of bits. None of them, however, were box-office blockbusters, nor are they now considered "important" films, two musts if you're going to have a major movie career, certainly in today's market. But I tried. I suppose I did a lot better than some in this most difficult of professions, but, alas, my star only twinkled briefly. Living and pain may have eventually made me a better actor, but it was a stiff price.

In looking back, I've tried to recall what made me the happiest, what brought me the most personal satisfaction? While I loved making films and there was a superficial charge in seeing myself up on that large screen, my real satisfaction came from my stage work. Whether I was making $10,000 a week or nothing at all, I look to *Vieux Carre* and *Confessions of a Nightingale* as the high points in my career. Finally, I considered myself a real actor. And life's experiences were responsible for that hard-earned realization. But ultimately, I don't think I was given the opportunities to be the artist I was capable of being. I regret that.

Throughout much of my career I've been fortunate where the critics are concerned. But that's a toss of the dice, a real crap shoot. One notice may be positive, the next negative, yet they've witnessed the same performance. It boils down to individual taste and judgment. But I've often wondered what would have happened if the first review I'd gotten on *Confessions of a Nightingale* had been a pan, like David Richards' *Washington Post* notice? It would have destroyed me. I would never have continued with the play, thereby missing out on the greatest and most rewarding experience of my whole career. The "little show" that kept growing, that became my life, my bread-earner, winning me not only great critical acclaim and many awards, but most importantly, gave me back my self-respect. The fact that it has also earned me close to a quarter of a million dollars over the years isn't to be sneezed at either. Not a bad return on a presentation only scheduled to play one weekend. Of course the secret is not to take reviews too seriously, but most actors egos are fragile and we don't heed that advice. Certainly this one didn't.

Do I have any advice for the young actor? Make sure acting is something you need to do, not just something you want to do. Don't do it if you can possibly be content doing something else. It's a cruel and often heartbreaking profession, with more rejections than acceptances. Chances for success are not on your side. Any other profession, if you work and study, you are usually guaranteed at least a livelihood. Not so as an actor. You can be the very best and still not be working.

And while it's great to have other actors as friends, usually they can't (or don't) help you in your career, so I'd advise you to cultivate writers, directors and producers if given the opportunity. And for practical purposes, it wouldn't hurt to throw in a lawyer, doctor, plumber, electrician, dentist and banker. They'll be needed too along the way. And, disheartening though it may be, in Hollywood it's deemed more important to have played a scene on *Seinfeld* than to have given a wonderful performance in a play. Sad, but true. To succeed as an actor you must have a real need, desire, ambition, guts and luck. The latter plays a far more important role than you think. But miracles do happen and perhaps the angels will smile on you. You'll be up and you'll be down, but remember that neither place is permanent.

Personally, I owe so much to Tennessee Williams. How could I have possibly known that he would play such an important role in my life, a powerful force in my evolvement? From the very first he was there. The revelation of seeing my first Broadway play, *The Glass Menagerie*. Winning an acting scholarship by attempting to play his *Moony's Kid Don't Cry*. Quitting acting after I thought I'd been a failure in *Camino Real*. And giving me back my career and life with *Vieux Carre* and *Confessions of a Nightingale*. Without his even knowing it, he was there. At the beginning, the middle, and the end. Remarkable.

So, in the final analysis, if I had my life to live over again, would I do it any differently? You bet. For one, I'd try to be less punishing of myself. Would I make the same mistakes? Perhaps. But I hope I would be wiser.

* * * * *

They say when you're dying that your whole life flashes before you. In attempting to put these words to paper, my life has certainly flashed before me.

Does that mean ...?

Until that inevitable moment arrives, I will don my white suit one more time and let the nightingales sing ....

> Thank you, thank you. You act as if you think something wonderful is about to happen ...

—The End—

CREDITS

MOTION PICTURES

The Proud and the Profane (Par./1956) William Holden, Deborah Kerr
Crime In the Streets (AA/1956) John Cassavetes, James Whitmore, Sal Mineo
Somebody Up There Likes Me (MGM/1956) Paul Newman, Pier Angeli
The Catered Affair (MGM/1956) Bette Davis, Ernest Borgnine, Debbie Reynolds
The Last Wagon (20th-Fox/1956) Richard Widmark, Felicia Farr, Susan Kohner
The Return of Dracula (UA/1958) Francis Lederer, Norma Eberhardt
10 North Frederick (20th-Fox/1958) Gary Cooper, Diane Varsi, Suzy Parker
The Remarkable Mr. Pennypacker (Fox/1959) Clifton Webb, Dorothy McGuire
The Big Fisherman (Buena Vista/1959) Howard Keel, Susan Kohner, John Saxon
Young Jesse James (Fox/1960) Title role / with Willard Parker, Merry Anders
The Lost World (Fox/1960) Claude Rains, Michael Rennie, Jill St. John
The Plunderers (AA/1960) Jeff Chandler, John Saxon, Dolores Hart
Arizona Raiders (Col./1965) Audie Murphy, Buster Crabbe, Ben Cooper
Track of Thunder (UA/1967) Tommy Kirk, Brenda Benet, Faith Domergue
Dogpound Shuffle (Ind./1974) Ron Moody, David Soul, Pamela McMyler
La Ilegal (Mexican film, 1976)
Write to Kill (Ind./1985) Scott Valentine, France Nuyen

MOVIES-FOR-TELEVISION

The Andersonville Trial (Directed by George C. Scott) William Shatner, Richard
Basehart, Cameron Mitchell, Jack Cassidy, Martin Sheen, Buddy Ebsen
North and South: Part II
Jealousy (Directed by Jeffrey Bloom) Angie Dickinson, David Carradine, Susan Tyrrell
Danielle Steel's Secrets (Dir. Peter Hunt) Christopher Plummer, Linda Purl
Hart to Hart Returns ((Dir. Peter Hunt) Robert Wagner, Stefanie Powers

TELEVISION APPEARANCES (A partial listing)

The Nanny (1998) with Fran Drescher
Days of Our Lives (1998) as Judge Wells
Seinfeld with Jerry Seinfeld, Jason Alexander
Harry and the Hendersons (two-parter) Bruce Davison
Cheers with Ted Danson, Kirstie Alley, Woody Harrelson, Roger Rees
Veronica Clare with Laura Robinson, Lois Chiles (Title role as "Mr. Duvall")
Days of Our Lives (Series regular as 'Howard Hawkins')
Dynasty with John Forsythe, Emma Samms, Maxwell Caulfield
The Colbys with Barbara Stanwyck, Charlton Heston, Emma Samms, Maxwell
    Caulfield, Stephanie Beacham, Katharine Ross (Series regular as Dr. Parris)
Wiseguy (Six episodes as Sen. Pickering) with Ken Wahl, Jonathan Banks
Silk Stalkings with Rob Estes, Mitzi Kapture

Juarez with Benjamin Bratt
Shades of L.A. (Title role in "Teacher from Hell")
The George Carlin Show
Medical Center with Chad Everett, Arthur Hill, Stephanie Zimbalist
The Rockford Files with James Garner
The Long Hot Summer with Nancy Malone, Roy Thinnes
Judd for the Defense with Carl Betz, Coleen Gray
One Step Beyond with Zina Bethune
This Is the Life (Starred in ten episodes)
Bonanza (two episodes) with Michael Landon, Lorne Greene
Markham with Ray Milland (Title role as "The Nephew")
The Rebel with Nick Adams
Bourbon Street Beat with Richard Long, Mary Tyler Moore
Cheyenne with Clint Walker, Nancy Gates
Wagon Train (two episodes) with Robert Horton, Dean Jones, Everett Sloane
Bronco with Ty Hardin
Lawman with John Russell, Peter Brown, Peggie Castle
Broken Arrow (3 episodes) John Lupton, Michael Ansara
The Millionaire with Barbara Eden, Marian Seldes
Perry Mason (two episodes) Raymond Burr, Barbara Hale
Combat with Vic Morrow, Rick Jason
Whirlybirds with Craig Hill, Kenneth Tobey
M-Squad with Lee Marvin (Title role as "The Second Best Killer")
Dr. Christian with Macdonald Carey
4-Star Playhouse - "That Woman" with Ida Lupino
Schlitz Playhouse - "For Better, For Worse" with Bette Davis, John Williams
Schlitz Playhouse - "Honor Thy Father" with Paul Douglas
Ford Theatre - "Front Page Father" with Charles Bickford
Telephone Time - "The Churchill Club" with Martin Milner
General Hospital
Father Knows Best with Robert Young, Jane Wyatt, Billy Gray
Matinee Theatre - "When the Bough Breaks" with Betty Lynn, James Lydon
State Trooper with Rod Cameron
Crossroads with Richard Carlson
Navy Log with Chuck Connors
Lamp Unto My Feet with Nancy Malone, Steve McQueen, Robert Loggia
Danger
Big Story
Robert Montgomery Presents
Studio One
I Remember Mama with Peggy Wood, Dick Van Patten
The Danny Thomas Show with Danny Thomas, Sherry Jackson
College Bowl with Chico Marx, Ann Crowley, Barbara Ruick
The Peter Lind Hayes-Mary Healy Show

The Faye Emerson Show
Ed Sullivan's Toast of the Town with Kate Smith
Ed Sullivan's Toast of the Town with Douglas Fairbanks Jr.
etc.

STAGE APPEARANCES

Ah, Wilderness! (Houston Civic Theatre)
The Damask Cheek (Jewish Community Center, Houston)
Junior Miss (Texas State Hotel, Houston)
George Washington Slept Here (Houston Little Theatre)
A Midsummer Night's Dream (Houston Little Theatre)
The Cradle Song (Houston Little Theatre)
Doctor Knock (Houston Little Theatre
You Never Can Tell (Houston Little Theatre)
The Tempest (Houston Little Theatre)
Little Women (Houston Little Theatre)
Love Possessed Juana (Houston Little Theatre)
The Man Who Came to Dinner (Irvine Studio, NYC)
Hello Out There (Little Stages, Houston)
Rope (Irvine Studio, NY)
Bury the Dead (Irvine Studio, NY)
Winterset (Irvine Studio, NY)
Arsenic and Old Lace (Litchfield Summer Theatre, Conn.) with Bela Lugosi
Room Service (Litchfield) with Jackie Coogan
The Petrified Forest (Litchfield)
Good News (Houston Musical Theatre) with Ann Crowley, Biff McGuire
The New Moon (Houston Musical Theatre) with Marguerite Piazza, Sterling Holloway
Season with Ginger (Alley Theatre, Houston)
You Never Can Tell (Woodstock Playhouse, NY) with Jack Sydow, Van Williams
An Inspector Calls (Woodstock) with Van Williams, Jack Sydow, Anna Leonard
The Climate of Eden (Martin Beck Theatre, NY) Rosemary Harris, John Cromwell
The Grass Harp (Circle-In-the-Square, NY) Clarice Blackburn, Ruth Attaway
Stalag 17 (National tour) with George Tobias
Sabrina Fair (Elitch's Gardens, Denver) Margot Stevenson, Laurence Hugo
The Crucible (Elitch's Gardens) with Laurence Hugo, Margot Stevenson
My Three Angels (Elitch's Gardens)
The Vinegar Tree (Palm Beach Playhouse) with Shirley Booth
Here Today (Palm Beach Playhouse) with Faye Emerson
Saint Joan (Palm Beach Playhouse) with Jan Sterling, Romney Brent
Compulsion (Omnibus Center Theatre, L.A.) Donald Buka, Patricia Huston, Ted Knight
Kataki (Laguna Summer Theatre) with Dale Ishimoto
The Sea Gull (Hollywood Center Theatre) with Jennifer West
Long Day's Journey Into Night (Alley Theatre, Houston) with Virginia Payne
The Caretaker (Beverly Hills Playhouse) with Tom Troupe, Richard Bull

Entertaining Mr. Sloane (Beverly Hills Playhouse) Richard Bull, Barbara Collentine
Bernardine (Alley Theatre, Houston)
The Knack (Alley Theatre, Houston)
The Miracle Worker (Sombrero Playhouse, Phoenix) with Eileen Brennan
Long Day's Journey Into Night (Orange County) with Gertrude Flynn, Jody McCrea
Who's Afraid of Virginia Woolf? (Orange County) with Henry Beckman
Joan of Arc at the Stake (L.A. Music Center) with Dorothy McGuire
Mourning Becomes Electra (Alley Theatre, Houston) with Lillian Evans
The Night Thoreau Spent In Jail (Alley Theatre) with Michael Moriarty
Our Town (Alley Theatre)
Camino Real (Alley Theatre)
How Does Your Garden Grow? (Cast Theatre, L.A.) with Bill Gamble
Naomi Court (Pilot Theatre, L.A.) Mary Jo Catlett, Nathaniel Christian
Vieux Carre (Beverly Hills Playhouse) Karen Kondazian, Robert Wightman,
    Michael Nader
Confessions of a Nightingale (Audrey Wood Playhouse, NY; Beverly Hills
    Playhouse; National tour, etc.)
Bus Stop (Pasadena Playhouse) with Lea Thompson

AWARDS

Theatre World Award - "Most Promising New Broadway Personality" (1952)
    for performance in Moss Hart's *The Climate of Eden.*
Golden Globe Award nomination - "Most Promising New Actor" (1958)
    for performance in the film, *Ten North Frederick.*
Golden Globe Award nomination - "Best Supporting Actor" (1960)
    for performance in the film, *The Plunderers.*
Drama-Logue Award - "Best Actor" (1982) for performance in stage production
    of *Naomi Court.*
For performance in *Vieux Carre* (1983)
    Los Angeles Drama Critics Circle Award - "Best Actor"
    L.A. Weekly Award - "Best Actor"
    Drama-Logue Award - "Best Actor"
    Robby Award - "Best Actor"
    Daily Variety's Critic's Choice - "Best Actor"
    Daily News Critic's Choice - "Best Supporting Actor"
    Frontiers Critic's Choice - "Best Actor"
    L.A. Edge Critic's Choice - "Best Actor"

For performance in *Confessions of a Nightingale* (1985)
    Los Angeles Drama Critics Circle Award - "Best Actor"
    L.A. Weekly Award - "Best Actor"
    Drama-Logue Award - "Best Actor"
    Robby Award - Best Actor"

AGLA Media Award - "Best Actor"
The Oscar Wilde Award - "Best Actor"

For performance in *Confessions of a Nightingale* (1987)
Los Angeles Times' Critic's Choice - "Best of '87"
San Diego Drama-Logue Award - "Best Actor"
San Diego Theatre Critics Circle - "Best Touring Show" nomination

For performance in *Bus Stop* (1990)
Robby Award nomination - "Best Supporting Actor"

For *Confessions of a Nightingale*
Official U.S. representative at the Edinburgh International Festival, Scotland (1987)
Official U.S. representative at the Israel International Festival, Jerusalem (1988)

K

Kanes, Jonathan, 269
Kashfi, Anna, 96-97
Kastner, Elliott, 192-93, 254
Kataki (play), 133-35, 189, 256
Katselas, Milton, 220, 222, 232, 235-
    37, 239, 243, 250
Katz, Natasha, 246
Kaufman, George S., 20, 41
Kaye, Danny, 41
Kazan, Elia, 34, 61-62, 75, 152, 186
Kearns, Michael, 224, 229, 234
Keel, Howard, 122
Keeler, Ruby, 210
Keith, Brian, 69
Kelly, Gene, 199, 212
Kelly, Grace, 48, 50, 55, *211*, 212
Kennedy, Arthur, 62
Kent, Paul, 180
Kerr, Deborah, *55*, 56, 75
Kerr, John, 48, 57, 61, 75
Kerr, Sondra, 127-28
Kerwin, Brian, 204, 250, 254, 261
Keyes, Evelyn, 212
Kiley, Richard, 48
Kilgallen, Dorothy, 60
Kimmel, Joel, 250, 270
King, Perry, 246
King and I, The (play), 43
King Lear (play), 153
Kings Go Forth (film), 112
Kinsolving, Lee, 145
Kirk, Tommy, 178-79
Kiser, Terry, 227
Kitt, Eartha, 114
Klansman, The (film), 191
Knack, The (play), 7, 167-68, 172
Knight, Shirley, 116, 118, 145, 147,
    150, 186
Knight, Ted, 127
Knock on Any Door (film), 19
Knotts, Don, 158
Kohner, Paul, 77, 121-25, 127-28,
    130, 133, 142, 152, 254
Kohner, Susan, 76-77, 116, 121,
    124-25
Kondazian, Karen, 204, 219-20, 232,
    238
Kopell, Bernie, 127
Kristien, Dale, 250
Kundera, 1

L

Ladd, Alan, 121, 143
Ladd, David, 121
Lady in the Dark (play), 41
Lake, Veronica, 49

LaMaak, Jan, 183
Lamas, Fernando, 139, 205
Lambert, Gavin, 84-85
Lamont, Michael, 270
Lamour, Dorothy, 80
Lamp Unto My Feet (TV show), 57,
    70, 170
Lancaster, Burt, 11, 28, 48, 125-26,
    170
Landon, Alfred, 199
Landon, Dodie, 116
Landon, Michael, 75-76, 116, 195
Landres, Paul, 97
Lane, Burton, 268
Lane, Nathan, 250
Lane, Priscilla, 93
Lange, Hope, 214, 218
Langella, Frank, 249-50
Langner, Lawrence, 36
Lansbury, Angela, 170
Lanza, Mario, 51
Larsen, Michael, 270
Last Summer at Bluefish Cove
    (play), 233
Last Time I Saw Paris, The (film), 73
"Last Time I Saw Paris, The" (song),
    28
Last Wagon, The (film), 75-77, *78*,
    79-80, 101, 106, 114, 135
Laughton, Charles, 65, 153
Laura (play), 22
Laven, Arnold, 70
Law and Order (TV series), 260
Lawman, The (TV series), 135
Lawrence, Gertrude, 41, 112
Lawrence, Jack, 242-43, 245-46, 248-
    49
Lawrence, Jerome, 130, 152-53, 178,
    183, 237, 252
Lawrence, Naomi, 130
Lawrence, Richard, 247-48
Leachman, Cloris, 70, 199-200
Lean, David, 30
Lederer, Francis, 98
Lee, Peggy, 192, 254-55
Lee, Robert E., 130, 152, 183
Lee, Rowland, V., 122-23
Leigh, Janet, 151, 193, 197, 209, 212
Leigh, Vivien, 5, 112, 164, 271
Lembeck, Harvey, 49
Lemmon, Jack, 77, 151, 199, 231,
    272
Lenya, Lotte, 84
Leonard, Eric, 220, 232, 235-36, 239,
    243, 250
Leonard, Lu, 250

Lerner, Alan Jay, 214, 268
Lesher, Matthew, 254, 259
Letter to Three Wives, A (film), 5
Letter, The (film), 69, 271
Lettice & Lovage (play), 250
Levin, Meyer, 127-28
Levy, Jules, 97
Liberace, 164
Liebling, William, 37
Lieutenant, The (TV series), 179
Lindsay, Margaret, 89
Lion in Winter, The (play), 270
Lipton, James, 43-44
Little Foxes, The (film), 69
Little Night Music, A (play), 231
Little Women (play), 12-14
Live Spelled Backwards (play), 178
Lloyd, Suzanne, 125
Lochte, Dick, 240
Lockwood, Gary, 179
Loewe, Frederick, 268
Loggia, Robert, 57, 70, 170
Lombard, Carole, 153
Long Day's Journey Into Night
    (play), 46, 154, 156, 168-69
Long Hot Summer, The (film), 169
Long Hot Summer, The (TV series),
    169, 229
Look After Lulu (play), 150
Look Homeward, Angel (play), 95,
    240
Losch, Tilly, 84-85, 142
"Losing My Mind" (song), 271
Lost Horizon (film), 166
Lost Weekend, The (film), 99
Lost World, The (film), 139-42
Lost World, The (book), 139
Love Boat, The (TV series), 127
Love Me Tender (film), 148
Love Possessed Juana (play), 12
Loy, Myrna, 190, 204
Loynd, Ray, 239, 255
Ludlum, Edward, 127-28, 133
Luft, Sid, 68
Lugosi, Bela, 22
*Lullaby of Broadway: the Life &
    Lyrics of Al Dubin* (play), 250
Lundmark, Bill, 81-82, 98, 100, 157
Lunt, Alfred, 50
Lupino, Ida, *88*, 89
Lydon, James, 80
Lynley, Carol, 110
Lynn, Betty, 80, 198

M

M-Squad (TV series), 90
Ma Perkins (radio series), 155

Toast of the Town (TV show), 28-29
Tobey, Kenneth, 98
Tobias, George, 49
Tomlin, Lily, 247
*Tonight Show with Johnny Carson,
The* (TV series), 212-13
Topper (film), 58
Torrey, Roger, 143
Touch of Class, A (film), 193, 212
Tovar, Lupita, 77
Track of Thunder (film), 178
Tracy, Spencer, 99-101, 202-203
Trapper John (TV series), 89, 203, 229
Treasure of the Sierra Madre, The
(film), 272
Trevor, Claire, 93, 145
Trip to Bountiful, A (film), 271
Trouble in Tahiti (opera), 250
Troupe, Tom, 147, 153-54, 158-59, 177, 205, 270
Tryon, Tom, 108
Tsacrios, Nick, 218, 270
Tucker, Forrest, 108-109
Tully, Tom, 105
Turner, Lana, 5, 77, 122, 165, 204
Tyrrell, Susan, 226

U

Ullmann, Liv, 193, 212, 272
Ultimate Seduction, The (book), 236, 241, 243
Umeki, Miyoshi, 106
Unforgiven, The (film), 125, 170
Ustinov, Peter, 144-45

V

Vance, Nina, 11-12, 23, 25, 154-55, 167, 182-83, 186-87, 206, 240
Van Cleve, Edith ("Edie") (agent), 38-40, 45, 48, 50, 52
Van Doren, Mamie, 180
Van Druten, John, 11, 22
Van Dyke, Dick, 209
Van Fleet, Jo, 95
Varsi, Diane, 104-106, 108-109, 116, 120
Vaughan, Frankie, 152
Ventura, Clyde, 219-20, 222, 232, 234, 237
Verdon, Gwen, 48
Veronica Clare (TV series), 263
Victor/Victoria (film), 212, 231
Vidal, Gore, 71
Vieux Carre (play), 219-24, 227-28, 231, 234-35, 276-78
Vinegar Tree, The (play), 52

Virginian, The (TV series), 195
Voice of the Turtle, The (play), 22
von Stroheim, Erich, 86

W

Wagner, Robert, 100-101, 107, 198, 263
Wagon Train (TV series), 121, 135
Wahl, Ken, 261
Wald, Jerry, 110, 257
Walken, Christopher, 43
Walken, Ken, 43
Walker, Clint, 135, 195
Walker, Robert, 43
Wallace, Jean, 195
Wallace, Jimmie, 18-20, 54
Wallach, Eli, 38, 48, 60, 186
Walsh, Barbara, 210
Warfield, Polly, 217
Warfield, William, 148
Warhol, Andy, 214
Warner, John (Senator), 205
Watch on the Rhine (film), 127
Watch on the Rhine (play), 127
Wayland, Len, 49, 155
Wayne, John, 52, 63, 168, 262
Webb, Clifton, 65, 110-12
Wedding Breakfast (play), 30
Weill, Kurt, 31, 41, 84
Weissmuller, Johnny, 79
Weld, Jo, 115
Weld, Tuesday, 101, 115, 172
Welles, Orson, 85, 120, 169
Wertmuller, Lina, 193
West, Jennifer, 152
West, Mae, 203-204, 236
West Side Story (film), 70, 110
West Side Story (play), 247
What's My Line? (TV series), 27, 35, 60
Whirlybirds (TV series), 98, 133
White, Jane, 43
Whitman, Stuart, 104-105, 108, 116
Whitmore, James, 69, 251
Who's Afraid of Virginia Woolf?
(film), 205
Who's Afraid of Virginia Woolf?
(play), 161, 169, 265, 271
Widmark, Richard, 75, 77, 78, 199
Wightman, Robert, 220-21, 232
Wilcox, Rosemary, 9
Wilde, Cornel, 17-18, 195-96
Wilder, Billy, 99
Wilder, Thornton, 99
Williams, Billy Dee, 199
Williams, Dakin, 252

Williams, Esther, 79, 205
Williams, John, 91, 92
Williams, Tennessee, 10, 15-18, 33-38, 46, 48, 83, 139, 165-66, 178, 186-87, 204, 218-22, 224, 226, 228, 230, 232, 235-36, 238-39, 241-42, 245, 247-48, 251-53, 257, 261-63, 268, 271, 274, 278
Willkie, Wendell, 199
Willson, Henry, 58, 63, 66-67, 96-97, 118, 150
Wilson, Dennis, 226
Wilson, Lanford, 250, 262
Wilson, Scott, 210-11
Wincelberg, Shimon, 133, 135
Winters, Shelley, 193, 212, *213*, 226-27
Winterset (play), 21
Wise, Robert, 70
Wiseguy (TV series), 261
Witney, William, 170
Wizard of Oz, The (film), 157
Wolfe, Thomas, 154
Wong, B. D., 250
Wood, Audrey, 34, 37
Wood, Natalie, 56, 107, 110, 112, 114, 178, 198
Woodard, Charlayne, 260
Woodward, Joanne, 112, 114, 169, 204
Woolley, Monty, 43
Wright, Anita Peters, 21
Written on the Wind (film), 66-67
Wuthering Heights (film), 104, 271
Wyatt, Jane, 80
Wyler, William, 56-57, 73, 130
Wyman, Jane, 4-6, 67
Wyngarden, Virginia, 269

Y

You Can't Take It with You (play), 41
You Never Can Tell (play), 12, 29
Young Jesse James (film), 136, *137, 138*, 139
Young, Gig, 89
Young, Robert, 80, 164
Young, Roland, 58

Z

Zanuck, Darryl F., 40, 65, 120
Zanuck, Richard, 120
Zimbalist, Efrem, Jr., 121
Zimbalist, Stephanie, 210
Zoo Story, The (play), 265
Zorina, Vera, 84
Zugsmith, Albert, 66-67